Georgia McDermott is a food stylist, food photographer, recipe developer and blogger. Georgia writes, cooks and photographs gluten-free, FODMAP-friendly and pescetarian recipes on her blog and is the author of the bestselling cookbook *FODMAP Friendly*.

georgeats.com
georgeats

Also by Georgia McDermott:

FODMAP
FRIENDLY

Intolerance-Friendly Kitchen

Georgia McDermott

LANTERN

an imprint of
PENGUIN BOOKS

CONTENTS

INTRODUCTION

It can often feel like food intolerances and a love of good food are mutually exclusive. Garlic, onion and wheat are arguably the defining pillars of cooking, after all. I'd wager a bet that they're in about 90% of the recipes in cookbooks and on the internet. So what do you eat when you're left without them?

I stood at this precipice seven or so years ago when I finally acquiesced to a doctor's suggestion to try the FODMAP diet. I had been eating a gluten-free, low-dairy and low-fructose diet to manage a series of debilitating symptoms, but was reluctant to go all the way. I had (and still have) gastroparesis, long-term small intestinal bacterial overgrowth (SIBO) and a host of other digestive ailments. They were (and still are) impacting my life on a daily basis. It was finally time to do something serious about it.

I have always been fascinated by the science of why a recipe works, so I took quite quickly to experimenting with gluten-free, FODMAP-friendly flours. I went so far as to document my earnest (and oft unappealing) creations on a secret account I had on a small but growing app called Instagram.

Gluten-free baking has burgeoned from relative obscurity since I began posting photos of 'unique'-looking baked goods way back when. A constant in the evolution, however, has been the idea that you need to combine as many gluten-free flours and starches as you can to create an edible result. What's more? You'll need gums. Lots of them. Without gluten, starches and gums are heralded as the two ingredients that can hold things together and replicate wheat as best as possible. The catch? Neither ingredient is known for being particularly friendly towards or helpful for digestive systems in distress.

I'm not a dietician, a doctor or a nutritionist. These recipes are not superfood packed, low sugar or low fat. They are classic sweet and savoury baking basics, made as FODMAP friendly, digestive-system friendly and inclusive as possible for all of us on the dietary fringe. Like having water in between wines, these recipes are responsible fun for those with food intolerances and digestive issues: the cakes and baked goods you've missed, without the starches and gums you (often) don't need.

A life of bland, boring food seems to be the foregone conclusion when considering a life without onion, garlic and wheat, but after nearly a decade of dealing with my own food intolerances and digestive illness, I want you to know that this is not the case. I hope this book shows you that with a little creativity, good food and dietary intolerances can go hand in hand.

Happy baking,
George

BAKING LINGO

GENERAL

SINGLE FLOUR

Single-flour recipes do what they say on the tin: they use a single flour. Although we've been led to believe that gluten-free baking requires a minimum of 4.7 different flours per recipe, that isn't always the case. The benefit of a single-flour recipe is namely the ease of it. It's quick, straightforward and you need naught but a single flour! The caveat here, though, is that said single flour should be the best quality you can find, as a stale and gritty variety has nowhere to hide, and you will be able to taste it in your bake.

CREAMING BUTTER AND SUGAR

Creaming butter and sugar is the act of beating soft, room-temperature butter and sugar together at a high speed until they become light in colour and texture. This is a critical baking technique – as you beat, you're creating tiny little air bubbles within the mixture, aerating the ingredients as you go. These air bubbles will provide lift and lightness to your cake or cookies. Failure to cream butter correctly can result in a sunken, dense, oily or otherwise generally unpleasant result.

Although recipes often specify that creaming takes 2–3 minutes, I find this heavily dependent on the season. In summer? Sure, creaming might only take 3 minutes. In winter, however, it can take as long as 20 minutes, maybe more. My advice is to go by sight and texture, rather than time. The mixture should be a very pale yellow, almost white. It should feel light and fluffy, not dense. My preferred way of telling when butter and sugar are well creamed is scraping down the bowl of my stand mixer with a spatula. If I meet any resistance from firm butter or I struggle to scrape the sides or bottom, I know the mixture isn't fully creamed. If I meet no resistance and can slide the spatula around and through the fluffy mixture with absolute ease, I know it's done.

STEAM BAKING

Steam baking is a helpful tool in the arsenal of a gluten-free baker. It sounds more complicated than it is: all it involves is adding a small oven-proof container of boiling water to your oven 10 minutes before baking. This creates a steamy environment that encourages lift and rise in baked goods. It is particularly helpful when baking bread, either sourdough or yeasted.

It is also a really helpful tool for extending the freshness of your gluten-free baked goods. If you've ever eaten anything gluten free, you'll know it can become rock hard very, very easily. Reheating stale goods in a steamy environment (a steamy oven or a microwave) gives them an injection of moisture that restores them to their former glory.

TENTING

A few recipes in this book suggest tenting a baked good with foil to prevent overbrowning. This is just using a piece of foil to create a little tent for the dish as it bakes. Elevating the top of the foil (like a tent) means that it won't adhere to the top of the baked good and damage the surface. Loosely tenting allows airflow underneath the foil, which will prevent condensation and promote even cooking.

COVERING

Where I have simply said 'cover your dough', I have left it open for you to decide what to cover it with. In an effort to cut down both my use and recommendations to use plastic film, I have only specified it where truly necessary, such as wrapping the croissant dough. In other instances, such as making sourdough, suitable alternatives include using a reusable ziplock bag or creating a lid by placing a plate flush up against a bowl.

SCALDING

Scalding flour is simply the process of mixing boiling water into flour. This results in starch gelatinisation, which makes the dough elastic and flexible. It is an extremely efficient way of giving gluten-free dough some much-needed stretchiness. Make the dumpling dough on page 260 to see scalding in action.

LAMINATION

Laminating is the process whereby a block of butter is encased in a lean dough and then repeatedly rolled out, folded and rolled out again. The aim of the game is to create tiny, thin layers of butter in the dough. When baked, laminated dough expands and puffs as the butter melts and the liquid evaporates. The result is a light, flaky and buttery pastry. Puff pastry and croissants both utilise lamination, although the gluten-free varieties don't get quite as lofty as their regular counterparts.

ENRICHED

Generally related to bread or bready products, this describes a dough that has eggs, butter, cream or another similar ingredient added. Brioche is an example of an enriched dough, as is the enriched bread on page 230.

FODMAP

Are you unfamiliar with FODMAP? Firstly, welcome! Secondly, I hope you can't feel my seething envy from where you're sitting.

FODMAPs (a group of short-chain carbohydrates) are components in some foods that tend to cause digestive distress. These include ingredients such as onion, garlic, wheat, legumes and some fruits, to name my personal worst offenders. The recipes in this book are designed to be FODMAP friendly (that is, devoid of as many FODMAP-containing ingredients as possible), as well as gluten free. It's worth noting that I am not a dietician – merely a fellow digestively challenged food lover who likes developing recipes. The concept of the FODMAP diet was created by the research team at Monash University, including Sue Shepherd. They are the ultimate resource for all things FODMAP, as they regularly test a variety of foods and their FODMAP thresholds. I highly recommend buying their FODMAP smartphone app for detailed lists of everyday foods and their FODMAP content. I use it every day.

SOURDOUGH TERMS

Let it be known: I'm not a bread or sourdough expert. I am naught but a sourdough enthusiast who is fascinated by the magic that is making something from nothing. I'm sure you could find someone to explain these terms in a more professional way, but here are my definitions.

PRE-FERMENT

A mixture of active, bubbly sourdough starter, flour and water. Consider your pre-ferment as an extension of feeding your starter – one last meal to strengthen the culture and to develop flavour. There are a few other names for this such as levain, but pre-ferment is the term I use.

DISCARD

Sourdough discard is the sourdough starter that you would normally throw out (or discard) before feeding your starter. It hasn't been fed for a day or so, so it is tangy in flavour and highly acidic. This is important in recipes that contain bicarbonate of soda. The bicarbonate of soda works with the

acid content to nullify the acidic flavour and create leavening. The sourdough pancakes on page 160 use this reaction to make them nice and fluffy.

Because sourdough starter contains a lot of flavour, discard is also used in recipes that don't need leavening (like the sourdough brownies on page 162). The sourdough discard provides a complexity of flavour, and does not need to be active because it is not providing any lift.

PROOFING

The act of waiting for your bread to rise through the action of the yeast or sourdough starter. Proofing a yeasted loaf is a lot more predictable than a sourdough. Sourdough requires a watchful eye and some practice. Indicators of a good proof are a puffy, slightly jiggly dough and a good rise (maybe not doubled but a visible increase). You should be able to poke the dough and feel the airiness of it underneath. Proofing is dependent on many things: your starter, the climate where you live and in your kitchen, and the starchiness of your recipe. Loaves proof faster in summer as the cultures thrive in the heat. They also proof faster with higher starch recipes because of the easily accessible food source for the starter.

FRIDGE PROOF

Because of the unpredictable nature of proofing, it can sometimes be tricky to proof around your schedule. Enter: the fridge proof. Proofing your bread in the fridge slows fermentation right down to a more predictable rate. It also allows you to proof bread for longer – up to a day in some cases.

Fridge proofing offers the gluten-free baker a few more benefits besides flexibility. Firstly, it firms up the loaf and sets it a little, so it stands taller and rises better as it bakes. It is a particularly helpful tool if you're experimenting with high-hydration loaves, which tend to spread out when you remove them from the banneton. Overly hydrated loaves can spread outwards instead of upwards; a fridge proof will help prevent that.

Secondly (and most importantly), a fridge proof positively impacts the taste, as slow proofing develops flavour. If you don't like your bread to be sour, proceed with a little caution as it does develop the sourness.

AUTOLYSIS

Autolysis is a process more commonly used in regular sourdough baking, where it can assist with gluten bonds and extensibility. Although a newer technique to me, I have found that it softens gluten-free flours and increases their rate of absorption. A high liquid content in a loaf (see hydration percentage) leads to a softer, more open crumb. Autolysis is helpful because it enables you to add more liquid to your loaf without needing to add more psyllium husk, and without your dough becoming a sloppy mess.

I find an autolyse can resolve a sticky or gummy crumb in many cases, so you can experiment with it in other sourdough loaves if you have the time. Keep in mind that starches are a highly digestible food source for sourdough cultures and they will ferment a lot more quickly than a wholegrain flour or a loaf without starches. An autolyse for my 'white bread' sourdough (page 199), for example, would only need an hour or two as opposed to overnight. See the sourdough cinnamon raisin loaf on page 150 for an example of a short autolyse recipe. For an overnight autolyse, see the starch-free sourdough on page 206.

BAKER'S PERCENTAGE

The percentage of each ingredient in a recipe relative to the amount of flour. For example, if your bread recipe uses 100 g of flour and 100 g of water, it would be classified as a 100% hydration loaf. I don't use baker's percentages explicitly in my bread recipes as I find the inclusion of maths in anything confronting and offensive. I do use the formula to assess the hydration of all my loaves, though.

HYDRATION PERCENTAGE

Simply put, this is the percentage of water and/ or liquid ingredients in your loaf. It is based on baker's percentages and the percentage is relative to the flour content of the loaf. While a sourdough using regular flour might be 60–80% hydration, I find gluten-free sourdough needs to be at least 110%, if not more (so, for example, if you have 100 g of flour, you would need 110 g of water). This does depend on the flours used – starches need less hydration, whereas wholegrain flours need more. This is why you will see a hydration discrepancy between loaves such as my 'white bread' sourdough (page 199) and my starch-free one (page 206).

So, why would you want to push the hydration percentage? First and foremost, to create an edible bread. A dough that is insufficiently hydrated will bake up as dry as my mouth after a night of margaritas. In that vein, I suppose, is the second point: a high-hydration loaf should result in an open and light crumb, whereas a lower hydration loaf is more likely to result in a denser, finely knitted crumb (see below).

It should be noted that psyllium husk is essential for high-level hydration. Psyllium husk is a binder that absorbs lots of water, holding the dough together, giving it structure and keeping it moist. See page 11 for more information.

CRUMB

A few more terms before I end up defining every word in the English language. The crumb of a loaf describes the little air holes in it. An open crumb has bigger, more open holes. Open crumb can signal a higher hydration, as discussed above, but it can also mean that the bread was nicely proofed and the sourdough nice and active. An open crumb is pleasant to eat and it is often considered an important signifier of a good loaf (variety dependent, of course). It should be noted that a gluten-free sourdough crumb will never be as open as the crumb of a regular bread, although a higher starch content (and the added elasticity) will help.

LAME

A sharp blade used for scoring your sourdough loaves. Scoring is an important step: it tells the dough where you want it to rise as it bakes. Without scoring, the air in the loaf will break out wherever it can to the detriment of rise and height on the loaf. It's also just more likely to look ugly, you know? A lame is easily purchased online, but a really sharp, non-serrated knife will also work.

SCORING

As we have touched on, scoring a loaf serves both aesthetic and mechanical functions. A nicely scored loaf looks pretty and is all part of the fun, as far as I'm concerned. It also indicates to the dough where it should push up and expand as it bakes, which means you are controlling what happens in the oven (more so than with an unscored loaf, at least). You can experiment with fancy scoring, or keep it simple with a slice down the middle.

BANNETON

A bread-proofing basket, often made of cane. Bannetons can be any shape and will give your loaf those lovely ridges on the crust. If you don't have a banneton, you can use a bowl with a clean, dry, plain tea towel that has been well floured with rice flour. Dyes and fibres can adhere to the crust of the loaf, so keep the fancy tea towels for another day.

PASTRY TERMS

PUFF PASTRY

In my eyes, puff pastry is the crème de la crème of the pastry world. It is made by gently rolling and layering a block of butter into pastry dough, known as lamination. Each time the pastry is folded and rolled, thin layers of butter are formed in the dough. Then, when the pastry hits the hot oven, the water in the butter creates steam, puffing the pastry upwards. The result is a flaky, buttery and dramatically layered piece of pastry. Puff pastry is a challenging yet highly rewarding product. It is also great practice for the final boss – croissant dough.

ROUGH PUFF

The idea and appeal of rough puff is to achieve the delicious benefits of puff pastry without the time-consuming lamination process. Butter is rubbed into the flour with your fingers, as opposed to being added in a block (or beurrage). Because there are fewer even and controlled layers of butter, the results aren't quite as flaky and grandiose. They are, however, still buttery and delicious. It's a great pastry to learn the basics on.

ENRICHED PASTRY

Pastry that contains a fat other than butter is considered enriched pastry. The sour cream pastry on page 38 is one example. The benefit of enriching a pastry in gluten-free baking is that it becomes much more flexible and easy to handle than a purely butter-based pastry.

SHORTCRUST PASTRY

Unlike the other pastry styles mentioned, shortcrust does not aspire to be puffed and flaky. Shortened, if you will, by the inclusion of egg, shortcrust is a crumbly and buttery style of pastry most often used for tart crusts.

CROISSANT DOUGH

Although it's laminated like puff pastry, croissant dough is an entirely different sort of pastry. The primary difference? It is yeasted, meaning it has a leavening ingredient that other pastry does not. The yeast works in conjunction with the laminated butter to provide lift, height and structure to your croissants. For that reason, croissants are a balancing act of temperatures. Your workspace needs to be cool enough that the butter stays solid, yet warm enough that the yeast activates and proofs. This the most complex sort of pastry, but the finished product speaks for itself.

CHOUX PASTRY

Choux is a little different again! Choux pastry is made by cooking milk, butter and flour to form a thick roux. Once cooled, eggs are whisked in to create a magical dough that puffs up to form cavernous pastries in the oven. Once piped with a sweet filling, you'll find it impossible to stop at just one. Eclairs (see page 58), cream puffs (see page 61) and profiteroles are examples of desserts that are made with choux pastry.

THE GLUTEN-FREE PANTRY

Gluten-free baking, unlike baking with wheat, can often require a small arsenal of alternative flours. Here I will show you how to keep that arsenal to a minimum, while still exploring the flavours and capabilities of gluten-free and FODMAP-friendly wholegrains.

I have ordered the flours in terms of how I experience their absorption – thirstiest to least thirsty. By thirst, I don't mean the trap variety (although I would support them in that endeavour) – I mean how much liquid they need to properly hydrate and create a nice baked good. Your order of thirstiness might be a little different, depending on where you live and where you buy your flours. My hope is that this guide gives you a little assistance if you're trying to substitute flours.

WHOLEGRAIN FLOURS

BROWN RICE FLOUR

In my experience, brown rice flour is the thirstiest of the alternative grains. I also find that it isn't quite as multi-purpose as white rice flour because it behaves a little differently, needs extra hydration and tastes a little wholegrain. With all that said, it is still a great base on which to build a gluten-free recipe. It holds up well as the sole flour in a number of recipes.

WHITE RICE FLOUR

A real backbone flour, white rice flour can be used in essentially any application. It is second only to brown rice flour in its thirstiness – that is, the degree to which it requires liquids to be edible. Regardless, it performs incredibly well in both sweet and savoury situations. One caveat: cheaper or stale rice flours have a very distinct taste to them, so it's really essential to buy a good-quality variety to avoid it. I recommend buying from a bulk food store, if you can, as their stock tends to be fresher. White rice flour is a great performer in single-flour recipes.

BUCKWHEAT FLOUR (LIGHT)

First and foremost: buckwheat has no relation to wheat whatsoever. It is related to rhubarb and is completely, utterly gluten free. The flavour is nutty, strong and can be somewhat polarising. That said, it is an excellent flour for baking due to its almost gluten-esque qualities. If you've used buckwheat flour, you'll know that it becomes quite glue-like when mixed with liquid. This quality, when mixed with other flours, provides great structure and elasticity to gluten-free baked goods. In Australia, we generally only have light buckwheat flour, which is what I have used in all these recipes.

MILLET FLOUR

Millet is a sweet grain and flour that can produce some very pleasant baked goods when used in small amounts. In large amounts it can be quite bitter, and I find it goes rancid quite quickly. For that reason, I only use millet flour in a few recipes and in small amounts.

QUINOA FLOUR

Quinoa flour has as many haters as it does fans. The trick, I've learned, is to toast it. This really settles any bitterness and provides a nutty, almost Graham cracker–like flavour. I decided to keep the number of quinoa recipes on the lower end of the scale so as to keep the peace.

SORGHUM FLOUR (SWEET WHITE)

If I had to choose a favourite child, it would be sorghum flour. Lightly sweet and almost wheat-like in taste, sorghum makes for a lovely addition to anything you can throw it in. It's a little harder to find, but I daresay it will become easier to buy locally as demand picks up.

It should be noted that the absorptive qualities of sorghum flour can vary dramatically depending on where you buy it. Bob's Red Mill sweet white sorghum is a lot less thirsty than sorghum flour purchased at an Indian grocer. I'm not sure what causes the discrepancy, but I used sorghum flour from Bob's Red Mill for all my work in this book. Sorghum can work well in single-flour recipes, but I find the end product can be a little crumbly without a sufficient amount of binding. It can also have a slight bitterness in large amounts.

IVORY AND BROWN TEFF FLOUR

A little newer to the mainstream, teff flour can be purchased in ivory or brown varieties, which both lend a pleasantly nutty flavour to baked goods. It does produce a darker baked good than rice flour or sorghum, so keep that in mind if aesthetics are important to you. I haven't tested teff flour in single-flour recipes because it is generally quite tricky to find. I have found them to be the least absorptive flours of the bunch.

STARCHES

TAPIOCA FLOUR/STARCH

Tapioca flour/starch is the white rice flour of the starch world: a true workhorse. It lightens up wholegrain flours and provides stretch and elasticity in a very un-elastic world. Although there might be a minor difference, I use tapioca flour and tapioca starch interchangeably. In some applications, tapioca flour promotes spreading.

POTATO STARCH

There is a lot of confusion in the realm of labelling potato starch, it would seem. So, my personal rule is this: if it's snow white in colour and feels squeaky to the touch, it's potato starch. If it's yellow and looks and feels more like polenta or millet flour, it's potato flour.

Potato starch is an almost stodgy starch. It performs really well in breads, seemingly drawing in moisture. Potato starch doesn't spread like tapioca.

GLUTINOUS RICE FLOUR

Totally unlike gluten and unlike rice flour, this one is in a league all of its own. It's the main ingredient in mochi, which I think is quite telling as to its qualities. I don't use it too often in this book, although it is the saviour of the scones on page 68. Either way, it's easily purchased in the Asian section of the supermarket or in Asian grocers.

CORNSTARCH/CORNFLOUR

Most people are familiar with cornstarch (also called cornflour here in Australia) for its thickening quality and ability to create a crisp end product. Given that corn is a common allergen, I try not to use it except when necessary and offer alternatives for those who can't have it.

BINDERS

PSYLLIUM HUSK

My gluten-free binding hero and soon to be yours too, psyllium husk can sometimes be marketed as a 'digestive aid'. In the small quantities included in these recipes, it should be well tolerated by those with sensitive tummies. Psyllium husk has an amazing ability to absorb a seemingly infinite amount of water, which is always welcome in gluten-free baking. It provides structure, elasticity and binding – it is basically the gluten of the gluten-free world. There is no substitution for psyllium in either form and you can expect a hot mess if you try to omit it.

PSYLLIUM HUSK POWDER

Psyllium husk powder is simply powdered psyllium husk, but it absorbs much more liquid in this form. Although I have always worked with psyllium husk, I can concede that the powder has its perks. Because of its finer texture and extra absorption power, you can use less powder with less of an impact on the aesthetic of the product. If the labelling on the packet is vague, have a look at the actual product: regular psyllium husk looks like little flakes, whereas the powder looks very much like a powder.

Psyllium husk powder is also useful for intricate baked goods; namely, the croissants on page 44. Because it is much finer, it doesn't interfere with the butter lamination process like the husks do. This means more even layers of butter in your dough, and more lift for your croissants.

XANTHAN GUM

Xanthan gum is the most common of the gums and can quite easily be purchased at supermarkets these days. While it does perform some almost miraculous functions, it can cause digestive upset in some people. Therefore, I like to keep it to a minimum and offer alternatives whenever possible. I find it paradoxical that we would cut out gluten to aid ailing digestive systems, only to load up on gums. Xanthan gum is a treat ingredient for me.

OTHER ITEMS

EXTRA-LARGE EGGS

I use extra-large eggs for all my baking. Gluten-free goods really benefit from the binding and hydration capabilities that they provide and these recipes have all been tested with extra-large eggs. Each cracked egg weighs approximately 50 g. In Australia, a dozen extra-large eggs come in the 700 g minimum weight pack.

TAMARI OR GLUTEN-FREE DARK SOY

Tamari is a gluten-free soy sauce that is available at all supermarkets, either in the Asian section or the health-food aisle. Gluten-free dark soy sauce is used interchangeably in this book, and is becoming easy to find at supermarkets across Australia. The advantage of using gluten-free dark soy is the colour it provides, giving a slight aesthetic advantage in some dishes (like the Not quite Dan Dan noodles on page 254).

ASAFOETIDA

A powder used regularly in Indian cuisine, asafoetida tastes quite a lot like cooked onion and garlic. For those of us with fructose issues, it can go a long way to adding that rich and layered flavour that FODMAP dishes can lack. Not all asafoetida powder is gluten free, though, so make sure you check the labels.

SPRING ONION GREENS

You will notice that there are a lot of spring onion greens in this book. Because the oligo-fructans are located in the bulb, Monash

University (see page 2) states that the greens can be eaten freely and without restraint. They, like asafoetida, go a long way to creating an onion-like depth of flavour.

BUTTER

Butter is such a critical ingredient in this book. Conveniently and contrary to popular belief, it has an almost negligible lactose content. My personal toxic trait is that I find unsalted butter a disappointing concept and I am reticent to purchase or recommend it unless strictly required. I can concede that there are instances where it is necessary, and I have specified such instances. You can, of course, use the style you prefer.

PLANT-BASED BUTTER

Different plant-based/vegan butters are made differently and thus can yield varying results. My best suggestion is to choose a brand with 80% fat per 100 g, or as close to this as possible. This is roughly the same fat percentage as regular butter, leaving you in the best possible position to produce a delicious end product. I recommend reading the labels of all plant-based butter, too, to check for any weird or unpleasant ingredients. It would have taken me another year to test all these recipes with plant-based butter and my zippered pants would not allow that. I have specified the recipes that have been tested with plant-based butter. You can attempt the others, but I have not tested them.

MILK AND YOGHURT

Milk and yoghurt can be complex ingredients when it comes to gluten-free and FODMAP requirements. In my recipes, I often specify 'FODMAP-friendly milk/yoghurt of choice' in the belief that you will have a preferred variety that suits your needs. In terms of milk, full-cream, lactose-free and soy are most popular at my house, and I like to use full-cream, lactose-free

yoghurt. Keep in mind that inulin and chicory are often added to specialty dairy products and these are a FODMAP no-go, so make sure you read the labels carefully.

SOY MILK

Soy milk can be consumed on a FODMAP diet – there's a simple trick to finding a variety that works for you. Soy milk made with soy protein is given the green light by Monash University (see page 2), and is low in oligo-fructans. Soy milk made with whole soy beans is high FODMAP, even in smaller amounts. If you enjoy using soy milk (like I do), check the labels and buy a variety made with soy protein.

NUTS

I have included as many recipes as I could without added nuts, provided you steer clear of any nut milks or plant-based butters containing nuts. Keep in mind, though, that nuts can sneak in anywhere in the manufacturing process, and nut allergies can be life threatening. If you're cooking for someone with a nut allergy, make sure you buy ingredients that guarantee they contain no traces of nuts.

DOUGH ENHANCERS

I once read that dough enhancers are like coffee for yeast and I liked it so much that I have been regurgitating that line ever since. They are an easy to way to add some extra oomph to a yeasted baked good and can strengthen the yeast, help the dough rise and improve taste and texture. I often use ginger powder (available at the supermarket), pure vitamin C powder (available at the pharmacy) and apple cider vinegar. Experiment and see what you like and what works for you. Keep in mind, though, that vitamin C powder and apple cider vinegar interact and cancel each other out, so don't use them together.

TIPS FOR THIS COOKBOOK

The past decade of experimenting has taught me that gluten-free flours can be particularly unforgiving. There is barely room for winging it in regular baking, and even less when it comes to gluten free. As such, I am passionate about ensuring you have every little detail you need to be set up for baking success. Follow these tips and you'll be well on your way.

BAKING EQUIPMENT

If you don't have the same size cake pan as I've suggested, always use an alternative that is smaller, or only a centimetre or two bigger. Using a 26 cm cake tin when I've suggested a 20 cm one is the fastest way to end up with a pancake. When you're using a different-sized pan, expect to adjust the cooking time to suit.

COOKING TIMES

Every oven is different. Think of the times outlined as a guide, and go by sight and smell. Is it nicely browned? Firm to the touch, if it should be? Does the texture match what I've described? Is there a delightful smell of baked goods in the air? All of these are signs your bake is finished or nearly there.

MEASURING

I hate to be a nag (I don't at all) but it's not worth investing in a single flour if you don't have a kitchen scale to weigh it on. Gluten-free baking, like fame, is a fickle beast, and gram measurements are the only ones that are remotely accurate. These days kitchen scales are inexpensive and easy to buy. If you email me with a recipe fail, the first question I'll ask is if you weighed the ingredients, rather than dumping a 'cup' in and hoping for the best. I have included cup measurements really just so you can eyeball whether or not you need to go to the shops before baking.

FLOURS

Try to source the best quality flours possible (see more about flours on page 8). They needn't break the bank, but if you use gritty, stale flour, you will inevitably end up with gritty, stale baked goods. This is of particular importance for the single-flour recipes in this book – the taste of bad flour will inevitably shine through. If I had to choose one flour to splurge on, it would be rice flour. That stale, musky smell of supermarket flour? That's what your end product will taste like. Good quality, fresh, finely milled rice flour is always the way to go, as it incorporates more seamlessly into baked goods.

The absorbency of flours varies from batch to batch, country to country. Intuition in the kitchen is absolutely vital to success. If your dough looks dry when I've written that it should look like pancake batter, trust your dough and add more liquid. Always be open to making adjustments where necessary. I have tested and tested and tested each of these recipes, but I can't try all brands of flour, so if your dishes don't seem to be working out, consider your flour. You can always reach out to me and we can workshop what the issue might be – I love to chat gluten-free baking science.

That said, there are no two ways about it: substituting different flours in a recipe will create a different and perhaps less than ideal result. Unless I have suggested an alternative, I recommend using the flours specified for best results. I understand that availability can be difficult, but each recipe has been designed for the absorption qualities of the flour or flours used. Feel free to experiment, but don't be mad if the results no longer look like the picture.

BEST RECIPES FOR . . .

AN EGG ALLERGY:

Spinach, water chestnut and tofu dumplings (page 264)
'Sausage' and caramelised fennel pizzas (page 236)

AN OPTION WITHOUT HIGH-STARCH FLOURS:

Rough puff pastry (page 168)
Starch-free sourdough (page 206)
Wholegrain single-flour carrot cake (page 116)
Vanilla birthday cake with brown butter chocolate
    buttercream (page 110)

A GRAIN-FREE OPTION:

Grain-free choc-chip cookies (page 128)
Molten chocolate cakes (page 91)

A VEGAN OPTION:

Small-batch vegan blueberry muffins (page 120)
Vegan chocolate cake (page 108)
Scones for everyone (page 68)
Tofu and ginger dumpling filling (page 263)
Vietnamese spring rolls (page 278)

A BEGINNER'S RECIPE:

Banana cake with vanilla cream cheese icing (page 122)
Rough puff pastry (page 168)
Gum-free 'wheat' tortillas (page 188)
Sourdough flatbread (page 196)

AN EASY BREAKFAST:

Oatless porridge (page 24)
Seedy no-bake breakfast bars (page 28)

A WEEKEND BREAKFAST:

Crumpets (page 26)
Weekend waffles (page 30)
Ricotta pancakes (page 33)

A FOOLPROOF DESSERT:

Best ever brownies (page 130)
Banana cake with vanilla cream cheese icing (page 122)
Any-flour-you-like brownie cookies (page 140)

A CELEBRATION:

Easiest ever chocolate layer cake (page 104)
Burnt Basque cheesecake (page 72)

A PROJECT:

Yeasted croissants (page 44)
Traditional puff pastry (page 166)
Curried vegetable and paneer pie (page 170)
Cacio e pepe ravioli and brown butter sage sauce (page 244)

A GLUTEN-FREE CROISSANT FLEX:

Pains au chocolat (page 52)
Custard danishes (page 55)
Sourdough croissants (page 158)

A MIDWEEK DINNER:

Vegan taco mince (page 191)
Not quite Dan Dan noodles (page 254)
Vegetarian chow mein (page 257)
Vegetarian okonomiyaki (page 276)

A SLICE OF AUSTRALIANA:

Dark chocolate sandwich biscuits (page 136)
Lamingtons (page 125)
Passionfruit and lime yoyo biscuits (page 144)
Anzac-style biscuits (page 133)
Vanilla slice (page 42)
Sourdough Vegemite scrolls (page 217)
Vegetarian or vegan sausage rolls (page 172)

A SATISFYING BAKING MOMENT:

Chocolate babka (page 64)
Choux pastry (page 56)
Sourdough croissants (page 158)

AN INSTAGRAM PHOTO:

Lemon drizzle cake (page 112)

A FESTIVE TREAT:

Tiramisu (page 86)
Cheesecake with Graham cracker-style base (page 75)
Hot cross buns (page 71)
Sourdough cinnamon scrolls (page 153)

A GOOD SANDWICH:

'White bread' sourdough (page 199)
Everything dough (page 202)
Enriched bread (page 230)
Yeast-free buckwheat seed bread (page 239)

A BOUGIE SANDWICH:

Pickled jalapeño and cheddar sourdough (page 210)
Olive and rosemary 'supermarket' sourdough (page 214)

A PICNIC:

Tomato, red pesto, thyme and goat's
    cheese galette (page 175)
Sourdough baguettes (page 220)
Sourdough fougasse (page 208)

AROUND THE WORLD:

Empanadas (pages 182–185)
Laksa (page 253)
Dumplings (pages 260–269)
Tantanmen-style ramen (page 248)
Yorkshire puddings (page 186)
Not quite Dan Dan noodles (page 254)
Potato and pea samosas (page 273)

AN ESSENTIAL BASIC:

Lactose-free ricotta (page 100)
Gluten-free sourdough starter (page 148)
Low-lactose crème patissiere (page 96)
Vegan crème patissiere (page 99)
Chinese egg noodles (page 250)
Egg pasta (page 242)
Chilli oil (page 270)
Dumpling dipping sauce (page 271)
Cheat's imli chutney (page 275)

A SPOT OF CARB LOADING:

Flaky roti (page 176)
Chinese scallion pancakes (page 179)
Wholegrain sourdough pizza bases (page 222)
Wholegrain cacio e pepe scones (page 192)

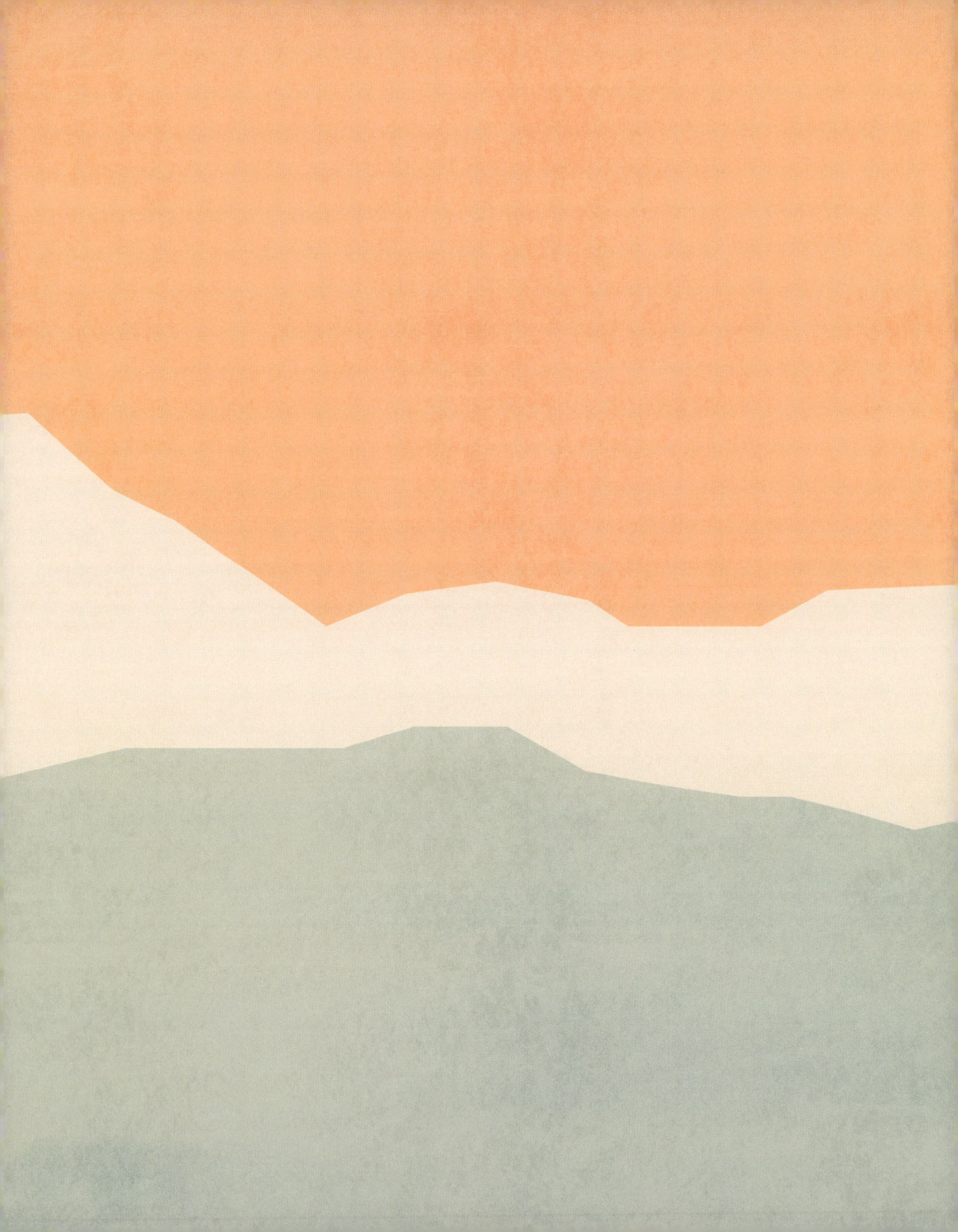

CHAPTER ONE

Breakfasts

Vegan breakfast banana bread

LACTOSE FREE
GUM FREE
EGG FREE
VEGAN
FODMAP FRIENDLY
GLUTEN FREE
DAIRY FREE

Serves: 8-10
Prep time: 25 minutes
Cook time: 40-55 minutes

The year 2020 taught us a few things, and one of them was the importance of a good banana bread. This version is refined sugar free, dairy free and vegan, which all sounds pretty good to me.

While the quantity of ripe banana in this bread is within FODMAP limits, it might not agree with some. If you don't get along with ripe bananas, use just ripe or slightly under-ripe ones instead. I find it can be helpful to roast these first to bring out their sweetness and flavour.

~~~~~

200 g (1 ¼ cups) fine white rice flour
60 g (½ cup) tapioca flour
2 ¼ teaspoons gluten-free baking powder
½ teaspoon bicarbonate of soda
1 teaspoon ground cinnamon
1 teaspoon ground nutmeg
200 g banana, ripe or just ripe (see intro) + 50 g extra for decoration (optional)
100 g light brown sugar
160 ml (⅔ cup) FODMAP-friendly plant-based milk of choice
80 ml (⅓ cup) oil (I have used vegetable and olive)
1 tablespoon vinegar (white or apple cider vinegar)
2 teaspoons vanilla bean paste
pinch of fine salt

NOTES

This banana bread will keep in an airtight container for up to 3-4 days.

You can mix in several things here: chocolate, nuts or berries. Just make sure any additions are vegan, low FODMAP and gluten free if they need to be.

1. Preheat oven to 180°C. Grease a 21.5 cm x 11.5 cm (base measurement) loaf pan.

2. Place flours, baking powder and soda, cinnamon and nutmeg in a large bowl and whisk to combine.

3. Mash the banana in a medium bowl, keeping some larger chunks for texture. Mix in the dry ingredients.

4. Mix the wet ingredients into the dry ingredients until just combined. Stir in any additions here if using (see notes). You can top the bread with some thinly sliced banana coins or slices, but this is optional.

5. Pour the mixture into the pan, sitting it on a baking tray. Cook for 40 minutes, or until the top is golden and a skewer inserted into the centre comes out clean. If necessary, cover with foil and continue to cook for a further 10-15 minutes, or until cooked through.

6. Set loaf aside to cool in pan for 5 minutes before transferring to a wire rack to cool completely. Slice and serve with vegan, FODMAP-friendly yoghurt if desired.

Choose your own ending pancakes

FREE FROM HIGH-STARCH FLOURS
GUM FREE
FODMAP FRIENDLY
GLUTEN FREE
DAIRY-FREE OPTION

Makes: 8 pancakes
Prep time: 5 minutes
Cook time: 25 minutes

80 g fine white rice flour or wholegrain flour of choice
80 g sorghum flour or wholegrain flour of choice
55 g (¼ cup) caster sugar, light brown sugar or other sugar of choice
1 teaspoon gluten-free baking powder
195 g (¾ cup) FODMAP-friendly yoghurt of choice (I have used lactose-free full cream and coconut)
2 teaspoons apple cider vinegar
1 teaspoon vanilla bean paste
3 extra-large eggs
2 tablespoons oil of choice (I used vegetable)
butter or oil, for cooking

TO FINISH:

toppings of choice

The only thing worse than starting a recipe before realising you're missing an ingredient? Starting a *breakfast* recipe before realising you're missing an ingredient. Enter: the choose your own ending pancake. They're easily customisable based on what you have on hand – choose any yoghurt, gluten-free wholegrain flour and granulated sugar you like.

~~~~~

1. Place flours, sugar and baking powder in a small bowl and whisk to combine.

2. In a large bowl, combine the yoghurt, vinegar, vanilla, eggs and oil and whisk until well combined. Whisk in flour mixture to form a smooth, spoonable batter. If the batter is too thick or thin, add a little milk or flour.

3. Heat a little butter or oil in a large non-stick frying pan over medium heat. Once the pan is heated thoroughly, spoon 2–3 tablespoons of batter into pan. Reduce heat and cook for 2–3 minutes, or until bubbles appear on top of pancake. Flip and cook for a further 2–3 minutes, or until pancake is golden and cooked through. Transfer pancake to a plate and repeat with remaining batter, greasing pan as necessary, to make 8 pancakes.

4. Serve warm or cold with toppings of choice. Leftover pancakes keep well in the fridge in an airtight container for a few days.

Oatless porridge

LACTOSE-FREE OPTION
FREE FROM HIGH-STARCH FLOURS
GUM FREE
VEGAN OPTION
FODMAP FRIENDLY
GLUTEN FREE

Makes: 1 large or 2 small serves
Prep time: 5 minutes
Cook time: 5 minutes

250 ml (1 cup) FODMAP-friendly milk of
   choice
2–3 teaspoons light brown sugar
20 g butter (or plant-based substitute)
2–3 tablespoons sorghum flour

TO FINISH:

toppings of choice (such as caramelised
   unripe banana, peanut butter and a
   sprinkle of cinnamon)

NOTES

As with regular porridge, you
can mix and match toppings.
My favourite combinations
are caramelised banana,
peanut butter and cinnamon;
or strawberries and almond
butter.

This recipe has been designed
around sorghum flour with
its wheat-like taste. I have not
tried it with any other flours.

Because it's so quick and easy
to make, I recommend making
this porridge just before you
intend to eat it. That said,
leftover porridge can be kept
in an airtight container in the
fridge for 1–2 days.

While I was busy trialling failed batches of choux pastry
(successful recipe on page 56), I realised that adding sorghum
flour to the formative stage of choux looked and tasted a
lot like porridge. A quick google told me I was not the first
to discover this: many different nationalities eat sorghum
porridge, particularly in Africa. This version is my 2-minute,
choux-inspired take.

1. Combine milk, sugar and butter in a small saucepan. Measure
   your sorghum flour into a small bowl and grab your whisk.

2. Warm the milk mixture over a medium heat until the butter
   has melted and milk begins to bubble. Whisking continuously,
   slowly add the sorghum flour until well combined. Do not
   worry if there are some small lumps – they are what makes
   this so texturally similar to oat porridge. Just make sure there
   aren't any giant lumps, as these will be unpleasant to eat.

3. Continue whisking until the porridge reaches your desired
   thickness, noting that it thickens a little as it cools.

4. Serve with suggested toppings or your preferred porridge
   toppings.

Crumpets

GUM FREE
EGG FREE
FODMAP FRIENDLY
GLUTEN FREE
FREE FROM HIGH-STARCH FLOURS
 OPTION
DAIRY-FREE OPTION
VEGAN OPTION

Makes: 6–7 crumpets
Prep time: 10 minutes
Proofing time: 60–90 minutes
Cook time: 15 minutes

2 teaspoons caster sugar
7.5 g (1 sachet) dried yeast
100 ml warm water
160 g (1 cup) fine white rice flour
30 g (¼ cup) potato starch
    (or additional white rice flour
    for option that is free from high-starch
    flours)
2 teaspoons psyllium husk
250 ml (1 cup) FODMAP-friendly milk of
    choice (I use lactose-free full cream)
2 teaspoons vegetable oil, plus extra for
    cooking
1 teaspoon bicarbonate of soda
100 ml water
¾ teaspoon fine salt

NOTES

If you want a quicker breakfast,
follow recipe up to step 3
the night before and proof
overnight in the fridge.

Crumpets keep well in an
airtight container in the fridge
for 3–4 days. They can also be
frozen and defrosted.

A crumpet with butter and a little honey immediately
transports me right back to my childhood – those gloriously
simple days when I didn't have to pay tax or watch people
dance on TikTok. Honey is low in fructose in 1 teaspoon serves,
but you can also use maple syrup or nix the sweetener and go
savoury.

~~~~~~

1. Combine sugar, yeast and warm water in a small bowl. Set aside
    in a warm spot to proof for 10 minutes. The top of the mixture
    should be slightly domed and very bubbly. If this doesn't happen,
    discard the mixture and start again (as the yeast is inactive).

2. Meanwhile, place flours and psyllium husk in a medium non-
    reactive bowl and whisk to combine.

3. Add the activated yeast mixture, milk and vegetable oil. Whisk
    to combine, then cover and set batter aside to proof in a
    warm, non-draughty place for 60–90 minutes. The proofing
    process is quicker in summer and slower in winter.

4. The batter is ready when it is bubbly, maybe slightly domed,
    and has risen tangibly. Combine the bicarbonate of soda,
    water and salt in a small bowl, then add it to the batter and
    whisk to combine. Rest the batter for 10 minutes.

5. Heat 1 tablespoon of oil in a non-stick frying pan over medium
    heat. Thoroughly grease your crumpet or egg rings (I like to
    use butter for this). Half fill the first crumpet ring. Reduce
    heat to low and cook for 5 or so minutes or until the edges
    start to set. Using tongs, remove ring and cook for a further
    1–2 minutes. When crumpet is almost cooked through, flip
    and cook for 1–2 minutes to lightly brown the top.

6. Repeat with remaining batter, 2–3 at a time if you have
    enough rings. If your first crumpet doesn't get any air holes,
    add a tablespoon of water before cooking the next crumpet.
    Repeat between each crumpet if necessary.

7. Allow crumpets to stand for 5–10 minutes before eating.
    This allows them to set, giving them a much better texture.
    Serve with whatever you enjoy – I can't go past butter and
    a teaspoon of honey.

Seedy no-bake breakfast bars

LACTOSE FREE
FREE FROM HIGH-STARCH FLOURS
GUM FREE
EGG FREE
VEGAN
FODMAP FRIENDLY
GLUTEN FREE

Makes: 12 bars
Prep time: 15 minutes
Cook time: 5 minutes
Chilling time: 2 hours or overnight

There are morning people, and then there's me: finally coherent at around 11.30am after coffee and a lengthy stint in my towel staring at the wall. These bars are constantly in my fridge as a set and forget breakfast snack, preserving the use of my two firing brain cells for other things. Can confirm: easily devoured in a towel.

~~~~~~

DRY INGREDIENTS:

25 g (2 cups) puffed buckwheat or rice
80 g (½ cup) pepitas
35 g (¼ cup) sunflower seeds
30 g (¼ cup) hemp seeds
2 tablespoons chia seeds
2 tablespoons linseeds (flaxseeds)

WET INGREDIENTS:

185 g (½ cup) rice malt syrup
140 g (½ cup) peanut, almond or
    sunflower seed butter
60 g (¼ cup) coconut oil, measured after
    melting
1 tablespoon pure maple syrup (optional)

NOTES

Rice malt syrup is an excellent binding sweetener, but I personally find it lacks in sweetness. The tablespoon of maple syrup is an optional addition for those who might be unaccustomed to the subtle sweetness of rice malt.

If you don't have access to rice malt syrup, fear not! You can use 140 g (½ cup) peanut butter, 110 g (½ cup) coconut oil or butter and 60 ml (¼ cup) maple syrup for the wet ingredients instead.

1. Combine the dry ingredients in a large bowl. You can dry toast them in a large frying pan over a medium heat first for extra flavour, but it's not compulsory.

2. Combine all wet ingredients in a small saucepan. Place over a medium–low heat and cook, whisking occasionally, until the mixture begins to bubble gently. The mixture should be smooth and cohesive.

3. Pour the peanut butter mixture over the dry ingredients. Use a spatula to scrape in all the wet ingredients – there is just enough liquid here to hold the bars together so you don't want to leave any behind. Stir thoroughly to coat all dry ingredients.

4. Line a 16 cm × 26 cm (base measurement) baking tin with plastic film, allowing excess to overhang the 2 long sides to form handles. Pour the mixture into prepared baking tin and use the spatula to smooth to an even layer. Fold excess plastic film over slice to cover. Using your hands, press down really firmly to pack the mixture in. Uncover the slice (so it doesn't sweat) and place in the fridge until cool and set, about 2 hours or up to overnight.

5. Cut slice into 12 bars and store in an airtight container for up to 2 weeks.

Weekend waffles

LACTOSE-FREE OPTION
GUM FREE
FODMAP FRIENDLY
GLUTEN FREE

Makes: 4 waffles
Prep time: 25 minutes
Cook time: 30 minutes

160 g (1 cup) fine white rice flour
60 g (½ cup) tapioca flour
1 teaspoon gluten-free baking powder
55 g (¼ cup) caster sugar
pinch of fine salt
250 ml (1 cup) FODMAP-friendly milk of choice
1 tablespoon lemon juice (or apple cider vinegar)
2 extra-large eggs, separated
125 ml (½ cup) vegetable oil
2 teaspoons vanilla bean paste, optional

TO FINISH:

toppings of choice

NOTES

Place cooked waffles on a wire rack to prevent steam being trapped. To aid in crispiness, you can also keep the waffles in a warm oven while you cook the rest.

These waffles can be frozen, but they won't be quite as fluffy and fresh upon reheating.

On an average weekday I'm barely awake enough to get down the stairs, so whipping egg whites to stiff peaks is truly out of the question. Enter the weekend waffle: for when you've had just enough coffee and sleep to dig out the hand beater from the back of the cupboard.

1. Place flours and baking powder in a large bowl and whisk to combine. Stir in sugar and salt.

2. Combine milk and lemon juice in a small bowl. This will form buttermilk, which helps the waffles rise and stay crisp.

3. Place egg whites in a large clean and dry bowl. Using electric beaters, beat until stiff peaks form. You should be able to invert the mixing bowl without the egg whites sliding out.

4. Add the egg yolks, vegetable oil and milk mixture and the vanilla bean paste, if using, to the flour mixture, whisking until completely smooth.

5. Bit by bit, add the egg whites into the batter and use a spatula to gently fold them in. Continue until the batter is mostly smooth, but light and bubbly.

6. Heat a waffle iron following manufacturer's instructions, making sure it is on the hottest setting. Once hot, lightly spray with oil. Ladle in enough batter to three quarters fill waffle iron, spreading the batter to every corner. Close and cook for 5–7 minutes or until waffle is golden brown and crisp around the edges. Transfer to a wire rack (see notes). Repeat to make 4 waffles, spraying with a little more oil between batches.

7. Serve immediately with toppings of choice. I like berries or caramelised bananas and FODMAP-friendly yoghurt (use your preferred style).

Ricotta pancakes

LOW LACTOSE
FREE FROM HIGH-STARCH FLOURS
GUM FREE
FODMAP FRIENDLY
GLUTEN FREE

Makes: 7–8 pancakes
Prep time: 20 minutes
Cook time: 15 minutes

100 g fine white rice flour
1 teaspoon gluten-free baking powder
¼ teaspoon bicarbonate of soda
3–4 tablespoons caster sugar (according to your penchant for sweetness)
¼ teaspoon fine salt
4 extra-large eggs, separated
200 g (1 cup) lactose-free ricotta (page 100)
125 ml (½ cup) FODMAP-friendly milk of choice
1 teaspoon vanilla bean paste
zest of ½–1 lemon, to taste
1 teaspoon white vinegar
butter or oil, to grease

TO FINISH:

toppings of choice

NOTES

Leftover pancakes keep really well in an airtight container in the fridge for 3–4 days.

If you have no issues with lactose, you can also use store-bought, firm deli ricotta for these pancakes.

These pancakes are the salve to my 2-year-old wound caused by watching my sister eat the iconic ricotta pancakes at Bill's in London the last time I visited her. My homage to the classic uses naught but a good quality, fresh and fine white rice flour and my lactose-free ricotta recipe on page 100 to keep the general FODMAP content low.

~~~~~~

1. Combine the flour, baking powder, bicarbonate of soda, sugar and salt in a large bowl. Place egg yolks, ricotta, milk, vanilla and lemon zest in a small bowl. Stir to break up the ricotta, leaving some texture.

2. Use an electric beater to beat egg whites in a clean dry bowl until stiff peaks form.

3. Add the ricotta mixture and vinegar to the flour mixture and whisk to combine. The batter will be quite thick and lumpy. Use a spatula to gently fold in one-third of the egg whites, being careful not to deflate them. Fold in remaining egg whites until they are just combined and the batter is mostly smooth and aerated.

4. Heat a large non-stick frying pan over medium heat. Grease with butter or oil, then add 1–2 tablespoons of batter per pancake. Cook for 1–2 minutes or until edges brown and the top starts to firm, then flip. Cook for a further 2–3 minutes or until cooked through. Repeat with remaining batter to make 7–8 pancakes, greasing pan as required.

5. Serve pancakes warm with your toppings of choice. I like slightly under-ripe banana slices with maple syrup and a dusting of icing sugar.

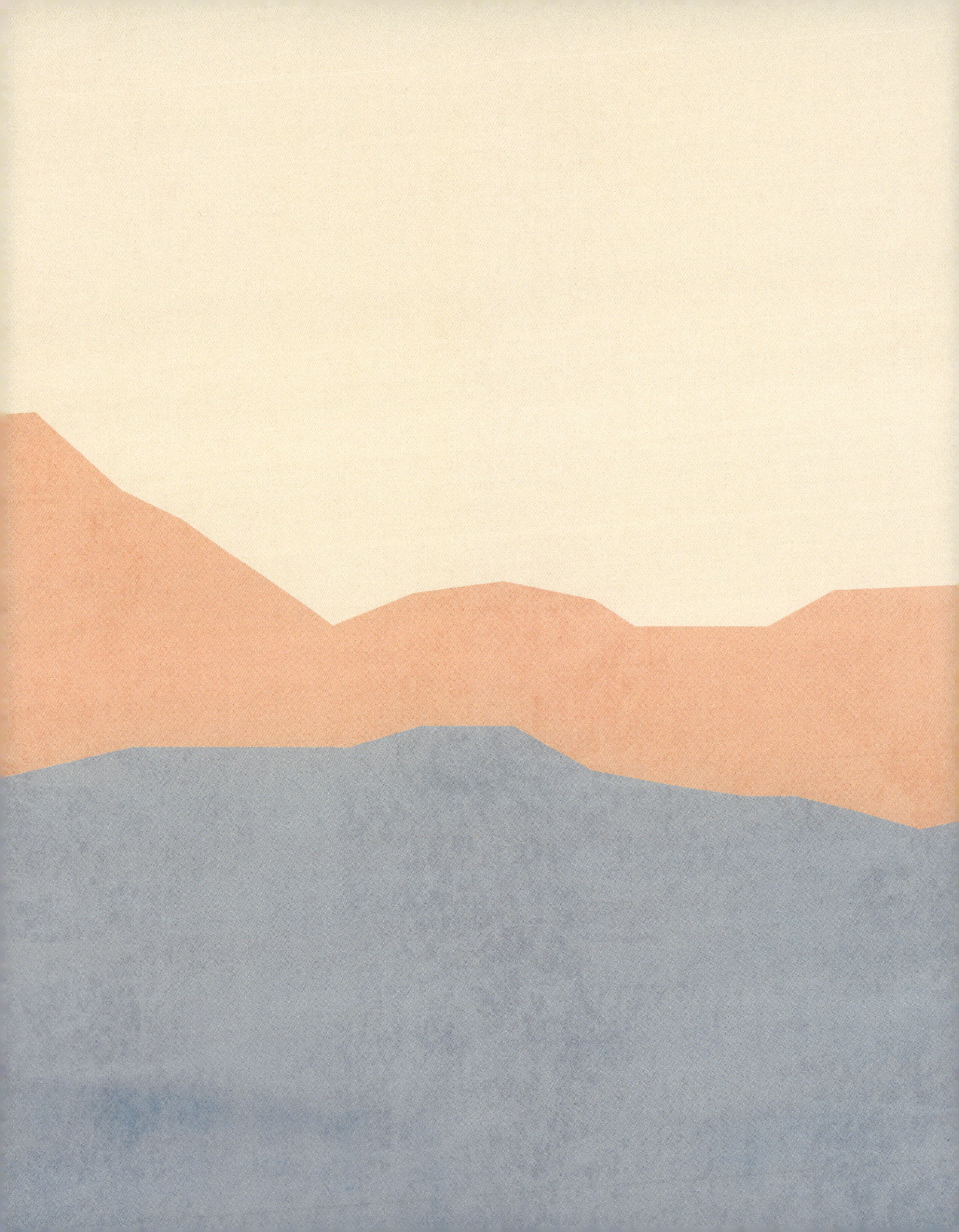

CHAPTER TWO

Sweet pastry

PAGES 35-61

Sweet shortcrust pastry

LOW LACTOSE
GLUTEN FREE
FODMAP FRIENDLY

Makes: 1 × 25 cm tart shell
Prep time: 10 minutes
Chilling time: 15–20 minutes
Cook time: 20 minutes

80 g (½ cup) fine white rice flour
60 g (½ cup) tapioca flour
50 g (½ cup) blanched almond meal
40 g (¼ cup) sorghum flour
80 g (⅓ cup) pure icing sugar
1 tablespoon psyllium husk powder
pinch of fine salt
100 g chilled butter, cut into cubes
1 extra-large egg

Given that I used to make shortcrust pastry purely out of almond meal, there's a certain irony to this recipe requiring the most flours of any in the book. This combination of flours provides lightness, structure and flavour, while the almond meal adds much-needed moisture and a hint of sweetness. It is worth the hunter-gatherer mission, I promise.

1. Combine flours, almond meal, icing sugar, psyllium husk and salt in a medium bowl. Add butter and, using your fingertips, rub in until mixture resembles coarse crumbs.

2. Use a fork to whisk in the egg. Get your hands in and work the dough until it comes together in a smooth ball. Add a teaspoon of water if it doesn't.

3. Cover dough with plastic film and place in fridge to firm, around 15–20 minutes. When the dough has chilled, you are ready to use your shortcrust pastry.

4. To bake, preheat the oven to 180°C. Roll the pastry out on a well-floured sheet of baking paper to a circle 6–7 cm larger than your 25 cm (base measurement) fluted tart tin. The pastry should be about ¼–½ centimetre thick. Invert the fluted tart tin onto the middle of the pastry. Place one hand under the baking paper and one atop the tin, then flip the pastry upright into the tart tin. Peel off the baking paper and allow the pastry to generously hang into the tin. Adhere pastry to the edges of the tin and trim off any excess. Use those trimmings to patch up any holes as necessary.

5. Use a fork to prick the pastry base thoroughly to allow air to escape. Bake for 20 minutes or until lightly golden. Remove from the oven and allow to cool and firm up before use.

Sour cream pastry

GLUTEN FREE
FODMAP-FRIENDLY OPTION

**Makes: enough pastry for 1 tart (base
   and top) or large galette**
Prep time: 15 minutes
Chilling time: 30 minutes

A life lesson, free of charge: putting sour cream in things inevitably makes them better. This pastry is incredibly easy and flakier than it should reasonably be, and that's thanks to the combination of butter and full-fat sour cream.

Currently there is only light lactose-free sour cream available in Australia. I really recommend buying regular, full-fat sour cream for this pastry as the high fat content and lower water content are what make it so flaky. Sour cream is FODMAP friendly in 2 tablespoon serves, so unless you eat half a pie you'll be golden. This recipe also works well with full-cream, lactose-free yoghurt instead of the sour cream. If you have a dairy allergy or a severe lactose intolerance, use the puff or rough puff pastry recipes on page 166 or 168 with vegan butter.

~~~~~~~~

FOR THE PASTRY:

240 g (1 ½ cups) fine white rice flour
120 g (1 cup) tapioca flour
1 teaspoon xanthan gum
1 teaspoon fine salt
125 g chilled butter, cut into cubes
75 g sour cream, chilled
iced water only as necessary

FOR A SWEET PASTRY OPTION:

100 g pure icing sugar

NOTES

The heat of your fingers will gradually warm even the coldest of butter, allowing you to rub it into the flour in little sheets. This is what makes the pastry puffy and flaky.

You can freeze the pastry, well wrapped in an airtight container. Allow to thaw before attempting to roll out.

1. Start by ensuring that all your liquid ingredients are super cold. Place the butter and sour cream in the freezer, and prepare some iced water.

2. Mix the flours, xanthan gum and salt together in a large bowl (or icing sugar if you're making a sweet pastry). Add the cubes of cold butter and coat them in the flour. Use your fingertips to gently rub the butter into the flour mixture. The idea is to leave small pockets of butter in the dough as these are what will create flakiness and provide lift. Continue until the mixture resembles coarse crumbs.

3. Add the sour cream and use a spoon or your hands to gently bring the dough together without crushing the butter chunks. It will get a little messy.

4. Add iced water, a tablespoon at a time. Using your hands again, bring the dough together between each addition and stop as soon as the dough is smooth. I have found this dough can take anywhere from 3 ½–5 tablespoons of water. Yours might be different but go by feel and stop as soon as it forms a ball.

5. Wrap dough in plastic film and chill in fridge for at least 30 minutes. Your pastry is then ready to roll out and use!

Rough puff pastry *without xanthan gum*

GUM FREE
GLUTEN FREE
FODMAP FRIENDLY

**Makes: 2 sheets (enough for 1 large
pastry-topped pie)**
Prep time: 30 minutes (spread out)
**Chilling time: 2 hours or up to
overnight**

Thanks to our old pal psyllium husk and a nifty trick called scalding (see page 2), it's possible to create a flaky, delicious rough puff pastry without xanthan gum. Initially, you'll curse my name as you attempt to cobble together an impossibly delicate and cracked lump of dough. After that magical sixth roll, though, all will be forgiven – a smooth and flexible pastry will emerge.

I've tested this recipe with all different varieties of gluten-free flours and they each work well. The general rule of thumb is to adhere to the given ratio of wholegrain to starch – 160 g wholegrain to 60 g starch. If you'd like to create an all-wholegrain pastry, use an extra teaspoon of psyllium husk in the scald, and expect a little less height on the baked product.

FOR THE SCALD:

3 teaspoons psyllium husk
1 tablespoon fine white rice flour
1 teaspoon butter, softened (or melted)
80ml (⅓ cup) boiling water

FOR THE PASTRY:

160 g (1 cup) fine white rice flour
60 g (½ cup) tapioca flour
1 teaspoon fine salt for savoury OR a
    pinch of salt and 55 g (¼ cup) caster
    sugar for sweet
150 g chilled butter, cut into cubes
2–4 tablespoons iced water, as necessary
flour, to dust (I generally use tapioca
    flour)

1. To make the scald, combine psyllium, flour and butter in a small bowl placed on a tea towel (to stop it moving as you whisk). Whisking continuously, gradually add boiling water until well combined and mixture forms a thick gel-like paste. Set aside to cool completely.

2. To make the pastry, combine the flours and salt (and sugar for sweet pastry) in a large bowl. Add the cooled scald and use your fingertips to rub in as you would rub butter into flour. Keep going until the mixture looks like shredded chicken (okay, maybe not the most suitable description to use in a vegetarian cookbook . . .).

3. Add the butter cubes and use your fingertips again to rub them into the pastry until only small butter chunks remain. Some small chunks are good - they will create the puff.

4. Add the iced water, tablespoon by tablespoon, and use your hands to gently combine to get a sense of how much water it needs. The dough needs to only just clump together without many dry, floury bits. Adding too much water will prevent the pastry from puffing nicely, so only add as much as necessary. Once the dough just comes together, transfer onto a large piece of plastic film and press into a square. Wrap and chill in fridge until solid, a few hours or up to overnight.

RECIPE CONTINUES >

NOTES

Rough puff keeps well, unused, for a day in the fridge. Leaving it in the fridge much longer will decrease its puff power. You can wrap puff pastry and freeze it for a month or two. Allow it to thaw before attempting to roll it out.

In a cold, winter kitchen, you can sometimes get away with laminating the pastry all in one go. In a hot summer one, you'll need to refrigerate the pastry between turns.

I've had mixed results with a vegan version, but if you have a brand of vegan spread you trust, you could substitute it for the regular butter in this recipe.

5. Generously flour a long sheet of baking paper or clean work surface. Use a rolling pin to gently bash the square of pastry into a slightly flatter and even shape. From there, use gentle pressure and even strokes to roll the pastry out into a longish rectangle. Length doesn't matter at this stage - just long enough that you can fold it like a business letter. Dust off any excess flour and roll the top third of dough down onto the middle, and then the bottom third of dough over the top of that. This is your first 'turn'. The dough will crack, bits will fall off, and you'll wonder if it will ever come together. Fret not! It will.

6. Repeat this process 5 more times, using as much flour as necessary. If the butter starts melting out at any point, wrap in plastic film and place in fridge for 10–15 minutes to firm.

7. By the sixth turn, the dough should be smooth and only crack a little when you fold it, if at all. Wrap in plastic film and place in fridge to chill for 30 minutes. After that, it is ready to roll out and use.

Vanilla slice

LOW-LACTOSE OPTION
GLUTEN FREE
FODMAP FRIENDLY
GUM-FREE OPTION

Makes: 10–12 medium slices
Prep time: 1 hour 30 minutes
Cook time: 40 minutes
Chilling time: a few hours or overnight

Although there's a recipe for crème patissiere in this book, I decided this version for vanilla slice needed its own space. A double batch of the original recipe, it also includes a special ingredient: agar agar powder. Agar is a vegetarian gelling agent, akin to gelatin. It is made of seaweed and these days it is widely available at supermarkets and health food stores. Without agar agar, the crème patissiere isn't thick and sturdy enough, which will result in a hot mess of a vanilla slice. With it, you'll achieve that sturdy yet wobbly vanilla slice that normal people talk about.

~~~~~~

1 quantity puff pastry (page 166) or rough puff pastry without xanthan gum (page 39), laminated

FOR THE DOUBLE BATCH OF CRÈME PATISSIERE:
875 ml (3 ½ cups) FODMAP-friendly milk of choice
130 g caster sugar
2 teaspoons powdered agar agar
40 g (⅓ cup) gluten-free cornflour, sieved
5 extra-large egg yolks, plus 2 whole extra-large eggs
75 g butter

TO FINISH:
1 egg, lightly beaten
pure icing sugar, to dust

NOTES
Vanilla slice can be kept in an airtight container in the fridge for 2 days.

1. To make the crème patissiere, follow instructions on page 96. Add the agar agar to the milk and caster sugar in the saucepan.

2. Continue with recipe, pouring the tempered egg mixture back into the saucepan.

3. Cook on your smallest cooking element, on a low heat, whisking constantly, until the mixture is really thick and smooth. It should easily coat the back of a spoon and fall off the spoon in drips, rather than a stream. This can take 15–20 minutes.

4. While the crème patissiere is cooling, preheat oven to 200°C. Line a large baking tray with baking paper. Place the pastry block onto a large piece of well-floured baking paper and divide into 2 pieces using a sharp knife. Set 1 piece of pastry aside (or in the fridge if your kitchen is warm). Roll the pastry out into a rectangle, about ¼ cm thick. Use the base of a 16 cm × 26 cm (base measurement) baking tin as a size guide (I like to leave a few extra centimetres as a margin of error). Repeat with the second block of pastry.

5. Place pastry rectangles on prepared tray, brush with beaten egg and bake for 15–20 minutes or until golden and puffed. You might need to do this in batches. Remove from oven and set aside to cool.

6. Once cooled, gently pick up 1 piece of pastry and place it in the base of the baking tin, trimming to fit.

7. Whisk the cooled crème patissiere to remove any lumps, and gently spoon over pastry base. Using a spatula, smooth surface and top with remaining pastry rectangle. Press firmly but gently to adhere the pastry to the crème patissiere.

8. Place slice in fridge to completely cool and firm, for a few hours or overnight. Dust with icing sugar, if you wish, before serving.

Yeasted croissants

LOW LACTOSE
GLUTEN FREE
FODMAP FRIENDLY

Makes: 6 small or 4 large croissants
Prep time: 30 minutes + 2–3 hours
**   rolling**
Proofing time: overnight + 2–3 hours
Cook time: 15–25 minutes

Second only to my cat Arthur and my extensive photographic catalogue of him sleeping, this croissant recipe is my pride and joy. It took me nearly 100 attempts (seriously) to nail down not only the recipe, but more importantly the technique. While they're certainly a labour of love and the technique takes some learning, you'll get to eat croissants at the end. Is there anything more motivating than that?

Croissants are fussy creatures and this recipe has been designed around specific ingredients. I like to make recipes as flexible as possible but, in this instance, I recommend sticking to the ones outlined, unsalted butter included.

～～～～

YEAST MIXTURE:

60 ml (¼ cup) warm full-cream, lactose-
    free milk
7.5 g (1 sachet) dried yeast
1 teaspoon caster sugar

FOR THE DOUGH:

120 g (¾ cup) fine white or brown
    rice flour
90 g (¾ cup) tapioca flour
60 g (½ cup) buckwheat flour
½ teaspoon xanthan gum
1 teaspoon gluten-free baking powder
15 g psyllium husk powder (see notes)
100 g caster sugar
¼ teaspoon fine salt
50 g unsalted butter, softened
60–125 ml (¼–½ cup) full-cream,
    lactose-free milk (see notes)
2 extra-large eggs

FOR THE BEURRAGE (BUTTER BLOCK):

150–200 g good quality unsalted butter

TO FINISH:
1 egg, lightly beaten

THE NIGHT BEFORE:

1. To make the yeast mixture, place the warm (not hot) milk in a small bowl. Sprinkle over the yeast and sugar and mix to combine. Set aside until bubbling and foamy, about 10 minutes.

2. To make the dough, combine the flours, xanthan gum, baking powder, psyllium, sugar and salt in the bowl of your stand mixer. Add the activated yeast. Using the paddle attachment, start mixing dough on low speed. Add the softened butter and continue mixing until combined. Add milk and eggs and mix until a relatively thick, batter-like dough forms. The dough will be a little thinner than a traditional croissant dough, but you should be able to pick it up and scrape it out of the bowl. If not, leave it for 10 minutes for the psyllium husk powder to absorb some liquid.

3. Transfer dough onto a large piece of plastic film. Wrap to cover and press it into a rectangle shape. Chill in fridge overnight.

RECIPE CONTINUES >

THE NEXT DAY:

4. Place the butter for the beurrage on a large sheet of baking paper and set aside to just slightly soften for 10–20 minutes, season dependent. Fold 1 side of paper over the butter block and use a rolling pin to bash the butter into a rectangle shape. Lay butter rectangle flat in the fridge while you work on the pastry.

5. Generously flour a large sheet of baking paper or a clean, dry bench and both sides of your dough. Gently roll dough out into a rectangle, double the length of your butter block. The idea here is to achieve an even layer of butter between every bit of the dough layers, as this is what helps the croissants to rise.

6. Dust excess flour off pastry and place your butter block on the bottom half of the rectangle. You should be able to cleanly fold the top half over the bottom, just pinching the sides and bottom to secure the butter in the dough. Pick dough up gently to ensure the bottom has adequate flour to prevent it sticking. Place it back down with the shorter side facing you.

7. Using gentle and even pressure, roll dough out into a rectangle, roughly 20 cm in length. The length doesn't matter too much – it just needs to be long enough to fold into thirds. If the dough cracks or the butter feels too solid, stop rolling and wait 5–10 minutes. Similarly, if the butter starts feeling soft or seeps out, transfer it straight to the fridge. We are trying to roll tiny thin sheets of butter into dough (that has no gluten!) without it melting, cracking or breaking, so you really need to concentrate on even, slow and considered pressure. If you hack at the dough, you can expect a very dense and unimpressive croissant.

8. Dust any excess flour off the pastry. Fold the top third into the middle of the pastry and the bottom third up over the top. This is called a business letter fold. Press dough down gently to secure with your rolling pin before wrapping in plastic film and placing in fridge for 10–30 minutes. This is to firm the butter up, so allow more time in a hot kitchen and less in a cool one. Congratulations! You have just completed your first turn.

9. Complete this process of rolling, folding and dusting two more times, letting the dough soften or putting it in the fridge as often as necessary. I like to complete my turns with the seams of the dough facing up, so they fold back into the pastry. It makes for a neater dough that's easier to handle. More lamination is not better in the case of croissants. If you exceed 3 folds you are on a fast track to a very time-consuming brioche. Make sure you keep count of how many turns you have done.

10. Generously flour a large sheet of baking paper or a clean, dry bench with tapioca flour. Lay out dough with the short side facing you. Once it warms to a good rolling temperature (you should have a sense of this by now), begin rolling it out into a long rectangle, about 7.5 mm–1 cm thick and the width of the baking paper. The longer the rectangle, the more rings you'll get on the finished product.

11. Use a small, sharp, non-serrated knife to trim the edges with a clean, swift action. Blunting the edges now will squash all those beautiful layers we've worked hard to create. Slice dough into 4–6 long triangles. Two triangles should equal 1 long rectangle so that the dough starts and finishes with the straight edges.

12. Gently pick up the first triangle, transferring the others to the fridge if they start to stick.

13. Turn the triangle over, dust off excess flour and cut a small 1–2 cm slit in the centre of the wide base. Flick the 2 edges of the slit outwards to the edges of the dough. From here, start rolling the croissant up reasonably tightly. Once you get to the end, leave the croissant tail hanging down. Don't tuck it underneath the croissant as you would with regular ones - if you do, the croissant will split down the middle as it bakes. Repeat with the remaining croissants.

RECIPE CONTINUES >

NOTES

Proofing croissants is somewhat of an art and requires a lot of intuition as it is dependent on so many factors unique to where you are baking. They need to be hot enough that the yeast becomes active and gives the croissants lift, but cool enough that the thin sheets of butter don't melt. Needless to say, the process is infinitely easier in winter when you can better control the temperature. I do not recommend making croissants in summer unless you have a cool kitchen, a willingness to fail and the patience of a saint.

Croissants are best on the day of baking, but leftover croissants can be kept in an airtight container at room temperature for 2 days, or made into almond croissants (page 51). Microwave or steam heat croissants before serving.

14. To proof, cover your croissants completely without the covering touching the croissants. I like to divide them into ceramic baking dishes and place in giant ziplock bags. Next, consider your kitchen and weather conditions. If it's hot, they will need less proofing time. Place them in a temperate zone (never in direct sunlight) and check on them every so often. If you see any leaking butter, pop them straight in the fridge. If you're baking in winter, place the ziplock bagged croissants in the oven with either the light on or a small baking dish of hot water at the base of the oven. Change the water every hour or so, checking on the croissants as you do.

15. Your croissants are proofed or close to proofed when they feel puffy and light to the touch. They might not look like they have expanded significantly, but the dough should feel springy and the tray of croissants a little lighter than you'd expect them to be. They might feel like crackling sherbet against your fingers when you touch them lightly. While this might only take an hour or two in summer, it can take most of the day in a cold, wintery kitchen, so be patient and don't panic.

16. Preheat oven to 180°C and line a large baking tray with baking paper. Carefully transfer croissants to prepared tray. Use a small paintbrush to brush pastry tops with beaten egg, being careful not to paint the exposed edges or you'll glue the layers together and stop the croissant from rising and becoming flaky.

17. Transfer croissants to fridge for 10 minutes to chill. Bake for 15–25 minutes or until golden brown and puffy. Some butter leaking is normal, but if yours are swimming, see the troubleshooting section for next time.

18. Gently transfer croissants to a wire rack to cool. They can be eaten warmish, but I give them at least an hour to set.

If your croissants leaked a lot of butter, this is a sign they were under-proofed. It can also suggest that the butter wasn't rolled into the dough with enough precision. Next time, proof them for longer and focus on even, considered rolling of the dough.

If your croissants didn't rise, they have not been proofed sufficiently. Proof them a little longer next time.

Is the inside of your croissant dense and brioche-like? This comes down to rolling technique. With practice you'll get there! A dense croissant can also be a sign that you have laminated the dough too many times, which results in the dough absorbing the butter rather than having distinct layers of it. Make sure you keep track of how many times you have laminated the dough.

Almond croissants

LOW LACTOSE
GLUTEN FREE
FODMAP FRIENDLY

Makes: 4–6 croissants
Prep time: 20 minutes
Cook time: 15 minutes

My hot take you didn't ask for: the only thing more addictive than a croissant is an almond croissant. And the only thing that matters in an almond croissant is the almond extract. Okay, so that's two hot takes you didn't ask for.

I would recommend making a batch of six small yeasted croissants (page 44) to make almond croissants as opposed to four larger. I have made many attempts to eat a large almond croissant and I found them quite overwhelming. You can also easily halve the ingredients for each component for a small batch of croissants.

~~~~~

4–6 baked gluten-free croissants, fresh or day-old (page 44)

FOR THE ALMOND SYRUP:

60 ml (¼ cup) water
55 g (¼ cup) caster sugar
½ teaspoon almond extract

FOR THE ALMOND FRANGIPANE:

30 g butter
50 g (½ cup) almond meal
35 g (¼ cup) pure icing sugar
1 extra-large egg
½ teaspoon almond extract

TO FINISH:

25 g flaked almonds

1. Gently cut the baked gluten-free croissants (page 44) in half lengthways.

2. To make the syrup, combine the water and sugar in a small saucepan and place over a medium heat. Cook, stirring, until the mixture thickens slightly and becomes syrupy. Stir in extract and remove from heat.

3. To make frangipane, combine butter, almond meal, sugar, egg and extract in a small bowl. Using electric beaters, beat until light and fluffy, about 2 minutes.

4. Preheat oven to 180°C. Arrange croissants on a baking tray. Brush insides of each croissant with syrup, leaving a little for the tops. Smear frangipane onto cut sides of each croissant and sandwich pieces together. The frangipane will leak if you add too much.

5. Brush tops of each croissant with remaining syrup and top that with a smear of the frangipane. It doesn't need to be too much, just enough to stick the almonds to.

6. Top each croissant with flaked almonds and bake for 10–15 minutes or until the frangipane has set and the almonds on top are lightly golden.

NOTES

You can serve warm or at room temperature. They are best eaten on the day of baking as croissants may already be a day old.

Pains au chocolat

LOW LACTOSE
FODMAP FRIENDLY
GLUTEN FREE

Makes: 8 pains au chocolat
Prep time: 30 minutes
Proofing time: overnight + 1-4 hours
Cook time: 25 minutes

1 quantity croissant pastry (page 44 for regular or page 158 for sourdough)
50-100 g 70% cocoa solids dark chocolate (I like to use buttons here so I can control how many I add to each pastry)

TO FINISH:
1 egg, lightly beaten

NOTES

Pastries keep well in an airtight container on the bench for 2–3 days but are best microwaved or steam baked after the first day.

Code for: another way for me talk about croissant dough. Sorry.

~~~~~~

1. Make the croissant dough as per instructions on pages 44-47, up to step 10. Once you have rolled out the rectangle of laminated dough, trim the edges. Then, cut dough lengthwise into 4 long rectangles and then across the centre, making 8 smaller rectangles.

2. Preheat oven to 180°C. Line a baking tray with baking paper.

3. Take the first rectangle of dough. With a short side facing you, arrange a thin line of chocolate horizontally across the dough, just above the bottom edge of the pastry. Don't be tempted to overstuff them with chocolate as it will just leak out the sides and burn.

4. Starting at the chocolate end, roll each pain au chocolat up into a log. Keep the roll reasonably tight so that chocolate doesn't spill out of the sides.

5. Proof the pains au chocolat for 1-4 hours, climate dependent, (see proofing notes on page 159) until doughy and puffy to the touch. Gently transfer to the prepared baking tray.

6. Brush pastry tops with beaten egg, being careful not to paint the exposed edges or you'll glue the layers together. Place in the fridge for 10-15 minutes to set the butter. Bake for 20-25 minutes or until golden and cooked through.

7. Transfer to a wire rack and set aside to cool for at least half an hour before eating. They can be eaten warm, but give the chocolate a little time to cool and the crumb time to set.

Custard danishes

LOW LACTOSE
FODMAP FRIENDLY
GLUTEN FREE

Makes: 12–15 danishes
Prep time: 30 minutes
Proofing time: overnight + 1–4 hours
Cook time: 20 minutes

Who me? Squeezing every last drop out of the croissant dough humanly possible? Absolutely. These danishes can also be made with the sourdough croissant recipe on page 158, finished as per the instructions here. You can use any sweet topping you can humanly conceive of, too, provided it meets your dietary requirements.

FOR THE DANISHES:

1 quantity croissant dough (page 44), rolled out to a 30cm × 45 cm rectangle on a sheet of baking paper

FOR THE CRÈME PATISSIERE:

180 ml (¾ cup) full-cream, lactose-free milk
30 g caster sugar
1 extra-large egg, plus 1 extra-large egg yolk
25 g gluten-free cornflour
25 g butter

TO FINISH:

1 egg, lightly beaten
2 punnets (250 g) raspberries or strawberries
2 tablespoons seedless raspberry or strawberry jam
1 tablespoon hot water

NOTES

Pastries are best eaten on the day they are made. Leftover pastries can be stored in an airtight container in the fridge. Reheat in the microwave or steam bake after first day.

1. Line 2 baking trays with baking paper. Cut the croissant dough rectangle into 9–12 even squares. Gently peel dough away from paper and place pastry squares on the prepared baking trays. Fold corners of each pastry square over and gently press to secure. You can also make opposing cuts in the corners of the pastry, then twist the ends over each other to create a fancy pastry border.

2. Place each baking tray in a giant ziplock bag and set aside to proof for 3–4 hours, climate dependent. See croissant recipe on page 159 for proofing suggestions tailored to different climates.

3. While the danishes are proofing, make the small batch crème patissiere as per instructions on page 96. Allow to cool completely before using.

4. Once pastries are fully proofed, preheat oven to 180°C. Take pastries out of ziplock bags and brush gently with beaten egg, being careful not to paint the exposed edges or you'll glue the layers together!

5. Spoon 1–2 teaspoons custard onto each pastry and top with berries. You can also add the berries fresh at the end, if you prefer. Bake for 20 minutes or until golden brown and cooked through. A little butter leakage is okay, but if there is a lot of butter on the tray there has been an issue with laminating or proofing. See the croissant troubleshooting (page 49) for more detail.

6. Transfer pastries to a wire rack to prevent bottoms from becoming soggy.

7. Mix the jam with a tablespoon of hot water to form a glaze. Brush the top of each danish with the glaze before serving.

Choux pastry

GUM FREE
FODMAP FRIENDLY
GLUTEN FREE
FREE FROM HIGH-STARCH FLOURS
 OPTION
LOW-LACTOSE OPTION

Makes: 7–8 eclairs or 10 cream puffs
Prep time: 15–20 minutes
Cook time: Depends on use

60 g fine white rice flour
10 g tapioca flour (or 10 g more white
 rice flour for option that is free from
 high-starch flours)
100–125 g eggs (2–3 extra-large eggs)
80 ml (⅓ cup) FODMAP-friendly milk of
 choice
80 ml (⅓ cup) water
50 g butter

Once you get into the swing of making choux pastry, it becomes kind of addictive. It never ceases to amaze me how a paste and some eggs can puff up in the oven to create such light and airy little morsels of deliciousness.

Choux pastry can be used to make eclairs (page 58) or cream puffs (page 61). And if you top your cream puffs with some melted chocolate, word is you have yourself a profiterole.

1. Preheat oven to 200°C. Line a baking tray with baking paper.

2. Place flour/s in a small bowl and whisk to combine. Weigh out your eggs into a small jug and whisk until well combined.

3. Combine milk, water and butter in a medium-sized saucepan and place over a medium heat. Allow the butter to melt. When the milk begins to bubble, add the flour and whisk vigorously until everything is well combined. It won't form a smooth paste like regular choux – it will look like dry mashed potatoes. Grab a wooden spoon and continue mixing over the heat for about 15–20 seconds to cook off some of the liquid. Remove from heat and allow to cool, so you don't scramble the eggs in the next step.

4. Add the egg a little at a time, stirring really well until each batch of egg incorporates. It will look like the egg will never amalgamate but keep mixing and I promise it will. Repeat with the next bit of egg.

5. The tricky thing with choux pastry is the amount of egg needed generally differs from batch to batch. The dough should look like stiff but silky mashed potatoes with a lot of cream. It should be a little shiny and still firm enough that it will hold shape when you pipe it. If in doubt, don't add more egg. Too much egg will result in flat discs of choux, as opposed to light puffs. Some batches will require the whole 125 g, some only 100 g (or less!). This depends on everything from the batches of flour to the humidity in your kitchen.

6. When you're happy with how your choux is looking, transfer to a piping bag or a ziplock bag with a tiny cut in a corner (which will be your piping nozzle). Pipe eight 10 cm x 3 cm (roughly) rectangular logs or 10 golf-ball-sized puffs onto prepared tray. I like to pipe a couple of layers to give them a bit of height. They should hopefully be holding their shape – if not, you might have added a bit too much egg (but bake them anyway!).

7. Bake for 15–20 minutes or until golden and puffed. Reduce oven temperature to 150°C, and bake for a further 10–20 minutes (or more) or until completely dry. The shells should be solid to the touch, not squishy or malleable. You might like to gently cover them with a piece of foil, tented so it doesn't touch the pastry, for the remaining time if they have turned sufficiently golden. Make sure there is space for air to circulate.

8. Remove the choux pastries from oven and use a skewer to quickly poke an air hole through the side of each pastry, stopping short of the other side. This will prevent pastries from collapsing as they cool. Allow pastries to cool completely on the tray. You are now ready to fill your choux pastry!

Eclairs

FODMAP FRIENDLY
GLUTEN FREE
LOW-LACTOSE OPTION

Makes: 8 eclairs
Prep time: 40 minutes
Cook time: 25–40 minutes

1 quantity choux pastry (page 56)

FOR THE CRÈME PATISSIERE FILLING
(alternatively use a batch of the
cream filling on page 61):
180 ml (¾ cup) full-cream, lactose-free
    milk
40–50 g caster sugar (use 50 g for a
    sweet tooth)
¼ teaspoon powdered agar agar
1 extra-large egg, plus 1 extra-large egg
    yolk
25 g gluten-free cornflour
25 g butter

FOR THE CHOCOLATE TOPPING:
100 g 70% cocoa solids dark chocolate
2 teaspoons coconut oil or butter

NOTES

Eclairs are best served on the
day of making but can be
stored in an airtight container
in the fridge for 1–2 days. You
can serve dusted with a little
icing sugar if you desire.

If you're partial to a very well
filled eclair, make double the
filling of your choice.

Will I win any awards for my choux pastry piping skills? No.
But will I be lauded for my chocolate icing finesse? Also no.
BUT am I just happy to be here, eating my body weight in
homemade-looking eclairs? Absolutely.

~~~~~~~

1. Prepare the crème patissiere following the instructions on
   page 96. Cover and place in fridge to completely cool.

2. Make a batch of choux pastry following instructions on page
   56, piping rectangular logs in step 6.

3. Preheat oven to 200°C. Line a large baking tray with baking
   paper. Grease the tray very lightly to stop the baking paper
   slipping as you pipe. Pipe eight 10 cm × 3 cm (roughly)
   rectangular logs onto the prepared tray. I like to pipe a couple
   of layers to give them a bit of height. They should hopefully
   be holding their shape; if not, you might have added a bit too
   much egg (but bake them anyway!).

4. Bake for 15–20 minutes or until golden and puffed.
   Reduce oven temperature to 150°C, and bake for a further
   10–20 minutes or until completely dry. You might like to
   lightly tent them with a piece of foil for the additional oven
   time if they have turned sufficiently golden. Make sure there is
   room for air to circulate.

5. Remove pastries from oven and, working quickly, use a skewer
   to poke an air hole on the side of each, stopping short of the
   other side. This will prevent pastries from collapsing as they
   cool. Allow pastries to cool completely on the tray.

6. Using a sharp, non-serrated knife, cut 2 holes in the bottom
   of each eclair. You'll use them to pipe in the crème patissiere.
   Leave space between, so the bottom of the eclair doesn't
   collapse. You can also simply slice each eclair lengthways and
   sandwich the filling between the pieces.

7. Spoon the crème patissiere into your piping bag and pipe into
   each hole until the eclair begins to puff up a little. Repeat until
   you have used all the pastry cream and eclair cases.

8. To make the chocolate topping, place chocolate and coconut oil in a heatproof bowl over a saucepan of simmering water, ensuring the bowl does not touch the water. Cook, stirring until chocolate is melted and smooth. Remove from heat. Dip the top side of each eclair in the melted chocolate and allow excess chocolate to drip off while inverted. Flip right-side up and place on a wire rack until chocolate has set.

9. Place the chocolate-covered eclair lids back onto their bases and serve. Eclairs are best eaten on the day of baking (see notes).

Cream puffs

GUM FREE
FODMAP FRIENDLY
GLUTEN FREE
LOW-LACTOSE OPTION

Makes: 10 cream puffs
Prep time: 30 minutes
Cook time: 25–40 minutes

The chef's kiss was invented for the glorious combination of light, airy pastry and subtly sweetened whipped cream, as far as I'm concerned.

Make sure you buy lactose-free whipping cream for this recipe – pouring cream won't whip. You can also use regular cream if you have no lactose concerns, or whipped coconut cream for a dairy-free option.

~~~~~~

1 quantity choux pastry (page 56)

FOR THE CREAM:

250 ml full-cream, lactose-free
    whipping cream
2 tablespoons pure icing sugar, sifted
½ teaspoon vanilla bean paste

OR

400 ml can coconut cream, refrigerated
    overnight before use
2 tablespoons pure icing sugar, sifted
1 teaspoon vanilla bean paste

TO FINISH:

icing sugar, to dust

1. Prepare the choux pastry as per instructions on page 56. When you get to step 6, pipe the pastry into 10 golf-ball-sized rounds. Bake following recipe instructions and set aside to cool completely.

2. To prepare the filling, using hand beaters, beat all ingredients for your chosen cream filling in a large bowl until soft peaks form. Set aside.

3. Transfer cream mixture to a piping bag. Use a sharp knife to cut a small hole in the bottom of each cooled pastry. You can also simply slice them in half and sandwich the filling.

4. Pipe some cream mixture into a pastry until it noticeably puffs up. Repeat with remaining puffs and cream. Dust with a little icing sugar to serve.

NOTES

Cream puffs are best eaten on the day you make them.

If you use the dairy-free coconut-cream option, make sure you choose a brand that doesn't contain inulin.

SWEET PASTRY

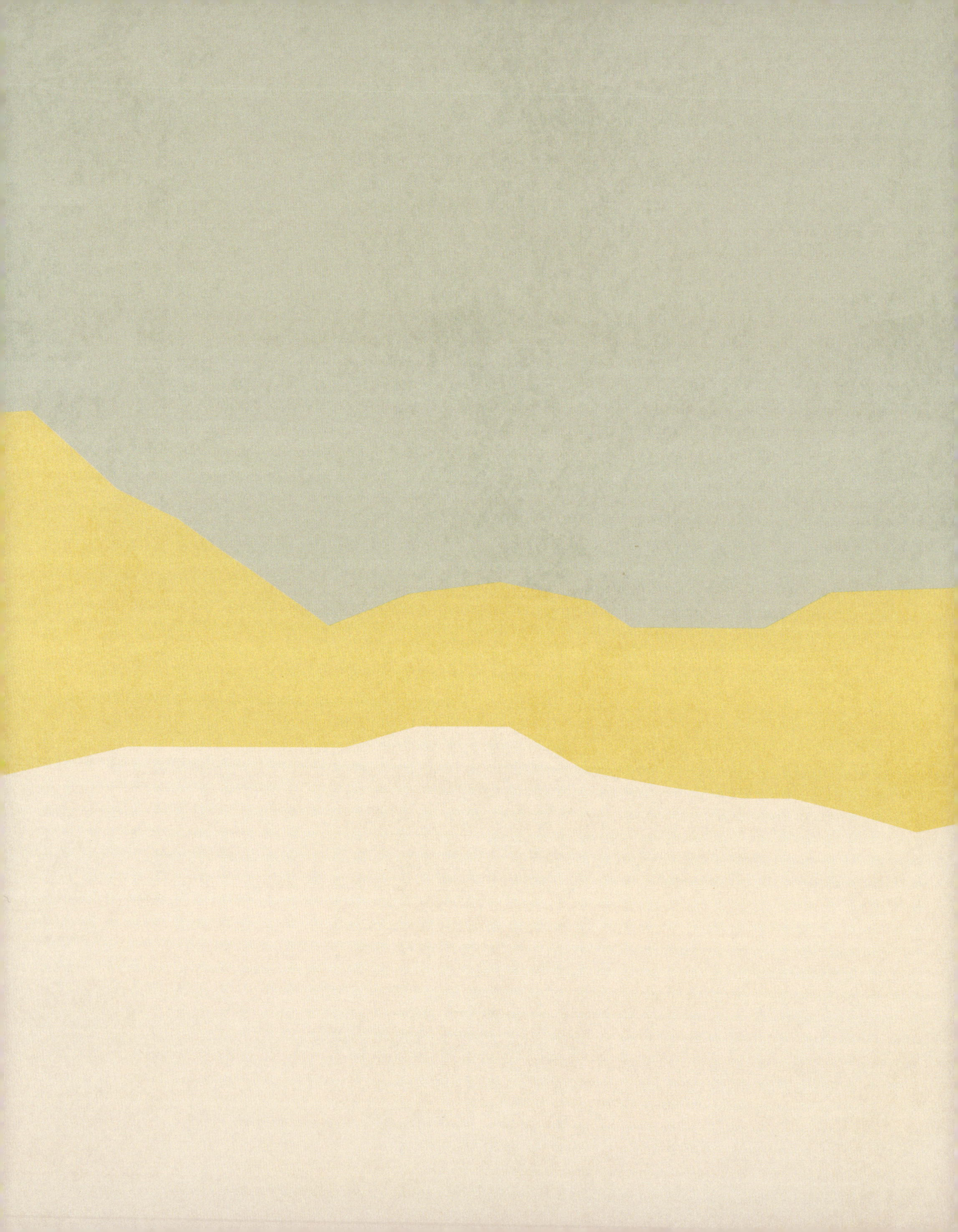

CHAPTER THREE

Sweet bakes

PAGES 63–77

Chocolate babka

FODMAP FRIENDLY
GLUTEN FREE

Serves: 8–10
Prep time: 45 minutes
Proofing time: overnight + 1–2 hours
Cook time: 1 hour

Because Elaine and Jerry were right – chocolate babka is the superior babka.

As you know by now, I don't throw xanthan gum into just anything. Its inclusion here is purposeful and extends beyond just giving the dough a bit of elasticity. Firstly, it holds the dough together so that it's easier (though not strictly easy) to form into a babka log. Secondly, it turns the dough from a soupy egg mixture into a viscous dough that is able to hold more liquid and fats, leading to a softer brioche.

~~~~~~

Oil for greasing

FOR THE BRIOCHE DOUGH:

80 ml (⅓ cup) warm full-cream, lactose-free milk or FODMAP-friendly milk of choice
7.5 g (1 sachet) dried yeast
125 g caster sugar + 1 teaspoon for the yeast mixture
160 g (1 cup) fine white rice flour
90 g (¾ cup) tapioca flour
1 teaspoon gluten-free baking powder
¼ teaspoon fine salt
2 tablespoons psyllium husk
1 teaspoon xanthan gum
4 extra-large eggs, at room temperature
150 g butter, softened and roughly chopped
1 teaspoon vanilla bean paste (optional)

FOR THE CHOCOLATE FILLING:

75 g butter
75 g 70% cocoa solids dark chocolate
40 g (¼ cup) pure icing sugar
1 tablespoon unsweetened cocoa powder (I used Dutch processed)

FOR THE SYRUP GLAZE:

2 tablespoons water
2 tablespoons caster sugar
pinch of ground cinnamon (optional)

THE NIGHT BEFORE:

1. Combine the warm milk, yeast and extra teaspoon of caster sugar in a small bowl and whisk to combine. Set aside for 10 minutes until the mixture is bubbling and foamy. If you have no action after 10 minutes, start again with new yeast.

2. Meanwhile, combine flours, remaining sugar, baking powder, salt, psyllium and xanthan gum in the bowl of your stand mixer. Add the yeast mixture and use the paddle attachment to mix the dough on low speed to combine. Add eggs one at a time, mixing well after each addition. The mixture should look like a stiff bread dough at this point.

3. With the speed on low, gradually add the chunks of soft butter until well combined. The mixture should be a light blond in colour and relatively thick yet fluffy. Add the vanilla bean paste, if using, and mix one last time to combine.

4. Cover mixture with plastic film and transfer to the fridge overnight. This will allow it to rise slowly and develop flavour. It will also firm up overnight, making it easier to roll out in the morning.

RECIPE CONTINUES >

THE NEXT MORNING:

5. To make the chocolate filling, place the butter and chocolate in a small heatproof bowl over a saucepan of simmering water, ensuring the base of the bowl is not touching the water. Cook, stirring occasionally, until the mixture is melted and combined. Whisk in the icing sugar and cocoa. Remove from heat.

6. Lightly grease a 21.5 cm x 11.5 cm (base measurement) steel loaf pan with butter. Grease a large piece of baking paper, roughly 40 cm long, with a scant 1 teaspoon of oil. Place the chilled babka dough on the paper. Lightly oil your hands and press or roll it out in a large rectangle.

7. The size of the rectangle isn't super important. I normally aim for approximately the size of the sheet of baking paper. Make sure the dough is reasonably thin (roughly ½–1 cm) but without any holes. Using the back of a spoon, spread the chocolate filling over the dough, leaving a small 1 cm margin on both long sides of the rectangle.

8. Turn the rectangle so 1 long side of the dough is facing you. Use the baking paper to lift the dough up over itself to start rolling up the log. Continue rolling the dough over itself until you're about 80% of the way there, then start rolling the section furthest away from you back over the log. Press to seal the seam, and then roll the log so the seam is on the bottom.

9. This dough is necessarily fragile and wet, so just do your best. Patch up any holes as best you can and know that babka always comes out gorgeous, irrespective of any hiccups along the way.

10. Use a sharp, well-oiled knife to cut the log in half lengthways and gently turn each piece so the chocolate is facing upwards. Some people like to refrigerate the log before doing this, but I find it's best to rip the band-aid off and get it done. The dough tends to break if the chocolate solidifies with refrigeration.

11. Cross the top ends of each log over each other, then continue intertwining them until you reach the end and have a braid. Shunt it in at the ends to condense the braid. As best you can (speed helps here) scoop under each end of the babka and plop it into the prepared loaf pan. Don't worry if it's a bit of a mess, it will still look glorious baked. Place in a ziplock bag and set aside to proof once more for 1–2 hours, season dependent.

12. 20 minutes before the babka is proofed, preheat oven to 180°C. When ready, remove from ziplock, lightly tent with foil and bake for 1 hour, or until deeply golden and still slightly soft to touch without feeling squidgy.

13. While you're waiting, prepare the sugar syrup. Combine sugar, water and cinnamon, if using, in a small saucepan and cook over a medium heat for 2–3 minutes or until sugar is dissolved and mixture becomes syrupy. Remove from heat.

14. When the babka is ready, remove it from the oven. Drizzle with the sugar syrup. Set aside to cool in pan for 20 minutes before running a knife around the edge and transferring to a wire rack. You can serve the babka warm from the oven, or it keeps well for 1–2 days in an airtight container. Any leftovers are best gently reheated in the microwave or a steamy, low-temperature oven.

Scones for everyone

LACTOSE FREE
EGG FREE
VEGAN
FODMAP FRIENDLY
GLUTEN FREE
GUM-FREE OPTION

Makes: 5–6 large scones
Prep time: 35 minutes
Chilling time: 25–30 minutes
Cook time: 25 minutes

160 g (1 cup) fine white rice flour
60 g (½ cup) glutinous rice flour
60 g (½ cup) potato starch
3 teaspoons gluten-free baking powder
½ teaspoon bicarbonate of soda
½ teaspoon xanthan gum or 2 teaspoons
    psyllium husk powder
40 g caster sugar
100 g plant-based butter (I used
    Nuttelex Buttery), cubed and chilled in
    freezer for 30 minutes
180–250 ml (¾–1 cup) FODMAP-
    friendly, plant-based milk of choice
    (see notes)
1 tablespoon white vinegar

TO FINISH:

1 tablespoon FODMAP-friendly plant-
    based milk mixed with 2 teaspoons
    pure maple syrup (see notes)
jam and whipped coconut cream
    (see page 61), to serve

There's a time and a place for recipes that avoid high-starch flours. Vegan, gluten-free scones are not one of those times or those places. Second only to croissants, scones have been my biggest challenge to date. While I'm happy to say I've cracked the case, I recommend sticking to the flours suggested. The glutinous rice flour and potato starch work like a charm to create a light and fluffy scone without spreading. This recipe also works well with regular butter and milk and a regular egg wash – the butter will only need to chill for 10 minutes or so before proceeding with the recipe.

~~~~~~

1. Preheat oven to 180°C. Line the base and side of a 20 cm (base measurement) round cake tin with baking paper.

2. Place the flours, baking powder, bicarbonate of soda, xanthan gum or psyllium husk and caster sugar in a large bowl and whisk to combine.

3. Using your fingertips, rub in the chilled butter until mixture resembles coarse crumbs.

4. In a small bowl, combine 180 ml milk and vinegar to form a buttermilk. Add the buttermilk to the flour mixture and stir to combine. The flour should be completely hydrated and the dough a little sticky. Add a little extra milk if required. Transfer the bowl of dough to fridge for 15–20 minutes to set the butter.

5. Lightly flour a clean, dry work surface with tapioca flour. Place dough on surface and use your hands to form a flat oval, about 7 cm x 10–15 cm long.

6. Using a 7-cm round cookie or scone cutter, cut 5–6 scones from dough, pushing the cutter straight down into the dough (don't twist), and flouring the cutter between scones. Alternatively, simply cut dough into 6 wedges. Transfer scones to prepared tin. Keeping them snug will help them to rise instead of spread.

7. Transfer scones to freezer for 10 minutes to firm up the butter one last time. Brush the scones with vegan egg wash and bake for 25 minutes or until golden and cooked through. Set aside to cool in tin for 10 minutes before serving. They're fragile while hot, so be careful! Best served within a few hours of baking and with lashings of jam and coconut cream.

NOTES

How much milk you add to your scone dough depends on the absorbency of your flours, your chosen butter and binder, and how you like your scones. If you prefer a drier scone that holds its shape, use less milk. If you like a soft and fluffy scone, use more.

For a vegan egg wash, combine 1–2 tablespoons plant-based milk with 2 teaspoons pure maple syrup (the sugar will caramelise in the oven and brown like an egg wash would). If you don't want to use maple syrup, plain milk is fine too.

NOTES

These buns keep well in an airtight container on the bench or in the fridge for 2–3 days. They can also be frozen and defrosted.

Hot cross buns

LACTOSE FREE
FREE FROM HIGH-STARCH FLOURS
GUM FREE
EGG FREE
VEGAN
FODMAP FRIENDLY
GLUTEN FREE

Makes: 8–9 buns
Prep time: 20 minutes
Proofing time: overnight + 1 hour
Cook time: 30 minutes

60 ml (¼ cup) FODMAP-friendly plant-
   based milk of choice, warm
1 teaspoon sugar (any type)
7.5 g (1 sachet) dried yeast
160 g (1 cup) fine brown rice flour
120 g (¾ cup) buckwheat flour
1 ½ tablespoons ground cinnamon
1 tablespoon ground nutmeg
150 g light or dark brown sugar
20 g psyllium husk
finely grated zest of 1 orange
125 ml (½ cup) olive or vegetable oil
500 ml (2 cups) water

FOR THE ADD-INS:

2 tablespoons good quality dried peel
2 tablespoons dairy-free chocolate chips
few sprigs of finely chopped rosemary
   (optional)

FOR THE CROSSES:

1 tablespoon tapioca flour
2 teaspoons buckwheat flour
½ teaspoon oil of choice
water, as needed to form a thick but
   flowing paste

FOR THE GLAZE:

pure maple syrup, or marmalade, melted

Year after year, the social media posts decrying how early the hot cross buns have landed in supermarkets leave me feeling deprived. That ends this year! While I didn't initially set out to create a vegan bun, I found they were the best of the bunch by happy coincidence. Using water and oil allows the spices to shine and keeps the buns moist for days.

~~~~~~

THE NIGHT BEFORE:

1. Place the warm milk and sugar in a small bowl and whisk to combine. Sprinkle over the yeast and set aside for 10 minutes, until the mixture is bubbling and foamy. If you have no action after 10 minutes, start again with new yeast.

2. Place flours, spices, brown sugar, psyllium and orange zest in a large bowl and whisk to combine. Add the activated yeast mixture, oil and water, whisking until smooth. Don't panic at how wet the dough looks – the psyllium husk will firm it up overnight. Cover and refrigerate overnight.

THE NEXT MORNING:

3. After the fridge rest, the dough should look spongy and be borderline wet. Stir in your add-in ingredients. Using oiled hands, divide mixture into 8 or 9 portions and quickly roll into balls. Place buns in a 20 x 30 cm baking dish, lightly greased or lined, or on a lined baking tray. Buns baked on a tray will lose more shape, but still taste delicious. Cover and leave to proof in a warm draught-free place for 1 hour, or until they have tangibly risen and feel light and puffy to the touch.

4. Preheat oven to 180°C. To make the crosses, combine flours and oil in a small bowl. Add enough water to make a thick but flowing paste. Transfer mixture to a piping bag. Pipe crosses onto the buns using even pressure and motion. I go for the 'homemade' look, as you can tell.

5. Bake buns for 25–30 minutes, or until lightly browned and baked through. Remove from oven and glaze with maple syrup or marmalade while still hot. Allow to cool for 10–15 minutes before eating.

Burnt Basque cheesecake

LACTOSE FREE
GUM FREE
FREE FROM HIGH-STARCH FLOURS
GRAIN FREE
FODMAP FRIENDLY
GLUTEN FREE

Serves: 8–10
Prep time: 25 minutes
Cook time: 40–60 minutes

1 kg lactose-free, full-fat cream cheese
4 extra-large eggs
250 ml (1 cup) lactose-free cream
275 g (1 ¼ cups) caster sugar
  (see notes)
pinch of fine salt
2–3 teaspoons vanilla bean paste
  (optional)
2–3 teaspoons lemon juice (optional)

Basque-style cheesecake is a straightforward yet impressive variety that hails from San Sebastian, Spain. It utilises high heat to form a deeply caramelised crust on both the top and bottom of the cheesecake. With the advent of lactose-free dairy, there's no reason why this delicacy can't be FODMAP friendly. Generally, a Basque cheesecake uses a bit of flour to stabilise the cream cheese, but I didn't find it necessary here. On the question of necessity, a note on the vanilla bean paste and lemon juice: they're optional and not in any way traditional, but I think they add a lovely complexity of flavour.

~~~~~~~

1. Allow the cream cheese, eggs and cream to come to room temperature before you begin. Soft cream cheese is essential for a smooth cheesecake.

2. Preheat oven to 220°C. Line a 24 cm (base measurement) round springform tin with 2 large overlapping pieces of baking paper, allowing excess to overhang and form handles. It can help to scrunch up the pieces of paper, so they sit compliantly in the tin.

3. Place cream cheese in a large bowl or bowl of your stand mixer. Using electric beaters or a stand mixer with paddle attachment, beat on medium–low speed until smooth. Add the sugar and continue beating until sugar has dissolved, scraping down sides of the bowl with a spatula as you go.

4. On low speed, add eggs one at a time, beating well after each addition. Scrape down bowl as necessary. Add cream, salt and optional flavourings. Scrape down bowl one last time before mixing until smooth.

RECIPE CONTINUES >

Everyone's oven is a little different, so it's important to keep an eye on your cheesecake and turn the heat down as necessary.

So too is everyone's cheesecake preference – if you prefer custardy innards, you can cook it for less than the specified time. Personally, I prefer to make my cheesecake the night before and allow it to firm up in the fridge before eating.

If you don't have a sweet tooth, you can drop the sugar back to 1 cup.

Cheesecake can be stored in an airtight container in the fridge for 2–3 days.

5. Pour batter into prepared tin. Gently bang pan against the benchtop to remove any bubbles. Place tin on a baking tray and bake for 40 minutes to 1 hour (see notes), checking every so often to ensure top is not browning too quickly. If it is, lower the heat a little or gently tent the cheesecake with foil and continue cooking. The cheesecake is cooked when the top is caramelised but there is still a bit of jiggle in the centre.

6. Turn the oven off and leave the cheesecake to cool with the door ajar. If you've tented the cheesecake with foil, make sure it has some air circulation so it doesn't sweat. Leave the cheesecake to cool, a few hours or up to overnight. You can easily serve this cheesecake as a standalone dessert, but it also works nicely with some berries.

Cheesecake with Graham cracker–style base

LOW LACTOSE
FREE FROM HIGH-STARCH FLOURS
GUM FREE
FODMAP FRIENDLY
GLUTEN FREE

Serves: 8–10
Prep time: 30 minutes
Cook time: 1 hour 30 minutes

With all due respect to myself and my previous cheesecake recipes, an almond meal base will never beat a Graham cracker base. That's why this version riffs on a Graham cracker recipe I developed. The toasted quinoa flour combines with the cinnamon to create a nutty, oat-like taste that I just can't get enough of.

Make sure your dairy ingredients are truly room temperature. This will avert disaster in the form of cold, lumpy cream cheese and a lumpy cheesecake. For this cheesecake you will need a 24 cm springform tin.

~~~~~~~~

FOR THE BASE:

100 g butter, softened
110 g (½ cup) caster sugar
80 g (½ cup) fine white rice flour
40 g (¼ cup + 1 tablespoon) toasted quinoa flour (see notes)
½ teaspoon ground cinnamon

FOR THE CHEESECAKE:

1 kg lactose-free, full-fat cream cheese, at room temperature
275 g (1 ¼ cups) caster sugar
4 extra-large eggs, at room temperature
250 ml (1 cup) lactose-free cream
1–2 teaspoons vanilla bean paste or extract (optional)
1 tablespoon lemon juice (optional)

1. Preheat the oven to 170°C. Grease and line base of a 24 cm (base measurement) round springform tin with baking paper.

2. To make the base, using electric beaters or a stand mixer with paddle attachment, beat butter and sugar in a medium bowl until light and fluffy. I find this highly dependent on the season and the temperature of the butter. The hotter the butter and kitchen, the faster it creams. Persist until you achieve the right consistency – it can take up to 15 minutes. Scrape down the bowl as often as necessary.

3. Combine flours and cinnamon in a medium bowl. Once the butter is creamed, add flour mixture to the butter mixture on a low speed. Scrape down the sides of the bowl and increase the speed to high. Beat until mixture starts to ball up. It should come together in chunky crumbs and shouldn't look dry.

RECIPE CONTINUES >

4. Press mixture into prepared tin and press firmly to form an even layer. Prick base with a fork to allow any trapped air to escape. Bake for 25–30 minutes or until golden brown. The base might feel soft but will firm up as it cools. Remove from oven and set aside to cool while you make the cheesecake.

5. To make the filling, place cream cheese in a large bowl or bowl of your stand mixer. Using electric beaters or a stand mixer with paddle attachment, beat cream cheese on low speed until smooth. Add sugar and continue to beat for a further 2–3 minutes or sugar has dissolved.

6. Scrape down sides and base of bowl with a spatula to ensure there are no lumps on the bottom. Add eggs one at a time, beating well and scraping down bowl after each addition. Add the cream and vanilla and lemon if you're using them, and beat on low speed until well combined.

7. Pour the smooth filling over the prepared base. Bake for 40 minutes to 1 hour or until sides are set but the middle is still slightly wobbly and the top is lightly golden.

8. Turn off the oven and leave the door ajar or open. Allow the cheesecake to cool slowly in the oven until it reaches room temperature. Slow cooling will help prevent the top of your cheesecake cracking. I find running a knife around the edge of the cheesecake after baking helps prevent cracking as it cools. For best results, make the cheesecake the night before (or the morning of) and allow it to set in the fridge after cooling.

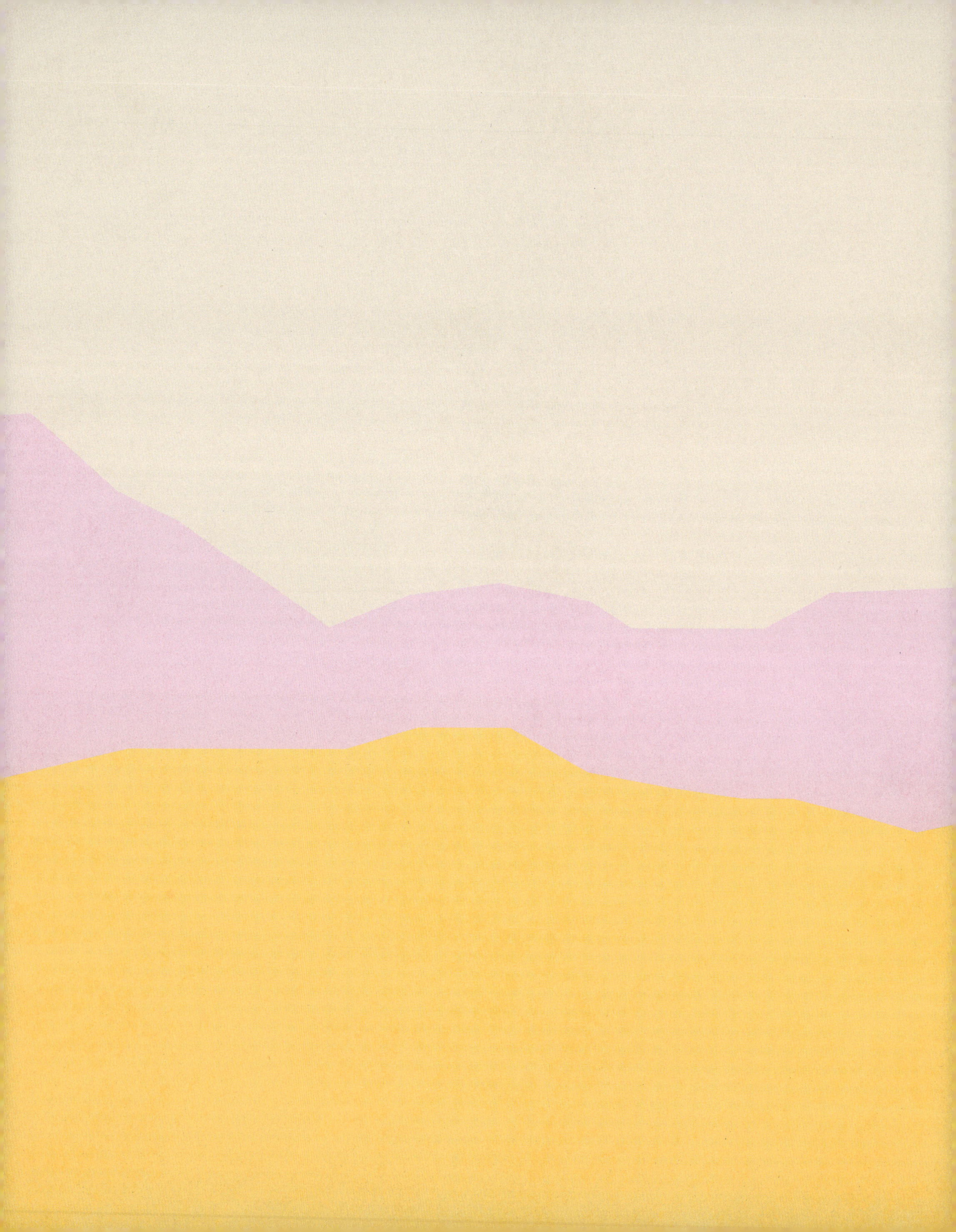

CHAPTER FOUR

Pies, tarts and puddings

Strawberry and rhubarb cobbler

LOW LACTOSE
FODMAP FRIENDLY
GLUTEN FREE

Serves: 8–10
Prep time: 45 minutes
Chilling time: 15–20 minutes
Cook time: 30 minutes

Consider this my petition to make the cobbler ubiquitous in the Australian dessert repertoire. A fruit pie topped with mini scone-like pastries – what's not to love? I am a strawberry fiend forever, but feel free to play around with a fruit that you enjoy or that's in season. Berries and rhubarb are generally the most FODMAP-friendly fruits.

~~~

FOR THE TOPPING:

120 g (1 cup) tapioca flour, plus extra
   to dust
120 g (¾ cup) fine white rice flour
2 teaspoons gluten-free baking powder
55 g (¼ cup) caster sugar
100 g chilled butter, cut into cubes
1 extra-large egg, lightly beaten
125 ml (½ cup + 1 tablespoon) full-
   cream, lactose-free cream
pinch of salt

FOR THE FILLING:

500 g fresh or frozen strawberries, hulled
   and chopped into bite-sized pieces
500 g rhubarb, chopped into bite-size
   pieces
2–3 tablespoons caster sugar
juice of 1 lemon
1–2 tablespoons gluten-free cornflour
   (see notes)
pinch of salt

TO FINISH:

1 egg, lightly beaten
granulated sugar, to sprinkle
lactose-free cream or ice-cream, to serve

1. To make the topping, combine the flours, baking powder, sugar and a pinch of salt in a large bowl. Using your fingertips, rub butter into flour mixture until it resembles coarse crumbs. Add the egg and stir to combine. Add the cream, 60 ml (¼ cup) at a time. Gently stir to combine after each addition. You don't want to crush the small chunks of butter, as they create flakiness. Once most of the cream has been incorporated (you might not need the last tablespoon), use your hands to gently bring the dough together into a ball. If the butter melts, transfer dough to the fridge for 10 minutes to firm it up.

2. Dust a clean work surface with extra flour. Place dough on surface and gently mould with your hands to form a rectangle, about 3 cm thick, dusting with extra flour as required.

3. Preheat oven to 200°C. Line a large baking tray with baking paper.

4. Using a 3–4 cm round cutter (see notes) cut 18–24 small rounds of dough, each about the size of a 50 cent piece. Continue flouring the cutter, reshaping and re-cutting until you have used all the dough. Place rounds on prepared tray and place in fridge or freezer for 15–20 minutes to firm up the butter.

RECIPE CONTINUES >

5. Meanwhile, to make the filling, place the chopped strawberries and rhubarb in a large bowl. Sprinkle over sugar and a pinch of salt and stir gently to combine. Set aside to macerate for 2–3 minutes. Stir in lemon juice. Add cornflour and toss to combine.

6. Transfer fruit mixture to a 28 cm/1.6 litre capacity baking dish. Brush chilled scones with beaten egg and arrange, in a close-knit pattern, over the fruit. Sprinkle the top with granulated sugar and bake for 10 minutes at 200°C, then reduce to 180°C and bake for a further 20 minutes or until the top is golden and the fruit bubbling.

7. Set aside to cool for 5–10 minutes before serving with lactose-free cream or ice-cream.

Not quite baklava

FODMAP FRIENDLY
GLUTEN FREE
LOW LACTOSE

Makes: 20 baklava pieces
Prep time: 30 minutes
Cook time: 1 hour

When I was at university, I ordered a small plate of baklava from a bakery on Sydney Road over the phone. Apparently, there was a misunderstanding because I turned up to a giant, family-sized tray with my name on it. Too awkward and embarrassed to correct the error, I dutifully paid for my 'entertaining platter' and spent the next week dining solely on baklava.

This recipe is my ode to that week of baklava. I couldn't quite make a gluten-free filo happen, so this not quite baklava recipe lacks the discernible pastry layers of the original version. It hits all the other notes, though; honeyed, buttery, rich and easily consumed for a week straight.

I have tried both varieties of puff pastry here and I find the xanthan gum version (regular or rough puff) works best. This is mainly because it is easier to roll into fine pieces and transfer into a baking dish.

1 quantity puff pastry or rough puff
   (pages 166 or 168)
tapioca flour, for dusting
100 g butter, melted

FOR THE NUT MIX:

300 g (3 cups) walnuts (see notes)
55 g (¼ cup) caster sugar
1 ½ tablespoons ground cinnamon
¾ teaspoon ground cloves

FOR THE SYRUP:

55 g (¼ cup) caster sugar
2–3 cloves
zest of ½ lemon (optional)
125 ml (½ cup) water
90 g (¼ cup) honey (see notes)

TO FINISH:

1 egg, lightly beaten

1. Prepare your pastry as per instructions on page 166 or 168. Once laminated, divide dough into 2 pieces. Cover with plastic film and refrigerate while you prepare the filling.

2. Process walnuts in a food processor until finely chopped. Place in a medium bowl, then add the sugar, cinnamon and cloves and stir to combine. Set aside.

3. Preheat oven to 200°C. Line the base of a 26 cm × 16 cm (base measurement) baking dish with baking paper.

4. Roll out the first piece of pastry to make 2 rectangles, the size of your baking dish. Lay 1 pastry rectangle in the base of prepared dish. If it breaks, just patch it as best you can. Brush the pastry liberally with melted butter and top with half the nut mixture. Repeat with remaining pastry rectangle, brush with some more melted butter and top with remaining nut mixture.

RECIPE CONTINUES >

Baklava keeps well, covered, in the fridge for several days.

I chose to use only walnuts in this baklava because I felt the FODMAP waters became too muddy with a mix of nuts. Traditionally, walnuts, pistachios and almonds are used, but I have had pine nuts in baklava too.

It is worth nothing that, contrary to popular belief, baklava doesn't actually contain a lot of honey. A small, FODMAP-friendly amount is added to the syrup for that rich and delicious baklava flavour. If you really don't want to use honey, you could try rice malt syrup, but it won't be quite the same.

5. Roll out second piece of pastry to make another 2 rectangles, the size of your baking dish. Add the first rectangle, then pour the remaining melted butter over the top. It might seem like a lot of butter, but it will seep into the nut layer during baking and make a beautifully decadent baklava.

6. Add the final layer of pastry and press down lightly to secure it to the butter layer. Brush the pastry with egg wash, then use a sharp, non-serrated knife to slice through the top 2 layers of pastry to create square or diamond baklava.

7. Bake for 20 minutes. Reduce oven temperature to 180°C and cook for a further 30–40 minutes, or until golden and crispy.

8. Meanwhile, to make the syrup, combine the sugar, cloves, lemon zest and water in a small saucepan. Cook, stirring, over a medium heat until sugar has dissolved and syrup has thickened slightly. Remove from heat and stir in honey. Transfer to fridge to cool.

9. Slowly pour the cooled syrup over the top of the hot baklava, letting it absorb before adding more. Allow baklava to cool completely before slicing and serving.

Tiramisu

LOW LACTOSE
FODMAP FRIENDLY
GLUTEN FREE

Serves: 6–8
Prep time: 1 hour
Cook time: 30–40 minutes

Tiramisu: because if cream, carbs, coffee and booze can't lift your spirits, there's probably not much that will. Tiramisu traditionally uses mascarpone and whipped eggs for the creamy layer and rum or Marsala for the alcohol. This version uses lactose-free whipping cream, gin or a FODMAP-friendly spirit of your choice, and gluten-free savoiardi to keep the FODMAP content low.

~~~~~~~

FOR THE SAVOIARDI:
(makes 30–40 biscuits)

4 extra-large eggs, separated
110 g (½ cup) caster sugar
1 teaspoon vanilla bean paste
80 g (½ cup) fine white rice flour
60 g (½ cup) tapioca flour
50 g (½ cup) almond meal
40 g (¼ cup) icing sugar (to finish)

FOR THE COFFEE MIXTURE:

125 ml (½ cup) fresh espresso coffee
2–3 tablespoons gin or FODMAP-friendly
  spirit of choice
310 ml (1 ¼ cups) hot water

FOR THE CREAM MIXTURE:

500 g (2 tubs) full-cream, lactose-free
  whipping cream
80 g (½ cup) pure icing sugar

TO FINISH:

70% cocoa solids dark chocolate, to grate
unsweetened cocoa powder, to dust

1. Preheat oven to 180°C. Line 2 large baking trays with baking paper. I like to lightly oil the trays first so the paper doesn't move when I pipe. Place flours in a small bowl and whisk to combine. Combine egg yolks, 55 g (¼ cup) caster sugar and the vanilla bean paste in a large bowl or stand mixer. Using electric beaters, beat on high speed until light and fluffy, about 5–10 minutes.

2. Place egg whites in a separate clean, dry bowl. Using clean electric beaters, beat until the whites become frothy, then gradually add the remaining caster sugar. Beat until stiff peaks form. Gently fold half the egg yolk mixture into the egg white mixture. Repeat with remaining half until just combined. Gently fold flour mixture into egg mixture until just combined.

3. Place your piping bag in a tall glass, and spoon mixture into the bag. I generally use a ziplock bag with a 2 cm hole cut in one corner. Twist the top to seal. Pipe mixture onto prepared trays to create roughly 10 cm × 3 cm biscuits. Sprinkle with icing sugar.

4. Bake savoiardi for 8 minutes, then swap the trays and bake for another 5 minutes. Turn the oven down to 150°C and bake for another 10 minutes or until the savoiardi are crisp or tops are golden. Set aside to cool completely on trays.

5. To make coffee mixture, combine all ingredients in a wide, shallow bowl. Set aside.

6. To make the cream mixture, combine cream and icing sugar in a large bowl and, using electric beaters, beat until light and fluffy.

NOTES

This recipe for savoiardi should make close to 40 biscuits, which is the perfect quantity for a 1.6 litre/28 cm dish. I have found that savoiardi batter often varies in the amount of biscuits it yields. I recommend keeping enough ingredients for another batch on hand, just in case. If your batch comes out with significantly fewer, make another half or whole batch to avoid getting caught out later. They keep well in an airtight container and are delicious dipped in espresso.

Tiramisu is best served the next day, when the flavours have had a chance to meld and the cream has set nicely. Leftover tiramisu keeps, covered, in the fridge for 1–2 days, if you can restrain yourself for that long.

7. Quickly soak one savoiardi at a time in the coffee liquor mixture. The crunchier the savoiardi, the longer you can leave them to soak. Arrange the soaked savoiardi in the base of a 1.6 litre capacity serving dish.

8. Once you have completely covered the base of the dish, top the savoiardi with half the cream mixture. It is more important to completely cover the top of the tiramisu (for aesthetics, anyway) so make sure you save enough for that.

9. Top the cream layer with a generous grating of dark chocolate (I like to use a microplane). I think this chocolate layer makes the difference between an okay tiramisu and an amazing one. Repeat with another layer of savoiardi (any leftover coffee mixture can be drizzled over the biscuits here) and then carefully spread over the remaining cream mixture. Finish with a super generous grating of the dark chocolate and dust with cocoa powder. Cover and refrigerate until ready to serve (see notes).

IF *cream, carbs,*
coffee AND *booze*
CAN'T LIFT YOUR *spirits,*
THERE'S PROBABLY
not much that will.

Molten chocolate cakes

LOW LACTOSE
GUM FREE
GRAIN FREE
FODMAP FRIENDLY
GLUTEN FREE

Makes: 6 cakes
Prep time: 20 minutes
Cook time: 12-15 minutes

150 g 70% cocoa solids dark chocolate
100 g butter
3 extra-large eggs
100 g caster sugar
¼ teaspoon fine salt, sieved
2 tablespoons unsweetened cocoa
   powder (I used Dutch processed),
   sieved, plus extra for the ramekins

NOTES

Cakes are best on the day of baking but can be stored in an airtight container in the fridge for 1–2 days. Gently reheat them in the microwave or a steamy oven to serve.

I might be an ~adult~ now, but the childlike wonder of watching someone spoon into a molten chocolate cake will never die, as far as I am concerned. These rich single-serving cakes are gluten free and grain free, which comes in handy when catering for a variety of dietary requirements at once.

1. Preheat oven to 180°C. Lightly grease six 8.5 cm (¾ cup capacity) ramekins or moulds. Dust them with cocoa to help prevent the cakes from sticking.

2. Place the chocolate and butter in a small heatproof bowl over a saucepan of simmering water, ensuring the base of the bowl is not touching the water. Cook, stirring occasionally, until melted and combined. Add the sieved salt and cocoa powder and stir into chocolate. Set aside to cool.

3. Place the eggs and caster sugar in a medium-sized clean, dry bowl. Using electric beaters or stand mixer with whisk attachment, beat until the mixture is pale yellow, light and foamy, about 5 minutes. Add a spoonful of the chocolate mixture to loosen egg mixture. Use a spatula to gently fold in remaining chocolate mixture until almost homogenous. A few little bits of egg are okay. Better to under-incorporate than to remove all the air.

4. Divide mixture between prepared ramekins (they will each be about half full) and place on a baking tray. Bake for 12–15 minutes or until cakes are still slightly molten in the centre. Cooking time can vary slightly depending on the size of your ramekins, so keep a close eye on them. The cakes are ready when they are set around the edges and squidgy in the middle.

5. Invert cakes onto plates, or save your sanity and simply serve in ramekins.

Fruit and custard tart

LOW LACTOSE
GUM FREE
FODMAP FRIENDLY
GLUTEN FREE

Serves: 8–10
Prep time: 1 hour
Cook time: 30 minutes

1 quantity crème patissiere, page 96
½ teaspoon powdered agar agar
1 quantity sweet shortcrust pastry, baked
   in a 25 cm fluted tart tin (page 36)

TO FINISH:
2–3 punnets (250–375 g) fresh
   strawberries (or berries of choice)
1 tablespoon seedless berry jam
1 tablespoon hot water
pure icing sugar, for dusting

NOTES

I have learned the hard way (many times) that it's better to buy more berries than you think you will need for a tart like this.

This tart is best on the day of assembly but keeps well in an airtight container for up to 2 days.

You can omit the berries and add a sprinkle of nutmeg for a somewhat inauthentic take on a classic Australian custard tart.

This tart is one of those nifty entertaining hacks that people who have their lives together seem to use. Each component of the tart can be prepared ahead of time, it's low fuss on the day, and it looks a lot more impressive than it realistically should. I've mentioned it in the notes but I'll say it twice: buy more berries than you think you will need — decorative berry arrangements are more art than science.

1. Prepare and bake the sweet shortcrust pastry as per the instructions on page 36. Set aside to cool.

2. Prepare the crème patissiere as per the instructions on page 96, adding the agar agar to the milk in step 1. This will help to set the custard and make the tart easier to slice and serve.

3. Pour the crème patissiere straight into the baked tart shell and smooth the surface with an offset spatula or knife. You can allow it to cool before topping with berries, or top while warm.

4. Arrange the strawberries over the tart, sitting upright, covering the custard. Combine the jam and hot water and mix until smooth. Carefully brush the berries with the jam mixture to give them a sheen and a little added sweetness. Sprinkle the tart with a little icing sugar before serving.

Strawberry and rhubarb pie

GLUTEN FREE
FODMAP-FRIENDLY OPTION

Serves: 8-10
Prep time: 1 hour + 30 minutes resting
Chilling time: 15-20 minutes
Cook time: 30-40 minutes

Childhood me knew of nothing more exciting than seeing a Nanna's Apple Pie box being pulled out of the freezer. This pie is my closest approximation, if you discount the fact that it contains no apples or gluten. You can play around with the fruit as you see fit. I really like using this sour cream pastry for pies because it's flaky yet compliant. This means you can make a decorative or lattice top without it puffing out of shape as it bakes. If lactose is an issue for you, use full-cream, lactose-free yoghurt instead of sour cream in the pastry.

~~~~~~~~

FOR THE SOUR CREAM PASTRY:

1 quantity sweet sour cream pastry (page 38), divided into 2 even rounds
tapioca flour, for dusting

FOR THE STRAWBERRY FILLING:

500 g fresh strawberries, hulled, halved (or quartered)
500 g rhubarb, washed and chopped into bite-size pieces
220 g (1 cup) caster sugar
2 tablespoons lemon juice
1-2 teaspoons vanilla bean paste
35 g (¼ cup) gluten-free cornflour

TO FINISH:

1 egg, lightly beaten
granulated sugar, to sprinkle (optional)
FODMAP-friendly ice-cream or custard, to serve

1. Grease a 20 cm diameter (base measurement) pie dish. Liberally dust a piece of baking paper with flour and place on a clean work surface. Place one of the pastry rounds in centre of paper and dust top with flour.

2. Gently roll out dough, dusting with a little more flour as often as necessary until you have a round of approximately 30 cm in diameter. Pick up the dough regularly to check it isn't sticking. Add more flour as often as necessary.

3. Place rolled pastry in freezer for 5 minutes to firm slightly. Carefully line prepared pie dish with pastry. Patch any tears as necessary and trim excess so there is equal overhang. Fold overhang to create a little wall of pastry the whole way around the edge of pie dish. Place pie base in fridge to chill.

4. Preheat oven to 200°C. To make the filling, combine all ingredients in a large bowl. Set aside to macerate for 5-10 minutes while the pastry cools. Spoon fruit into chilled pastry base.

5. Place second pastry round on a sheet of baking paper dusted with flour. Roll into a thin round, approximately 30 cm, so slightly larger than the top of the pie dish. Freeze pastry for 5 minutes.

6. You can create any design with the pastry over the filling, but I like to cut strips of pastry to make a lattice top. There are lots of videos online with different patterns to try out. Whatever you choose, secure the pastry by crimping it to the edges of your dish. Place pie on a baking tray and brush with beaten egg. Sprinkle with finishing sugar, if you're using it. Place in fridge to chill for 10-15 minutes.

7. Bake for 30–40 minutes or until the fruit is juicy and pastry is golden. You can place pie under the grill setting for a few minutes, watching carefully to ensure it does not burn, for extra colour.

8. Remove from oven and set aside to cool completely. Serve with FODMAP-friendly ice-cream or custard.

Low-lactose crème patissiere

GUM FREE
FODMAP FRIENDLY
GLUTEN FREE
LOW LACTOSE

Makes: approximately 2 ½ cups
Prep time: 5 minutes
Cook time: 10 minutes

430 ml (1 ¾ cups) lactose-free milk
75 g (⅓ cup) caster sugar
3 extra-large egg yolks, plus 1 whole
    extra-large egg
30 g (2 ½ tablespoons) gluten-free
    cornflour, sieved (see notes)
2 teaspoons vanilla bean paste
50 g butter

Crème patissiere is that rich and delicious custard often featured in baked desserts like danishes (page 55). This version uses lactose-free milk, which keeps the lactose content to a negligible amount. For a completely lactose-free version, use a plant-based butter. For a vegan version, see the recipe on page 99.

~

1. Heat milk in a medium heavy-bottomed saucepan over medium heat on your smallest stove element. Add roughly half of the caster sugar to the milk. Meanwhile, whisk egg yolks, whole egg, remaining sugar, sieved cornflour and vanilla together in a medium-sized heatproof bowl until smooth.

2. Once milk comes to just a simmer, remove from heat and transfer to a heatproof jug. Whisking constantly, slowly add the jug of hot milk to the egg and sugar mixture in a thin stream.

3. Pour the mixture back into the saucepan and return saucepan to a low heat. Continue whisking for anywhere from 3–10 minutes, or until the mixture thickens and begins to bubble. Once it is thick and easily coats the back of a spoon, remove from the heat and whisk in the butter.

4. Transfer crème patissiere to a heatproof bowl and cover surface with plastic film. This prevents a skin from forming. Allow to cool for 2–3 hours before using. Then, allow to come to room temperature and whisk vigorously before use.

Cornflour isn't always gluten free, so make sure you check the labels. Although cornflour is the absolute best option for this recipe, you can substitute potato starch if you have a corn allergy. I've found it results in a slightly less thick crème patissiere, but it works in a pinch. I found tapioca flour resulted in a slightly slimy-feeling custard, so I don't recommend it unless you're desperate.

Crème patissiere will keep, covered, in the fridge for 2 days, although it's incredibly addictive so I don't fancy its chances.

If your crème patissiere is a little lumpy, pass it through a sieve. Hot tip: don't put it in your blender. Learned that one the hard way.

Vegan crème patissiere

LACTOSE FREE
DAIRY FREE
GUM FREE
FODMAP FRIENDLY
GLUTEN FREE
VEGAN

Makes: 3 ½ cups
Prep time: 5 minutes
Cook time: 10 minutes

625 ml (2 ½ cups) plant-based milk
   of choice
75 g (⅓ cup) caster sugar
30–50 g gluten-free cornflour, sieved
   (see notes)
3 teaspoons vanilla bean paste
50 g plant-based butter

NOTES

Cornflour is not always gluten free, so make sure you check the labels. Although cornflour is the absolute best option for this recipe, you can substitute potato starch if you have a corn allergy. I've found it results in a slightly less thick crème patissiere, but it works in a pinch. I found tapioca flour resulted in a slightly slimy-feeling custard so I don't recommend it unless you're desperate. Use 30 g for a thinner crème patissiere and 50 g for a thick, sturdy crème patissiere.

A quick and easy vegan pastry cream recipe that can be used anywhere you would the regular variety. My serving suggestion: eat an offensive amount straight out of the bowl it is cooling in.

~~~~~~

1. Heat milk in a medium heavy-bottomed saucepan over medium heat. Meanwhile, whisk sugar, sieved cornflour and vanilla together in a medium heatproof bowl until smooth.

2. Once milk comes to just a simmer, remove from heat and transfer to a heatproof jug. Whisking constantly, slowly add the jug of hot milk to sugar mixture in a thin stream, ensuring there are no lumps of cornflour.

3. Pour the mixture back into the saucepan and return saucepan to a low heat. Continue whisking for 3–5 minutes, or until the mixture thickens and begins to bubble.

4. Remove from heat and whisk in butter until well combined. Transfer crème patissiere to a heatproof bowl and cover surface with plastic film. This prevents a skin from forming. Allow to cool for 2–3 hours. Then, allow to come to room temperature and whisk vigorously before use.

Lactose-free ricotta

GUM FREE
FODMAP FRIENDLY
GLUTEN FREE

Makes: 550–650 g ricotta
Prep time: 5 minutes + 20 minutes to
1 hour straining
Cook time: 15–30 minutes

As it's not technically sweet or savoury, I wasn't quite sure where in this book to place ricotta. It landed here due to its vague relation to crème patissiere. Regardless of vagaries, I love this simple recipe for lactose-free ricotta because it opens many more doors for people with lactose concerns. Use it in ravioli (à la page 244), in desserts, or just serve it with maple syrup and berries.

3 litres lactose-free, full-fat milk
1 ½ teaspoons fine salt (or to taste)
125 ml (½ cup) lemon juice (see notes),
    plus extra as required

NOTES

Instead of lemon juice you could also use white vinegar or apple cider vinegar, but they will leave more of an aftertaste.

If you have a food thermometer, heat the milk until it reaches 90°C.

Ricotta keeps 2–3 days in the fridge or can be frozen and defrosted (I checked). It can be used to make the ricotta pancakes (page 33) and the cacio e pepe ravioli (page 244). I also love it smeared on a good piece of sourdough.

To make a delicious spreadable whipped ricotta, simply pop the ricotta in your stand mixer and whisk until it is light and fluffy. You can also use a hand beater and add in any flavourings you see fit.

1. Place milk and salt in a large saucepan over a medium–low heat and bring to a gentle simmer. This will take about 10–15 minutes. I like to cook such a large quantity of milk in 2 batches as it makes it easier to control and avoid burning.

2. Once the milk is simmering, remove from the heat. Add lemon juice and gently stir to just combine. Set aside for 15 minutes. The mixture should have curdled and become obvious 'curds and whey' with ricotta-like lumps of milk and a semi-transparent lemon-coloured liquid.

3. If the liquid is still milky and completely opaque, return ricotta to a gentle heat until it begins to separate, and then remove from heat again. You can add a little extra lemon juice (1 tablespoon at a time) as an insurance policy, although this might affect the taste of the final product.

4. Gently pour ricotta into a sieve lined with muslin cloth or a nut milk bag. Discard the whey or use in smoothies or baking.

5. How long you strain the ricotta is up to you; it depends on how soft you like your ricotta. I like mine on the more spreadable side, so I either give it a good old squeeze and decant or strain it for a maximum of around 20 minutes. Anywhere from 20 minutes to 1 hour is a good ballpark. If you accidentally overstrain, you can add a little lactose-free milk to loosen it up.

6. Taste for salt levels and add more if necessary. Store in an airtight container in the fridge. Ricotta can also be frozen and defrosted when needed.

CHAPTER FIVE

Cakes

Easiest ever chocolate layer cake

FREE FROM HIGH-STARCH FLOURS
GUM FREE
FODMAP FRIENDLY
GLUTEN FREE
DAIRY-FREE OPTION

Serves: 8–10
Prep time: 20 minutes
Cook time: 30–40 minutes

This is the cake that piqued my interest in using single flours for baked goods. It's easy, delicious and stays moist for days as a result of the oil-based batter. It can easily be made dairy free by using plant milk in the batter and 150 g of plant-based butter for the icing (skip the browning step). If not, may I pre-empt your final question? Yes, browning the butter for the icing is worth it – it adds a nutty complexity that regular buttercream could only dream of.

～～～

FOR THE DRY INGREDIENTS:

220 g (1 cup) caster sugar
55 g (¼ cup) light brown sugar
200 g (1 ¼ cups) fine white rice flour
75 g (¾ cup) Dutch processed cocoa powder
2 teaspoons gluten-free baking powder
1 teaspoon bicarbonate of soda
1 ¼ teaspoons fine salt

FOR THE WET INGREDIENTS:

250 ml (1 cup) FODMAP-friendly milk of choice
1 tablespoon apple cider vinegar (or lemon juice)
180 ml (¾ cup) vegetable oil
60 ml (¼ cup) fresh espresso coffee or hot water
2 teaspoons vanilla bean paste
3 extra-large eggs
250 ml (1 cup) boiling water

FOR THE BROWN BUTTER CHOCOLATE BUTTERCREAM:

185 g butter
240 g (1 ½ cups) pure icing sugar
75 g (¾ cup) unsweetened cocoa powder (I used Dutch processed)
125 ml (½ cup) FODMAP-friendly milk of choice
pinch of salt
½ teaspoon vanilla bean paste (optional)

1. Preheat oven to 180°C. Line bases of two 20 cm (base measurement) round baking tins. See notes about which are best to use.

2. Place all the dry ingredients in a large bowl and whisk to combine.

3. Combine the milk and apple cider vinegar in a small bowl and set aside for 1–2 minutes. This will form a buttermilk. It might not curdle dramatically but the buttermilk will assist in flavour development, leavening and general fluffiness.

4. Add the buttermilk, oil, espresso, vanilla and eggs to the dry ingredients and whisk until it forms a smooth batter.

5. Add boiling water and whisk to combine. You might think you don't need to add any water, but you do! It blooms the cocoa, developing the chocolate flavour. It also creates a beautifully fluffy cake.

6. Pour mixture into prepared tins and bake for 30 minutes or until a skewer inserted into the centre comes out clean. Set cakes aside to cool in tin for 15–20 minutes before gently transferring to a wire rack to cool completely.

7. To make the buttercream, place the butter in a small saucepan and cook over a medium–low heat until deeply browned. It should be nutty and fragrant and the specks medium to dark brown in colour. Pour butter into a silicon cake pan and place in fridge or freezer to set.

NOTES

A cake pan as opposed to a springform tin is essential for this cake. Because the batter is so thin, it will leak through and wreak havoc if you attempt to use a springform tin. Trust me on that.

If you like to ice cakes generously, make one and a half batches of the icing recipe.

This cake keeps well in an airtight container in the fridge for 1–2 days.

8. Once set, break butter up. Beat with electric beaters in a large bowl or your stand mixer with whisk attachment until light and fluffy, scraping down sides of bowl as necessary. This will take 10–15 minutes.

9. Meanwhile, sift icing sugar and cocoa together into a medium bowl. I hate sieving so I wouldn't instruct you to do this unless it was totally necessary for a smooth icing, I promise.

10. On low speed, slowly add icing sugar mixture to butter mixture. Once the icing sugar has been incorporated, turn the mixer back up to high and beat until incorporated and fluffy. Slowly add milk until you reach a spreadable consistency – you may not need the full 125 ml. Add a pinch of salt and vanilla, if using (stop the machine to add vanilla or it gets tangled in the beaters), and mix until combined. Taste and adjust if necessary.

11. Time to assemble the cake. Use an offset spatula or flat-edged knife to ice the top of each round before stacking them and icing the edges. The recipe makes enough icing for a reasonably thin layer between each layer.

SOME OF LIFE'S
GREAT PLEASURES:
chocolate cake, chocolate buttercream
AND AN *infallible chocolate cake* RECIPE
THAT WON'T LEAVE YOU HANGING.

Vegan chocolate cake

EGG FREE
VEGAN
GUM FREE
FODMAP FRIENDLY
GLUTEN FREE

Serves: 8–10
Prep time: 15 minutes
Cook time: 30–35 minutes

As someone who has been known to eat butter on its own (apologies to all my non-elasticated pairs of pants), I am always in awe of how I almost prefer vegan cakes and muffins. Without butter or eggs, I find that flavours really shine. This cake is no exception: rich and uber chocolatey, it keeps exceedingly well due to the oil-based batter. Tapioca flour is essential here; in the absence of eggs or gums, it helps keep everything together.

FOR THE DRY INGREDIENTS:

120 g (¾ cup) fine white rice flour
30 g (¼ cup) tapioca flour
45 g Dutch processed cocoa powder
1 teaspoon gluten-free baking powder
½ teaspoon bicarbonate of soda
1 tablespoon psyllium husk

FOR THE WET INGREDIENTS:

½ cup FODMAP-friendly plant-based milk
    of choice
2 teaspoons acid (white vinegar,
    apple cider vinegar or lemon juice)
150 g (⅔ cup) light brown sugar
125 ml (½ cup) vegetable oil
2 tablespoons fresh espresso coffee
    (or extra boiling water)
180 ml (¾ cup) boiling water

FOR THE VEGAN CHOCOLATE
BUTTERCREAM:

100 g plant-based butter,
    thoroughly chilled
160 g (1 cup) pure icing sugar
45 g Dutch processed cocoa
pinch of fine salt
1–2 tablespoons FODMAP-friendly plant-
    based milk of choice

NOTES

This cake keeps well in an airtight container on the bench for 3–5 days, and can be frozen.

1. Preheat oven to 180°C. Grease a 20 cm (base measurement) round cake tin. As the batter is quite liquid, a springform pan isn't suitable here.

2. Place all the dry ingredients in a large bowl and whisk to combine.

3. In another medium bowl, combine milk and acid and set aside for 2 minutes to curdle. Add the sugar, oil and espresso and whisk to combine. Add wet ingredients to the dry ingredients and whisk until a smooth batter. It should feel lightly aerated under the whisk.

4. Add the boiling water and whisk to combine. This will bloom the cocoa and gelatinise the starches in the flours, helping hold the cake together.

5. Pour mixture into prepared tin and bake for 30–35 minutes or until a skewer inserted into the centre comes out clean. Set aside to cool in tin for 15–20 minutes before gently transferring to a wire rack to cool completely.

6. While the cake is baking, make the icing. Combine the plant-based butter and icing sugar in a large bowl or the bowl of your stand mixer. Use hand beaters or your stand mixer with paddle attachment to beat until light and fluffy. I find this process a lot quicker with plant-based butter. If it begins to melt at any time, chill for 10–15 minutes. Add the remaining ingredients and beat until combined. Taste and adjust according to your preferences.

7. Once the cake is completely cooled, ice it with the buttercream and serve.

Vanilla birthday cake with brown butter chocolate buttercream

GUM-FREE OPTION
FODMAP FRIENDLY
GLUTEN FREE
LOW LACTOSE
FREE FROM HIGH-STARCH FLOURS

Serves: 8-10
Prep time: 30-40 minutes
Cook time: 20 minutes

160 g (1 cup) fine white rice flour
2 teaspoons gluten-free baking powder
¼ teaspoon bicarbonate of soda
120 ml (½ cup) FODMAP-friendly milk of choice
65 g (¼ cup) full-cream, lactose-free yoghurt (I like pot set because it's nice and thick)
3 teaspoons vinegar (apple cider or white)
150 g butter, at room temperature
200 g caster sugar
2 teaspoons vegetable oil
2 extra-large eggs
1 teaspoon vanilla bean paste
1 quantity brown butter chocolate buttercream (page 104)
gluten-free sprinkles, to finish (optional)

NOTES

The milk and yoghurt mixture curdles quite dramatically when the acid is added, but it's nothing to worry about and won't affect the end result.

The cake can also be made in a 24 cm springform tin if you would like a round cake. It will need to bake for 30 minutes as opposed to 20 minutes, and I recommend lightly tenting it with foil for the last 10 minutes.

Call me vanilla (it wouldn't be the first time) but for me, nothing beats a good old vanilla cake. This one uses naught but a single flour and has two options for binding: either use yoghurt, or add ¼ cup extra milk and ½ teaspoon xanthan gum in its place. This vanilla gal loves an option.

1. Preheat the oven to 180°C. Grease and line a 16 cm × 26 cm (base measurement) rectangular baking tin.

2. Place flour, baking powder and bicarbonate of soda in a large bowl and whisk to combine. Set aside.

3. Combine the milk, yoghurt and vinegar in a small bowl and set aside for 2 minutes to curdle.

4. Place butter in a large bowl or the bowl of your stand mixer. Using electric beaters or your stand mixer with paddle attachment, beat on low speed until smooth. Add the sugar and oil and increase speed to medium–high. Beat mixture until it is pale and fluffy. This can take anywhere from 3-15 minutes, depending on the temperature of your butter and the season. Stop and scrape down the sides of bowl every few minutes.

5. Once the mixture is well creamed, reduce speed to low. Add eggs one at a time, beating well and scraping down sides of bowl after each addition. Allow each egg to fully incorporate before adding the next. Also add the vanilla bean paste.

6. Add about a third of the dry mixture and incorporate on low speed. Add half the yoghurt mixture and do the same. Repeat with the remaining flour and yoghurt, ending with flour. Don't worry if the batter looks a little split upon adding the yoghurt mixture – it will rectify itself when the flour is added. The mixture should be fluffy, thick and pale blond in colour.

7. Using a spatula, transfer batter to prepared tin and smooth top. Bake for 20 minutes, or until a skewer inserted into the centre comes out clean. You might need to cover the top with foil towards the end if it browns more than you'd like.

8. Set aside to cool in tin for 10–15 minutes before carefully transferring to a wire rack to cool completely. Once cooled, ice with the buttercream and top with sprinkles, if you're using them.

Lemon drizzle cake

LOW LACTOSE
GUM FREE
FODMAP FRIENDLY
GLUTEN FREE

Serves: 8–10
Prep time: 20 minutes
Cook time: 1 hour 10 minutes

160 g (1 cup) fine white or brown rice flour
1 teaspoon gluten-free baking powder
¼ teaspoon fine salt
200 g butter, at room temperature
200 g caster sugar
2 teaspoons vegetable oil
4 extra-large eggs, at room temperature
1 teaspoon vanilla bean paste or extract (optional)
60 ml (¼ cup) FODMAP-friendly milk of choice, warm

FOR THE LEMON SYRUP:

60 ml (¼ cup) lemon juice
55 g (¼ cup) caster sugar

FOR THE LEMON DRIZZLE ICING:

160 g (1 cup) pure icing sugar
1–2 tablespoons lemon juice
pinch of fine salt
finely grated lemon zest, to taste (optional)

Another day, another single-flour cake. As with the other single-floured numbers in this book, I don't recommend experimentation unless you're prepared to push through some potential kitchen flops.

~~~~~~

1. Preheat oven to 200°C. Grease and line a 21.5 cm x 11.5 cm (base measurement) steel loaf pan.

2. Place flour, baking powder and salt in a large bowl and whisk to combine. Sieve once and set aside.

3. Place butter in a large bowl or the bowl of your stand mixer. Using electric beaters or your stand mixer with paddle attachment, beat on low speed until smooth, soft and pliable. Add the sugar and oil. Increase speed to medium–high. Beat mixture until pale and fluffy. This can take anywhere from 3–15 minutes, depending on the temperature of your butter and the season. Stop and scrape down the sides of the bowl every few minutes.

4. Once the mixture is well creamed, reduce speed to low. Add eggs one at a time, beating well and scraping down sides of bowl after each addition. After the third and fourth eggs, the batter might look a little lumpy and split. This is normal – gluten-free baking requires more moisture than regular baking. Add the vanilla, if using, and mix to just combine.

5. Add the flour mixture in 3 batches while the mixer is running on low. In between each batch of flour, add a tablespoon of warm milk. Continue mixing on low until all the flour has been incorporated. Scrape down the bowl and mix one last time.

6. Using a spatula, transfer mixture to prepared tin and smooth the top. Reduce oven temperature to 160°C and bake for 1 hour 10 minutes or until a skewer inserted into the centre comes out clean. Set aside cake in tin while you make the syrup.

RECIPE CONTINUES >

NOTES

I recommend preheating the oven to 200°C and then reducing to 160°C to ensure the oven maintains its temperature. This helps prevent the cake from deflating.

Don't open the oven to check on the cake until about 1 hour into the cooking time (and even then, only if you must). It is cooked on a very gentle heat, so the risk of burning is low. The risk is high for deflating the centre of the cake by opening the oven, though, which is why I suggest not doing that. It can also help to leave the loaf to cool in the oven. If there's even a hint of undercooked centre, this will help keep it from deflating dramatically.

I recommend a steel loaf pan for this recipe – silicon doesn't have enough structure to keep the loaf from expanding outwards.

Cake will keep in an airtight container on the bench or in the fridge for up to 2 days.

7. Meanwhile, to make the lemon syrup, combine juice and sugar in a small saucepan over medium heat and cook, stirring, for 5 minutes or until slightly reduced. Set aside.

8. To make the drizzle icing (optional but delicious), place icing sugar in a small bowl. Gradually add lemon juice until you reached desired consistency. Add a pinch of salt to balance. You could also add some lemon zest here for an extra lemon hit.

9. Use a skewer to poke lots of little holes all over the cake (to absorb syrup). Slowly pour syrup over cake. Set cake aside to absorb syrup and cool completely in the tin.

10. Once cake is cool, remove from tin, top with lemon icing and serve.

Wholegrain single-flour carrot cake

LOW LACTOSE
FREE FROM HIGH-STARCH FLOURS
GUM FREE
FODMAP FRIENDLY
GLUTEN FREE

Serves: 8–10
Prep time: 20 minutes
Cook time: 40–50 minutes

You have to respect carrot cake for fighting its way to become a universally accepted cake made predominantly of vegetables. Truly inspirational stuff. This carrot cake uses a single wholegrain flour (hello, white rice flour) to create a delicious and easy end result.

~~~~~~~

400 g carrots, grated
1 teaspoon fine salt
200 g (1 ¼ cups) fine white rice flour
2 teaspoons ground cinnamon
1 teaspoon ground ginger
1 teaspoon ground nutmeg
1 teaspoon gluten-free baking powder
1 teaspoon bicarbonate of soda
4 extra-large eggs
200 g light brown sugar
125 ml (½ cup) FODMAP-friendly milk of choice
1 tablespoon apple cider vinegar or lemon juice
125 ml (½ cup) olive or vegetable oil
55 g (½ cup) walnuts, well chopped (optional)

FOR THE CREAM CHEESE ICING:

250 g lactose-free cream cheese, at room temperature
25 g butter, room temperature
160 g (1 cup) pure icing sugar, sieved
1 teaspoon vanilla bean paste
lemon juice, to taste
finely grated lemon zest (optional)

OPTIONAL TOPPINGS:

walnuts
icing sugar, dusted over cake

FOR CARROT CURLS (OPTIONAL):

2–3 large, straight carrots
½ cup caster sugar
½ cup water

1. Preheat oven to 180°C. Grease and line a 20 cm (base measurement) round cake tin.

2. Chop the grated carrot into relatively short pieces. I find grated carrot can sometimes be too long in carrot cake and it makes for a crumbly crumb. Place the grated carrot in a colander or sieve over the sink. Sprinkle over salt, and use your hands to rub in. This will start drawing moisture out of the carrots so you can wring out the excess. Set aside while you work on the rest of the cake.

3. Place flour, spices, baking powder and bicarbonate of soda in a large mixing bowl and whisk to combine. Crack eggs into a separate small bowl and whisk to combine. Place milk and vinegar in another small bowl and set aside for 2 minutes to make buttermilk – the mixture should start to curdle and thicken.

4. Give the carrots one last squeeze to rid them of all excess moisture. Add the eggs, oil and buttermilk to the flour mixture and stir until well combined. Add carrots and stir again until evenly distributed. Stir in walnuts, if using.

5. Transfer batter to prepared tin and smooth surface. Bake for 40–50 minutes, or until a skewer inserted into the centre comes out clean. Set cake aside to cool in the tin for 5 minutes before running a knife around the edges. Remove from the tin and set on a cooling rack to cool completely.

6. To make the icing, place cream cheese and butter in a large bowl or the bowl of your stand mixer. Using electric beaters or stand mixer with paddle attachment, beat at high speed until smooth and light. Add remaining ingredients and beat until well combined, scraping down sides of bowl as necessary. Taste and adjust according to your preferences.

7. Once cake is cooled, using an offset spatula or flat knife, spread icing over cake and decorate as desired (see optional toppings).

8. To make carrot curls, peel 2–3 carrots and discard the skins. Use a peeler to create long, thick, even carrot ribbons. In a small saucepan over a medium-low heat, add caster sugar and water and cook gently until the sugar dissolves. Add the carrot strips and cook for 10–15 minutes or until soft. Preheat the oven to 120°C and line two trays with baking paper. Space the carrot strips evenly on the trays. Sprinkle with granulated sugar if desired and bake for about 30 minutes or until carrot strips begin to appear translucent. Remove from oven and, working quickly, wrap each strip of carrot around the handle of a wooden spoon to create the curls. Allow to cool for 30 minutes or until set, then use to decorate.

NOTES

You can use brown rice flour or sorghum flour in place of fine white rice flour in these muffins. Sorghum will require 1 ¼ cups as opposed to 1 cup.

You can use FODMAP-friendly dairy-free butter and yoghurt to make them dairy free. I recommend using a plant-based butter with a high fat percentage and putting the batter in the fridge for 30 minutes before adding the blueberries and baking.

Adding ¼ teaspoon coriander powder is another way to make blueberry muffins taste more 'blueberry'. It works, I promise.

Muffins keep well in an airtight container for up to 3–4 days.

Blueberry muffins

FREE FROM HIGH-STARCH FLOURS
GUM FREE
FODMAP FRIENDLY
GLUTEN FREE
DAIRY-FREE OPTION

Makes: 9–12 muffins
Prep time: 30 minutes
Cook time: 25–35 minutes

The most important trick for deeply blueberry-flavoured muffins is one I learned from Izy Hossack of *Top with Cinnamon*. Spoiler alert: it's blueberry yoghurt. You can easily buy small, perfectly sized tubs of the stuff at most supermarkets. It's almost like the manufacturers are begging you to make blueberry muffins.

~~~~~

FOR THE BLUEBERRY COMPOTE:

125 g fresh or frozen blueberries
1 teaspoon caster sugar
splash of water

FOR THE BLUEBERRY MUFFINS:

125 g butter, at room temperature
110 g (½ cup) caster sugar
70 g (⅓ cup) brown sugar
160 g (1 cup) fine white rice flour
   (see notes for substitution options)
1 teaspoon gluten-free baking powder
½ teaspoon bicarbonate of soda
100 g FODMAP-friendly yoghurt (if you
   can, use blueberry yoghurt – it adds an
   incredible layer of flavour)
80 ml (⅓ cup) FODMAP-friendly milk of
   choice
2 teaspoons acid (lemon juice or
   white vinegar)
2 extra-large eggs, at room temperature
1 teaspoon vanilla bean paste or extract
2–3 tablespoons finishing sugar

1. To make the compote, place 100 g of the blueberries in a small saucepan with the caster sugar. Reserve remaining blueberries to add whole. Add a splash of water and cook over low heat until blueberries begin to soften and emit liquid. Use a fork to lightly smash the blueberries. Set aside to cool.

2. Preheat oven to 200°C. Grease 9–12 holes of a muffin tin (approximately 80 ml or ⅓ cup capacity) with butter and oil (this will ensure the blueberries do not stick).

3. Place butter in a large bowl or the bowl of your stand mixer. Using electric beaters or your stand mixer with paddle attachment, beat butter on medium–low speed until smooth. Add sugars and continue to beat, scraping down regularly, until the mixture is light and creamy. This can take anywhere from 3–15 minutes of beating, butter temperature and season dependent.

4. Meanwhile, combine flour, baking powder and bicarbonate of soda in a large bowl and whisk to combine. In a separate medium bowl whisk together the yoghurt, milk and acid.

5. Add eggs one at a time, beating well and scraping down sides of bowl after each addition. On low speed, add about a third of the flour mixture. Once incorporated, add half of the milk and yoghurt mixture and repeat, ending with flour. Once incorporated, add vanilla and beat to combine. Stir in the fresh blueberries, then gently fold in half the blueberry compote.

6. Divide mixture among prepared muffin holes. Top each muffin with some of the remaining blueberry compote. As an option, you can also sprinkle over some finishing sugar.

7. Bake, on lowest rack in oven, for 25–35 minutes, covering muffins with foil if browning too quickly (normally for the last 10 minutes of cooking time).

8. Set muffins aside to cool in tin before gently removing.

Small-batch vegan blueberry muffins

GUM FREE
EGG FREE
VEGAN
FODMAP FRIENDLY
GLUTEN FREE
FREE FROM HIGH-STARCH FLOURS

Makes: 5–7 muffins (see notes)
Prep time: 10 minutes
Cook time: 25 minutes

100 g fresh or frozen blueberries (see notes)
1 teaspoon caster sugar (if using frozen berries)
125 ml (½ cup) FODMAP-friendly plant-based milk of choice, plus extra as needed
3 teaspoons apple cider vinegar or lemon juice
160 g (1 cup) fine white rice flour
1 teaspoon gluten-free baking powder
½ teaspoon bicarbonate of soda
½ teaspoon psyllium husk
75 g FODMAP-friendly plant-based yoghurt (ideally blueberry flavour)
50 g plant-based butter, melted
100 g light brown sugar
1–2 tablespoons finishing sugar (optional)

These blueberry muffins are quick and easy with all the taste but none of the faff of their regular counterparts. They're also perfect for anyone with an egg allergy.

〰️

1. Preheat oven to 200°C. Grease 5–7 holes of a muffin tin (approximately 80 ml or ⅓ cup capacity) with plant-based butter and oil. Using both ensures the muffins won't stick to the pan.

2. If using frozen blueberries, gently cook them in a small saucepan with 1 teaspoon caster sugar until they thaw and release some juices. Turn off heat and set aside.

3. Combine milk and apple cider vinegar or lemon juice in a medium bowl. Set aside for 2 minutes to form buttermilk (mixture will curdle).

4. Place flour, baking powder, bicarbonate of soda and psyllium in a large bowl and whisk to combine.

5. Add the yoghurt, melted butter and sugar to the buttermilk and stir to combine.

6. Add the wet ingredients to the dry ingredients and whisk to combine. The mixture should be about the thickness of the yoghurt, and when left for a minute it should become a little bit light and bubbly. If the batter looks too dry, add a little extra milk.

7. If you're using frozen blueberries, gently squeeze them to remove excess liquid, as too much blueberry juice will result in grey muffins. Using a spatula, very gently fold in the blueberries (reserving a few for topping).

8. Divide batter among prepared muffin holes, filling each hole about three-quarters full. Top with the remaining blueberries and a sprinkle of finishing sugar, if using.

9. Bake muffins for 20–25 minutes or until browned and cooked through. Set aside to cool in tin for 5–10 minutes before gently transferring to a wire rack to cool completely.

NOTES

I recommend sticking with fine white rice flour for this recipe. I tried using brown rice flour and wasn't particularly impressed with the results.

Because these are quite fragile little muffins (aren't we all) I recommend using fresh blueberries where possible. If not, make sure you cook off the excess liquid and freezer ice in frozen blueberries.

I found that different yoghurt varieties yielded differing numbers of muffins. Some made 5, some made 7. If you need exactly 7 muffins, I recommend buying enough ingredients for a second batch, just in case.

Muffins keep well in an airtight container in the fridge for 3–4 days. They can also be frozen.

Banana cake with vanilla cream cheese icing

FREE FROM HIGH-STARCH FLOURS
GUM FREE
FODMAP FRIENDLY
GLUTEN FREE
LOW LACTOSE

Serves: 8–10
Prep time: 10 minutes
Cook time: 25–35 minutes

Before anyone starts, yes, this is a banana cake. In a FODMAP cookbook. Why? Well, because everyone loves banana cake. Also, because a single serve of ripe banana is 56 g, which means that you should be in the clear even if you do react to fructose. If you'd prefer, you could also use unripe bananas and safely eat 112 g of banana per serving. If you don't get along with ripe bananas, use just ripe or slightly under-ripe ones instead. I find it can be helpful to roast these first to bring out their sweetness and flavour.

~~~~~

FOR THE DRY INGREDIENTS:

160 g (1 cup) fine white rice flour
½ teaspoon gluten-free baking powder
¼ teaspoon bicarbonate of soda
¼ teaspoon fine salt

FOR THE WET INGREDIENTS:

300 g ripe bananas, weighed after
   peeling, roughly mashed (see intro)
100 g caster sugar
1 teaspoon vanilla bean paste (optional)
2 extra-large eggs
125 ml (½ cup) vegetable or olive oil
¼ cup FODMAP-friendly milk of choice
   (I used lactose-free full cream)

FOR THE VANILLA CREAM CHEESE ICING:

250 g lactose-free cream cheese, at
   room temperature
50 g butter, at room temperature
80 g (½ cup) pure icing sugar, sieved
1–2 teaspoons vanilla bean paste or extract
pinch of salt (optional)
squeeze of fresh lemon juice (optional)

> NOTES
>
> Cake can be kept in an airtight container in the fridge for 3–4 days.

1. Preheat oven to 180°C. Grease and line a 20 cm (base measurement) round cake tin.

2. Place all the dry ingredients in a large bowl and whisk to combine. In a separate medium bowl, place all the wet ingredients and whisk to combine. Add the wet ingredients to the dry ingredients and whisk to combine. The mixture will look thick, then thin out a little as you mix to become a batter-like consistency with some chunky banana bits.

3. Pour batter into prepared tin and bake for 25–35 minutes or until cooked through. Remove from the oven and set cake aside to cool in tin for 5 minutes before transferring to a wire rack to cool completely.

4. Meanwhile, make your icing (or make on the day you plan to serve your cake). Place cream cheese in a large bowl or the bowl of your stand mixer. Using electric beaters or stand mixer with paddle attachment, beat on low speed until smooth. Add butter and continue beating until completely smooth. Scrape down the sides and add icing sugar, vanilla, a pinch of salt and lemon, if using. Beat on a medium speed until smooth. You can continue beating on medium if you'd like a slightly whipped icing, or use it as is.

5. Using an offset spatula or the back of a spoon, spread icing over the cooled cake. Serve.

Lamingtons

FREE FROM HIGH-STARCH FLOURS
GUM-FREE OPTION
FODMAP FRIENDLY
GLUTEN FREE

Makes: 15 lamingtons
Prep time: 30 minutes + overnight
   cooling + assembling
Cook time: 20 minutes

FOR THE CAKE:

1 quantity vanilla birthday cake (see
   page 110), baked in a 16 cm × 26 cm
   (base measurement) baking tin and
   sliced into 15 squares

FOR THE CHOCOLATE TOPPING:

160 g (1 cup) pure icing sugar
80 g unsweetened cocoa powder
   (both Dutch and regular are fine)
25 g unsalted butter
125 ml (½ cup) water

TO FINISH:

100 g (1 ¼ cups) desiccated coconut

NOTES

Lamingtons keep well in an
airtight container for 2–3 days.

Desiccated coconut is
considered FODMAP friendly
in ½ cup servings. Provided you
don't eat half the lamingtons
in one sitting, they are well
within acceptable FODMAP
limits.

Lamingtons: because it would surely be a faux pas to publish a
baking book in Australia without some.

~~~~~~

1. Prepare the vanilla cake the night before you intend to make
    lamingtons, as slightly stale cake is far easier to dip into
    chocolate. Alternatively, you can prepare the cake on the
    same day, allow to cool, then cut and freeze the cake squares
    for 1 hour before dipping them.

2. To make the topping, combine icing sugar, cocoa, butter and
    boiling water in a medium bowl and whisk until smooth.

3. Have a baking tray ready for the lamingtons to sit on. Place
    coconut in a large shallow bowl. Using 2 forks, dip each cake
    square into chocolate mixture to coat. Allow excess chocolate
    mixture to drip off. Next, dip in coconut to cover all sides.
    Transfer to tray and repeat to make 15 lamingtons.

4. Allow lamingtons to set for an hour or two before eating
    (if you can).

CHAPTER SIX

Cookies

Grain-free choc-chip cookies

LOW LACTOSE
GRAIN FREE
GUM FREE
FODMAP FRIENDLY
GLUTEN FREE

Makes: 10–12 cookies
Prep time: 20 minutes + overnight
**   resting**
Cook time: 24–30 minutes

150 g butter
75 g light brown sugar
75 g caster sugar
150 g tiger nut flour
½ teaspoon fine salt
½ teaspoon gluten-free baking powder
½ teaspoon bicarbonate of soda
1 tablespoon FODMAP-friendly milk of
    choice
1 extra-large egg
1 teaspoon vanilla bean paste (optional)
100 g dark chocolate, chopped
sea salt, to finish (optional)

I didn't particularly want to include a new flour for a single recipe, but these cookies were simply too good to omit. Tiger nut flour is grain free (it's made from a type of tuber) and has a nutty and sweet flavour akin to almond meal. It's increasingly easy to find in supermarkets these days and it makes my favourite cookies to date. These cookies are FODMAP friendly in a 1 cookie serving size. Larger amounts of tiger nut flour (and thus these cookies) are best avoided if you have issues with fructans or galacto-oligosaccharides (GOS).

~~~~~~~~

THE NIGHT BEFORE:

1. Place butter in a small saucepan over medium–low heat. Cook, stirring occasionally, until butter is deep brown in colour and smells nutty. Weigh the browned butter – it should weigh 125 g or thereabouts. A little over is fine, but if it's significantly under, add a little extra butter.

2. Transfer brown butter to a medium-sized heatproof bowl. Add sugars and stir until well combined. Set aside to cool slightly.

3. Meanwhile, place tiger nut flour, salt, baking powder and bicarbonate of soda in a small bowl and whisk to combine.

4. Add the milk, egg and vanilla bean paste, if using, to the sugar mixture. Stir well to combine. Add the flour mixture and stir until completely combined. The texture of the dough should be smooth and thick, yet able to drip slowly off a spoon. Cover bowl and place in fridge overnight. The flavours will meld and the flour will soften during this time. I promise it is worth it.

THE NEXT DAY:

5. Preheat oven to 180°C. Line 2 baking trays with baking paper. Take the cookie dough out of the fridge and use a spoon to break it up. Add the chocolate chips, mix together and mould approximately 12 cookie dough balls with roughly equal amounts of chocolate.

6. Divide the cookie dough balls between the baking trays, leaving plenty of space between each cookie. Pop one tray in the fridge and the other in the oven for anywhere between 12 and 15 minutes, watching cookies closely and taking them out when they are done to your liking. Repeat with second tray.

7. Set cookies aside to cool completely on trays. Cookies will continue to firm as they cool.

Best ever brownies

GUM FREE
FREE FROM HIGH-STARCH FLOURS
FODMAP-FRIENDLY OPTION
GLUTEN FREE

Makes: 12 brownies
Prep time: 30 minutes
Cook time: 20–35 minutes

150 g butter
200 g 50–70% cocoa solids dark
    chocolate (see notes)
3 extra-large eggs
220 g (1 cup) caster sugar (or 110 g
    light brown and 110 g caster sugar)
pinch of salt
2 teaspoons vanilla bean paste
2 tablespoons Dutch processed cocoa
    powder
1 tablespoon hot water
1 tablespoon freshly brewed espresso
    coffee
100 g (1 cup) almond meal

The term 'best ever' gets bandied about with embarrassing frequency in the food blog world, but I feel these brownies truly warrant the moniker. They're rich, super fudgy and will inevitably become your go-to baked good for impressing fellow dietary requirement folk – and beyond!

1. Preheat oven to 180°C and line a 24 cm × 24 cm (base measurement) baking tin with baking paper.

2. Place butter and chocolate in a heatproof bowl over a saucepan of simmering water, ensuring base of bowl does not touch the water. Cook, stirring, until melted and well combined. Set aside to cool slightly.

3. Place eggs and sugar in a large bowl or bowl of your stand mixer. Using electric beaters or stand mixer with whisk attachment, beat on medium speed for 7–10 minutes or until the mixture is light (almost white) and fluffy. This will help create the crackly meringue surface.

4. Add the salt, vanilla bean paste and cocoa to the chocolate mixture. Pour the hot water and coffee over the cocoa to 'bloom' it – bring out the depth of the chocolate flavour. Stir until the additions are just mixed in with the chocolate and butter.

5. With the motor on a low speed, add the chocolate mixture to the egg mixture in a steady stream. Beat on low until well combined, about 1–2 minutes.

6. Add the almond meal and beat until just combined (be careful not to overbeat). Pour mixture into prepared pan and bake for 20–35 minutes, depending on how 'done' you like your brownies.

7. Set brownies aside to cool completely in tin before slicing.

NOTES

Brownies are best made the night before to allow them time to set before slicing. I also highly recommend keeping these in the fridge – when they're fresh from the oven they can be hard to eat for their fudginess.

I like to sprinkle my brownies with a little extra sea salt, but you do you.

If you don't want to use almonds, use 30 g (¼ cup) tapioca flour and 40 g (¼ cup) fine white rice flour in place of the almond meal. Bake time will be the lower end of the range specified.

50% dark chocolate will yield a shinier, more aesthetically pleasing brownie, but it does contain more milk solids. 70% dark chocolate will yield a more matte brownie but it contains less milk solids and is therefore a FODMAP-friendly choice.

Anzac-style biscuits

LOW LACTOSE
FREE FROM HIGH-STARCH FLOURS
GUM FREE
EGG FREE
FODMAP FRIENDLY
GLUTEN FREE

Makes: 9–10 small cookies
Prep time: 15 minutes
Cook time: 15 minutes

60–75 g fine white rice flour (see notes)
50 g desiccated coconut
75 g light brown sugar (use half caster sugar and half light brown sugar for a chewier cookie, see notes)
65 g (1 cup) quinoa flakes
100 g butter
2 tablespoons rice malt syrup
¾ teaspoon bicarbonate of soda

NOTES

You can adjust these biscuits according to your preference – use the smaller amount of flour and the caster sugar option for a thinner, chewier biscuit, or use the higher ratio of flour and all brown sugar for a thicker, crunchier one.

Sorghum flour and teff flour are suitable replacements for the rice flour. I suggest using the full 75 g as these flours are less absorbent than rice flour.

Biscuits will keep well in an airtight container for 1 week or more, although I dare you to make them last that long.

I've tried to keep these gluten-free Anzac-style biscuits as close to the original as possible. Using quinoa flakes in place of oats and rice malt instead of golden syrup, they're a FODMAP-friendly and gluten-free alternative to the real thing.

1. Preheat the oven to 150°C. Line 2 baking trays with baking paper.

2. Combine flour, coconut, sugar and quinoa flakes in a large bowl. Using clean hands, break up all the brown sugar bits.

3. Melt butter in a small saucepan over low heat. Add rice malt syrup and stir to combine. Add the bicarbonate of soda and cook until it bubbles and foams.

4. Add the butter mixture to dry ingredients and stir to combine. You will probably get three-quarters of the way there with a spoon, then use your hands to finish the job. The mixture might look crumbly and a little dry, but it should feel moist. If not, add a teaspoon of water.

5. Roll mixture into approximately 10 even-sized balls. You'll need to use a bit of pressure to bring them together. Place on prepared trays. Using heel of your hand, gently flatten biscuits slightly and coax back into a circular shape, patching up any cracks around the edges.

6. Bake for 6 or 7 minutes, before swapping trays. Continue to cook for a further 6 or 7 minutes or until golden brown and done to your liking. While the biscuits are hot, use your hands or a knife to gently adjust their shape if necessary.

7. Set biscuits aside to cool completely on trays.

COOKIES

Buckwheat choc-chip cookies

LOW LACTOSE
GUM FREE
FODMAP FRIENDLY
GLUTEN FREE
FREE FROM HIGH-STARCH FLOURS

Makes: 10–12 cookies
Prep time: 20 minutes + overnight resting
Cook time: 24–30 minutes

150 g butter
100 g light brown sugar
50 g caster sugar
150 g buckwheat flour
¼ teaspoon fine salt
¼ teaspoon bicarbonate of soda
1 extra-large egg
1 teaspoon vanilla bean paste
1 tablespoon FODMAP-friendly milk of choice (if needed)
75–100 g 70% cocoa solids dark chocolate, chopped

Quite frankly, cookies don't command enough respect given just how intricate the science behind them is. Each ingredient is purposefully chosen to promote a precise amount of spread and crispiness, right down to the amount of each type of sugar. For this reason, I don't recommend any substitution here.

~~~~~~~~~

THE NIGHT BEFORE:

1. Place butter in a small saucepan over medium–low heat. Cook, stirring occasionally, until butter is deep brown in colour and smells nutty. Weigh the browned butter into a medium-sized heatproof bowl. It should weigh 125 g or thereabouts. A little over is fine, but if it's significantly under, add a little extra butter.

2. Transfer brown butter to a medium-sized heatproof bowl. Add the sugars to the browned butter and stir until well combined. Set aside to cool slightly.

3. Meanwhile, place flour, salt and bicarbonate of soda in a small bowl and whisk to combine.

4. Add the egg and vanilla bean paste to the sugar mixture. Stir well to combine. Add the flour mixture and stir until completely combined. The texture of the dough should be smooth and thick, yet able to drip slowly off a spoon. If not, add the milk. Cover bowl and place in fridge overnight. The flavours will meld and the flour will soften during this time. I promise it is worth it.

NOTES

Cookies are best eaten on the day they are made but can be stored in an airtight container for 2–3 days.

The consistency and absorbency of buckwheat flour differs from brand to brand, so you might need to add more or less milk.

THE NEXT DAY:

5. Preheat oven to 180°C. Line 2 baking trays with baking paper. Take the cookie dough out of the fridge and use a spoon to break it up. Mix in chocolate chips, then mould approximately 12 cookie dough balls with roughly equal amounts of chocolate.

6. Divide the cookie dough balls between the baking trays, leaving plenty of space between each cookie – they spread considerably, in a good way. Pop 1 tray in the fridge and the other in the oven for anywhere between 12 and 15 minutes, watching cookies closely and taking them out when they are done to your liking. Repeat with second tray.

7. Set cookies aside to cool completely on trays. Cookies will continue to firm as they cool.

Dark chocolate sandwich biscuits

LOW LACTOSE
FREE FROM HIGH-STARCH FLOURS
GUM FREE
FODMAP FRIENDLY
GLUTEN FREE

Makes: 10–11 biscuit sandwiches
Prep time: 1 hour
Cook time: 30 minutes

Also known as: if you're into TimTams, you're into these chocolate sandwich biscuits. I've tried the biscuits using fine white rice flour, brown rice flour and buckwheat flour, all to success. Use the same amount (120 g) of any flour you substitute with.

FOR THE CHOCOLATE BISCUITS:

100 g butter, softened
110 g (½ cup) caster sugar
35 g (⅓ cup) Dutch processed cocoa powder, plus extra to dust
120 g sorghum flour (see page 10)
1 teaspoon gluten-free baking powder
1–2 teaspoons FODMAP-friendly milk of choice

FOR THE FILLING:

100 g butter, softened
125 g pure icing sugar
2 tablespoons Dutch processed cocoa powder
pinch of fine salt

FOR THE CHOCOLATE COATING:

200 g 70% cocoa solids dark chocolate
1–2 tablespoons coconut oil

NOTES

Biscuits keep well in an airtight container for up to 1 week, but they will absolutely disappear before then.

1. Preheat oven to 160°C. To make the biscuits, combine butter and sugar in a large bowl or bowl of your stand mixer. Using electric beaters or stand mixer with paddle attachment, beat on medium–high speed until light and fluffy. This can take anywhere from 3–15 minutes, butter temperature and season dependent.

2. Place cocoa, flour and baking powder in a small bowl and whisk to combine. With the motor running on low speed, add cocoa mixture to butter and sugar until well combined, scraping down sides of bowl as necessary. The mixture should become a reasonably stiff dough. Add just enough milk to form a smooth dough that doesn't crack as you roll it.

3. Dust a large sheet of baking paper with extra cocoa powder. Place dough on prepared paper and top with another equal sized sheet. Using your rolling pin, roll dough out to a thin rectangle, about 5 mm thick. The biscuits puff up during baking so they can be rolled a little thinner than you'd like them to end up. The biscuits are also served as a sandwich so you don't want to make them too thick.

4. Using a pizza wheel and/or a ruler and knife, gently cut sheet of dough into 10 cm × 3 cm rectangles. Aim for 20–22, which will make 10–11 biscuit sandwiches.

5. Place the sheet of cut biscuits on a large baking tray. Bake for 30 minutes or until completely cooked through. Set aside to cool completely on tray before gently snapping into individual biscuits.

6. Meanwhile, to make filling, place butter and sugar in a small bowl or bowl of your stand mixer. Using electric beaters or stand mixer with paddle attachment, beat until light and fluffy. Add the cocoa and a pinch of salt and beat until smooth and light brown in colour.

7. Sort biscuits into even-sized pairs. Add a decent smear of the buttercream and sandwich biscuits together. If your smear oozes out, you've used a little too much. Place sandwiched biscuits on a baking tray and place in fridge to set.

8. Meanwhile, place the chocolate and oil in a heatproof bowl over a saucepan of simmering water, ensuring base of bowl does not touch the water. Cook, stirring, until chocolate has melted and is smooth. Remove from heat.

9. Lightly grease a sheet of baking paper or some cooling racks. Using 2 forks, dip each biscuit sandwich into the chocolate mixture and turn to coat. Allow each biscuit to drain well or the last few will be chocolate deprived. Transfer to the greased sheet or rack and repeat with remaining sandwiches.

10. Transfer biscuits to fridge to set. After chocolate is set, they're ready to eat.

MY *favourite* SORT OF SANDWICH?
A *chocolate* SANDWICH!

Any-flour-you-like brownie cookies

LOW LACTOSE
GUM FREE
FREE FROM HIGH-STARCH FLOURS
  OPTION
FODMAP FRIENDLY
GLUTEN FREE

Makes: 12 cookies
Prep time: 15 minutes
Cook time: 20 minutes

75 g butter
200 g 70% cocoa solids dark chocolate
150 g caster sugar
2 extra-large eggs
2 tablespoons cocoa powder (Dutch
  processed or regular)
3–4 tablespoons any gluten-free flour
  (such as quinoa, buckwheat, sorghum,
  tapioca, fine white or brown rice
  flour – see notes)
¼ teaspoon gluten-free baking powder
¼–½ teaspoon fine salt
1 teaspoon vanilla bean paste (optional)
sea salt, to sprinkle

My favourite thing about these cookies (second to the fact they use any flour, very pantry-friendly) is that they're so fudgy rich that flour is rendered close to irrelevant by design. I like to top mine with a few sea salt flakes for a contrasted crunch, but they're also beautiful bare.

~~~~~~~~

1. Preheat oven to 180°C. Line 2 baking trays with baking paper. I like to lightly oil my trays beforehand so the baking paper doesn't slide around.

2. Place the butter in a small saucepan over medium–low heat. Cook, stirring occasionally, until butter is deep brown in colour and smells nutty. Weigh the browned butter. It should weigh 60 g or thereabouts. A little over is fine, but if it's significantly under, add a little extra butter.

3. Place chocolate in a heatproof bowl over a saucepan of simmering water, ensuring base of the bowl does not touch the water. Cook, stirring, until melted and smooth. Set aside.

4. Add the brown butter, sugar and eggs to a large bowl or the bowl of your stand mixer. Using electric beaters or stand mixer with whisk attachment, beat mixture for 7–10 minutes on medium–high speed or until light and fluffy.

5. Meanwhile, place cocoa, flour, baking powder and salt in a small bowl and whisk to combine.

6. With motor still running on low speed, add the melted chocolate to the egg mixture and beat until well combined. Add flour mixture, one spoon at a time, continuing to beat until all the flour is combined, scraping down sides of bowl as necessary.

7. Add vanilla, with motor off, then continue to beat until combined. The batter should be thick, but still slightly thinner than a traditional cookie dough, and fall off the beaters or whisk in ribbons.

RECIPE CONTINUES >

Cookies are best stored in an airtight container in the fridge.

White and brown rice flours are the most absorbent, so you can use 2–3 tablespoons instead of 3–4.

8. Using 2 spoons, scoop roughly 1 ½ tablespoons of batter per cookie onto the prepared tray, leaving a little space for spread. Set aside for 10 minutes – the cookies will form a skin during this time, which will help create a flaky, shiny top.

9. Sprinkle each cookie with a little sea salt. Place both trays in the oven and cook for 7–10 minutes or until tops are crackly but cookies are still soft. Swap trays and continue to bake for an additional 7–12 minutes or until cookies are done.

10. Set cookies aside to cool completely on trays. Cookies will continue to firm as they cool.

Passionfruit and lime yoyo biscuits

LOW LACTOSE
EGG-FREE OPTION
FODMAP FRIENDLY
GLUTEN FREE

Makes: 10–11 biscuit sandwiches
Prep time: 20 minutes
Cook time: 30 minutes

The yoyo, also known as the dry and sandy biscuit sandwich on the deli counter of your youth, gets a glow up thanks to a zesty lime and passionfruit buttercream. The annatto in store-bought custard powder is what gives yoyos their trademark colouring, but you can leave it out if you're making your own custard powder (see notes).

～～～～～

FOR THE YOYO BISCUITS:

150 g butter
65 g pure icing sugar
75 g (½ cup) gluten-free custard powder (see notes)
100 g fine white rice flour
30 g (¼ cup) tapioca flour
¼ teaspoon xanthan gum (optional)

FOR THE PASSIONFRUIT AND LIME BUTTERCREAM:

75 g butter
120 g (¾ cup) pure icing sugar
¼ cup fresh passionfruit pulp
pinch of salt
zest of ½ a lime and 1–2 teaspoons lime juice, to taste

1. Preheat oven to 170°C. Line 1 large or 2 small baking trays with baking paper.

2. To make the biscuits, place butter, icing sugar and custard powder in a large bowl or bowl of your stand mixer. Using electric beaters or a stand mixer with paddle attachment, beat until light and fluffy – anywhere from 3–15 minutes. The mixture should be pale in colour, and fluffy and light if you scoop a little up. Scrape down the sides of the bowl as you go and don't rush it – this airiness is integral to light cookies.

3. Meanwhile, place flours and xanthan gum (if you're using it) in a small bowl and whisk to combine.

4. With the motor running on low speed, add flour mixture until well combined, scraping down sides of the bowl as necessary. The mixture should be moist but not too tacky. You should be able to roll it in your hands to create the biscuit balls. If you can't, transfer it to the fridge for 10 minutes and then lightly flour your hands with tapioca flour.

5. Roll 2-teaspoon portions of dough into smooth balls. Place on prepared tray(s), then use the heel of your hand to gently press into reasonably thin biscuits, about ¼–½ cm thick and the size of a 50 cent piece. Because they are to be sandwiched, you don't want them to be too thick. Aim for 20–22 individual biscuits. Cup each biscuit gently as you press down to prevent the edges from cracking.

6. Use a thin-pronged fork to create the traditional indents in the top of each biscuit. Bake biscuits for 15 minutes, then swap the trays and bake for another 15 minutes. They should feel dry and airy to the touch when they are done. Set aside to cool completely on tray(s). The biscuits will continue to firm as they cool.

7. To make the buttercream, place butter and sugar in a small bowl or bowl of your stand mixer. Using electric beaters or stand mixer with paddle attachment, beat until light and fluffy. Scrape down sides of bowl. Add passionfruit, a pinch of salt, lime zest and juice and beat again until combined. Adjust according to your taste.

8. Sort biscuits into even-sized pairs. Add a decent smear of the buttercream and sandwich biscuits together. If your smear oozes out, you've used a little too much. Eat right away or transfer to the fridge so the buttercream firms up.

NOTES

You can buy gluten-free custard powder at supermarkets these days. I used an egg-free version that was predominantly made of cornflour and milk powder. If you can't find it, there are recipes online for making your own custard powder.

I had mixed results using plant-based butter in this recipe. You can try it if you have a brand that you trust, but you will likely need to refrigerate the yoyo dough for longer than the recipe specifies before rolling it out.

I found that a little bit of xanthan gum promotes a smoother, more aesthetically pleasing yoyo top. Yoyos do tend to come out of the oven with bubbly, slightly mottled tops, although this is just a sign the creamed butter is doing what it is supposed to do – provide lift to the cookies. If you want to minimise this, use the xanthan gum. If not, they're still great without it.

Biscuits keep well in an airtight container in the fridge for up to 1 week.

Sweet sourdough

Gluten-free sourdough starter

1 tablespoon sorghum flour
1 tablespoon quinoa flour, untoasted
filtered water, enough to make a paste
   consistency

Sourdough starter is such a magic ingredient (just look at the sourdough croissants!) and I highly recommend making one. It will change the game regardless, but particularly if you're plant based and gluten free. Much to the disdain of people who like precise measurements, I prefer to go mostly by sight with my starter these days. Because all gluten-free flours have different absorbencies (even batch to batch) it's rather difficult to pinpoint an exact hydration. Personally, I find a combination of wholegrain and high protein (sorghum and quinoa flour) to be optimal for getting a starter going quickly.

TROUBLESHOOTING

SMELL

Starters generally move through a series of smells before they're ready to bake with. A rotten egg or sulphuric smell is common as your starter grows. An alcohol or nail polish remover smell is common throughout all stages, and indicates that the starter is hungry. If you encounter this smell, give your starter some extra flour and water. A range of funky smells is normal – this is fermenting, after all. Hold your nerve!

APPEARANCE

My ideal starter looks like thick, bubbly yoghurt. The top of the starter should not look dry or crusty, nor should it have a layer of liquid on top, though this can appear sometimes. It is known as hooch and is often accompanied with an alcohol smell. Hooch can range from a light colour to a deep brown or grey. It's harmless and can be poured off or stirred back into the starter, but it is a sign that you need to feed your starter more.

Sometimes a furry layer can form on top of your starter. Most often this is Kahm yeast, a harmless mould that can form when the starter has too much contact with the air. It can safely be scraped off your starter. Something that shouldn't be scraped off? Pink mould. This is an indicator that some nasties have infiltrated your starter. If you see pink mould, it is best to discard the starter and begin again.

WHEN TO QUIT

This is the age-old question when it comes to sourdough starter. Sometimes, despite our best efforts, starters inexplicably fail. It has happened to most of us at some point (me included). If your starter has not formed any bubbles or changed in smell after day 10–12, think about starting again.

QUICK TIPS

Starters can feel intimidating, but they shouldn't! If you feed your starter consistently, you are well on your way. Consistency is more important than precision.

Temperature is critical. Starters grow and thrive in warm (but not excessively warm) climates. Give your starter more love and heat sources in winter. If you live in a tropical climate, consider keeping your starter in the fridge once it is established.

Buckwheat flour looks impressive in a starter (it almost appears to have a gluten-like quality) but it becomes mouldy and generally unwieldy far quicker than other flours. I don't recommend using buckwheat in a starter for this reason.

If anything feels or looks really wrong, throw it away. Better safe than sorry!

If you use a glass jar, you will need to 'burp' your jar (open it to allow gases to escape) every day or so. The gases build up as a by-product of fermentation and might eventually create enough pressure to crack the jar if you don't allow them to escape.

1. Combine the ingredients for your starter in a large, clean, sterilised jar or glass vessel. I like to use a glass measuring jug inside a sealed ziplock bag. Starters need to be covered but have space to allow the gases to escape. I find a ziplock bag is a good balance between keeping bugs out and allowing the starter to breathe.

2. Feed the starter with 1 tablespoon sorghum, 1 tablespoon quinoa flour and water twice a day, ideally in the morning and evening. Yeast doesn't grow without sufficient moisture, so make sure your starter is the consistency of paste or yoghurt each time you feed it. This means adding less or more water each feed as necessary.

3. After 3–4 days of feeding, your starter should have started to change in texture and smell, though this may vary depending on the weather/climate where you live. Ideally you will be able to see some small bubbles on the sides of the jar (this is why a glass vessel is useful). You might also be able to tell where the starter has grown to after feeding by looking at the flour on the sides of the jar. It should start to rise after feeding, and fall back down before the next feed. The smell of your starter could be anything from a mild, bready smell to an alcohol or rotten-egg smell. All are normal: see the troubleshooting tips opposite for more.

4. Once your starter shows some of these signs of life, it is time to start discarding about half the starter every day or two. Discarding serves two purposes: it removes some of the waste products involved in the growth of your starter culture, and it makes room for fresh food to replenish and continue growing the starter. You don't necessarily have to throw the starter away – there are plenty of recipes online that use discarded starter.

5. Continue to feed your starter twice a day. If you have fed the starter in the morning, I recommend discarding (and then feeding) at the end of the day.

6. From around day 7, your starter should rise and fall after feeding, smell pleasantly bready or yeasty, and have a significant number of bubbles. It should feel lighter than it looks, and it should pop as you stir it. Getting to this stage takes longer in winter, so be patient and consider giving your starter a heat source like a sunny windowsill. When your starter meets all of these criteria, you are ready to bake. If it doesn't, see the troubleshooting section.

Sourdough cinnamon raisin loaf

DAIRY FREE
GUM FREE
EGG FREE
VEGAN
FODMAP FRIENDLY
GLUTEN FREE

Serves: 8–10
Prep time: 40 minutes
Proofing time: overnight fermentation + 3–4 hours fermentation + 2–3 hours
Cook time: 1 hour 20–30 minutes

Hear me out before you lay into me for including raisins – firstly, they're FODMAP friendly in 1 tablespoon serves per sitting. Secondly, they are seriously good in this bread. I've been baking sourdough for a while now, but even I was shocked by how much the addition of cinnamon and raisins elevates the entire loaf.

This recipe uses a pre-ferment for strength and sourness as well as an autolyse for a soft crumb and infused cinnamon flavour. If you can't find brown teff flour, you could likely add the cinnamon and raisins to any plain sourdough loaf in the book, although it is well worth seeking out for its nutty flavour and nutritional profile.

~~~

FOR THE PRE-FERMENT:

130 g gluten-free sourdough starter, thick and active
100 g brown teff flour
150 g water

FOR THE LOAF:

175 g brown teff flour
100 g potato starch
75 g sorghum flour
10 g fine salt
300–350 g water
1 tablespoon olive oil
2–3 tablespoons pure maple syrup
1 ½ tablespoons ground cinnamon
¼ teaspoon ground ginger
¼ teaspoon vitamin C powder or apple cider vinegar
75–100 g raisins
20–25 g psyllium husk, plus 5 g extra if needed

THE NIGHT BEFORE:

1. Make the pre-ferment by combining the starter, flour and 150 g water in a non-reactive bowl. Cover and set aside on the bench overnight.

THE NEXT MORNING:

2. The next morning, weigh out your flours in a non-reactive mixing bowl. Pour roughly half of the flour into the pre-ferment from the night before. Add 150 g water and mix to combine.

3. Now, to make the autolyse (see page 4), combine the remaining flour with 150–200 g water, along with the oil, maple syrup, cinnamon, ground ginger and vitamin C powder or apple cider vinegar. Cover and set aside both bowls for 3–4 hours.

4. After 3–4 hours, the pre-ferment bowl should be bubbly and a little rounded on top. There should be a thin layer of water on top of the autolyse bowl. Measure the salt into the autolyse bowl and stir to combine.

RECIPE CONTINUES >

Store cut-side down on the bench for a couple of days, after which time it is best eaten as toast. Slices can be frozen and defrosted.

Make sure you use raisins as opposed to sultanas, which are only FODMAP friendly in 2 teaspoon serves, as opposed to 1 tablespoon for raisins.

5. Add the autolyse to the bowl with the pre-ferment and whisk to combine. Add the raisins and psyllium husk and stir again, then cover with a plate and set aside for 20 minutes. At this stage it will be a soupy consistency – don't panic! Give the psyllium husk time to do its work.

6. After 20 minutes, you should be able to scoop mixture out of the bowl with your hands, even if it doesn't hold its form. If you can't, stir in another 5 g psyllium husk and wait 5–10 minutes. Don't add too much or you will have a sticky loaf.

7. Once ready, scoop dough into a 21.5 cm × 11.5 cm steel loaf pan and use a moistened hand to flatten the top. Place tin into a large ziplock bag and set aside to proof in a warm draught-free place for around 2–3 hours.

8. Preheat oven to its highest setting and place oven rack in middle of oven. Half fill a small baking dish with boiling water and place in base of oven 10 minutes before ready to bake.

9. Place loaf in the oven and reduce oven temperature to 220°C. Bake for 20 minutes, then reduce oven to 180°C and bake for a further 40 minutes. Remove baking dish from oven and continue to bake for 20–30 minutes or until the top is golden and the loaf feels really firm to the touch. If the top of your bread is becoming too golden, loosely cover with foil.

10. Remove loaf from oven and set aside to cool on a wire rack. Alternatively, you can allow to cool in the oven by carefully removing bread from tin and placing it straight on the oven rack, with the oven off.

11. Allow bread to cool completely before cutting to prevent it becoming gummy.

Sourdough cinnamon scrolls

GUM FREE
EGG FREE
FODMAP FRIENDLY
GLUTEN FREE
VEGAN OPTION

Makes: 12 scrolls
Prep time: 45 minutes
**Proofing time: overnight fermentation
     + 1–3 hours**
Cook time: 30–40 minutes

'Addictive!' 'Delicious!' 'Would make again!' These are just some of the phrases I have uttered about my own recipe for these cinnamon scrolls. Because it's not inherently important to the structure, you can use plant milk and/or plant-based butter in this recipe. That said, plant-based butters are quite varied in ingredients and fat content, so choose a brand you trust.

FOR THE DRY INGREDIENTS:

150 g sorghum flour
150 g tapioca flour
150 g fine white rice flour
100 g caster sugar
¼ teaspoon ground ginger
¼ teaspoon vitamin C powder or apple
   cider vinegar
25 g psyllium husk

FOR THE WET INGREDIENTS:

130 g gluten-free sourdough starter,
   thick, active and fed 3–4 hours prior
250 ml (1 cup) FODMAP-friendly milk of
   choice
230 g water
100 g butter, melted

FOR THE CINNAMON FILLING:

2 tablespoons ground cinnamon
¾–1 cup brown sugar
100 g butter, melted

FOR ROLLING OUT:

vegetable oil
a long piece of thread or fine string, for
   cutting rolls

THE NIGHT BEFORE:

1. Combine the dry ingredients and wet ingredients in a large, non-reactive bowl and whisk until well combined. Cover and set aside on the bench overnight. Alternatively, place dough in the fridge. Keep in mind, it will take longer to proof in the morning.

THE NEXT DAY:

2. Oil or butter a rectangular baking dish approximately 30 cm x 20 cm (base measurement). Check your dough – it should be noticeably bubbly and light. If you kept it in the fridge overnight, allow to warm on the bench for 1 hour. Alternatively, if the dough looks dry or like it hasn't risen, add 50 g more water and work it through with your hands. Allow dough to sit in a warm spot for 1 hour before continuing.

3. Thoroughly grease a large sheet of baking paper. Divide dough into 2 even-sized portions. Cover one, and place the other portion onto the oiled baking paper. Use your hands to spread dough into a large rectangle with smooth edges, about 1 cm thick and with sides approximately 30 cm x 35–40 cm.

4. To make the filling, combine all ingredients in a medium bowl. Spoon half the filling over the top of the dough, then use a spatula or back of a spoon to gently and evenly spread it out, leaving a 1 cm margin on the long edges of the rectangle.

RECIPE CONTINUES >

<u>FOR THE GLAZE (OPTIONAL):</u>

75 g lactose-free cream cheese, at room
   temperature

75 g butter, at room temperature

75 g pure icing sugar

1 tablespoon FODMAP-friendly milk of
   choice

1 teaspoon vanilla bean paste or extract

pinch of salt

NOTES

Scrolls keep well in an airtight
container for 2–3 days. If they
start to get stale, microwave
individually or pop them in the
oven with a steam bath.

5. Turn baking paper so a long edge is facing you. Starting from
    the side closest to you, roll the dough over itself, using the
    baking paper to keep the roll nice and tight. Once you get
    80% of the way there, roll the furthest edge back towards you
    to create the full log. Carefully roll the log of dough over so
    that it sits seam side down.

6. Gently thread your piece of string underneath the log.
    Roughly eyeball or measure the dough into six even pieces.
    Think of the thread as your knife and, holding one end of
    the string in each hand, pull in opposing directions to slice
    through one-sixth of the dough. Sit that first cinnamon scroll
    upright and mould it with your hands by pressing down
    gently. Place roll into prepared dish and repeat to make 6
    cinnamon scrolls. Tuck the seam of each scroll against the
    side of the dish or another scroll, to prevent them from
    unfurling during the baking process.

7. Repeat with second ball of dough to make 12 scrolls in total.

8. Cover the dish of scrolls (I like to use and reuse a giant ziplock
    bag) and allow to proof for 1–3 hours (climate dependent)
    until a little puffy to the touch. They will not have doubled, but
    should look a little bigger.

9. Preheat oven to 180°C. Bake scrolls for 30–40 minutes or
    until cooked through and lightly golden on top. You can brush
    them with a little melted butter, if you like, but it is not strictly
    necessary.

10. To make the glaze, using electric beaters, beat the cream
    cheese and butter in a medium bowl until light and fluffy.
    Add the icing sugar, milk, vanilla and a pinch of salt and beat
    until combined. Taste and adjust for sweetness, salt and your
    desired thickness.

11. Spoon cream cheese glaze over scrolls (allow to cool in the
    tray first if you prefer a thick glaze), or eat them as they are.

Vegan sourdough chocolate muffins

DAIRY FREE
LACTOSE FREE
FREE FROM HIGH-STARCH FLOURS
GUM FREE
EGG FREE
VEGAN
FODMAP FRIENDLY
GLUTEN FREE

Makes: 8–10 muffins
Prep time: 15 minutes
Cook time: 20 minutes

My two champions, sourdough starter and psyllium husk, join forces to make these rich and delicious vegan chocolate muffins. Easy to make and even easier to eat.

~~~~~~

FOR THE DRY INGREDIENTS:

60 g (½ cup) fine white rice flour
40 g (⅓ cup + 1 tablespoon) Dutch
    processed cocoa powder
1 teaspoon gluten-free baking powder
¾ teaspoon bicarbonate of soda
½ teaspoon fine salt
2 teaspoons psyllium husk

FOR THE WET INGREDIENTS:

125 g light brown sugar
80 ml (⅓ cup) FODMAP-friendly plant-
    based milk of choice
130 g (½ cup) gluten-free sourdough
    starter, thick and active
125 ml (½ cup) vegetable or olive oil
1 teaspoon vanilla bean paste
125 ml (½ cup) boiling water

1. Preheat oven to 180°C and grease eight 80 ml (⅓ cup) capacity muffin holes. I like to grease with both plant-based butter and oil. Vegan muffins can be difficult to remove once cooked.

2. Combine all the dry ingredients in a large bowl and whisk to combine. Combine wet ingredients in a second bowl and whisk to combine. Add wet ingredients to dry ingredients (finishing with the boiling water) and whisk until mixture forms a thin but viscous batter.

3. Divide mixture between prepared muffin holes. If you have more batter remaining, grease 1 or 2 more holes to use it up. Bake for 20 minutes or until muffins are baked through and a skewer inserted into the centre comes out clean. Set aside to cool in tin for 15–20 minutes before gently transferring muffins to a wire rack to cool completely.

NOTES

Muffins keep well in an
airtight container for 2–3 days.

Sourdough croissants

GUM FREE
EGG-FREE OPTION
FODMAP FRIENDLY
GLUTEN FREE
VEGAN OPTION

Makes: 4 large or 6 small croissants
Prep time: 1 hour
Proofing time: overnight + 8-10 hours,
    season dependent (see proofing
    options)
Cook time: 20-30 minutes

This recipe was really a late-stage addition after having spent so much time on the regular croissants. The benefits are many: it's egg free if you use an alternative wash, gum free and can even be made vegan by using a plant-based stick butter! It's an extremely pleasant dough to handle even without gums, courtesy of sourdough magic.

This recipe assumes that your starter is well established (anything over a month or two), thick like Greek yoghurt and full of bubbles. Feed it 3–4 hours prior and allow it to reach full height before use.

~~~~~~~~

120 g (¾ cup) fine white or brown rice
    flour
90 g (¾ cup) tapioca flour
60 g (½ cup) buckwheat flour
125 g caster sugar
¼ teaspoon fine salt
20 g psyllium husk powder
50 g unsalted butter, at room
    temperature, roughly chopped
180 ml (¾ cup) FODMAP-friendly milk of
    choice, plus 60 ml (¼ cup) if needed
100 g gluten-free sourdough starter,
    thick and active, fed 3–4 hours prior
    to use

FOR THE BEURRAGE:
150-200 g unsalted butter

TO FINISH:
1 egg, beaten

NOTES

Store croissants in an airtight container on the bench for 2–3 days. Microwave or steam bake to reheat.

1-2 NIGHTS BEFORE:

1. Choose a proofing option (winter/cold weather or summer/humid weather) before you begin, so you can plan your time. Keep in mind that sourdough is a lot slower than yeast and can't be rushed. Combine the flours, sugar, salt and psyllium in the bowl of your stand mixer. Using the paddle attachment, incorporate the chunks of soft butter on low speed. Add the milk and starter and beat until a thick dough forms, about the consistency of playdough or pasta dough. If it is still bone dry, you can add another 60 ml (¼ cup) milk, but turn off your mixer and have a feel first. Runny dough is impossible to laminate so it should be quite stiff without being dry.

2. Shape dough into a rough rectangle and wrap in plastic film. Refrigerate overnight.

THE NEXT DAY:

3. Follow steps 4–9 on page 46 for the yeasted croissant dough. Once the dough is laminated, cut and roll it into croissants as per steps 10–13 on page 47.

4. Proof the croissants as per the proofing option you chose at the start of the recipe.

5. When your croissants are puffy and light to the touch, bake them as per steps 16–18 on page 48.

WINTER/COLD WEATHER PROOFING

Just before bed, follow the steps for rolling out and covering your croissants for proofing on page 47–48. Once they're covered, set them on the bench overnight for their slow rise. The next morning, assess the dough. If they are super puffy and soft to the touch, they are ready to bake. If not, transfer them to a cold oven on the middle rack. Boil the kettle and place a medium baking dish of hot or boiling water underneath. Check on them every hour and refresh the water. See the 'signs of a good proof' section to decide if they're ready. Be patient – mine have taken until 5 pm the next day to reach a good proof in winter.

SUMMER/HUMID WEATHER PROOFING

An overnight bench rise is likely too much for warm temperatures. Your croissants might over-proof or the butter might melt. In warm, humid weather, it's best to proof your croissants and bake them on the same day. Make sure you start the laminating process early on in the day so you have time to fit the whole process in. To summer proof, laminate your dough in the morning as per the 'next day' instructions on page 46, through to the 'rolling croissants' instructions on page 47 (steps 4–13). Cover as per 'proofing your croissants' on page 48 (steps 14–15). Set croissants on the bench to rise. Keep in mind that sourdough is a slower process and can take 8–10 hours, weather dependent. If it is really hot, you may need a few stints in the fridge to set the butter.

SIGNS OF A GOOD PROOF

I have found these croissants show more obvious signs of proofing than the non-sourdough ones. They puff visibly (but not dramatically) and they sometimes develop small bubbles of air under the skin that look kind of like little blisters.

When you pick up a fully proofed croissant, you can feel it: they are full of air and lighter than they look. The dough should feel puffy, smooth and a tiny bit moist. Dry croissants won't rise, so make sure they're completely covered while proofing.

Sourdough pancakes

GLUTEN FREE
FODMAP FRIENDLY
LOW LACTOSE
FREE FROM HIGH-STARCH FLOURS
  OPTION
DAIRY-FREE OPTION

Makes: 8 pancakes
Prep time: 15 minutes
Cook time: 15 minutes

Without an overwhelming amount of yoghurt or oil, gluten-free pancakes are generally a (literal) recipe for a sandy mouth. Enter: that sourdough starter magic. These pancakes are light, fluffy and a total pleasure to eat. They can easily be made dairy free, too, by using a plant-based butter. Thanks to a little baking science, the bicarbonate of soda cancels out most of the sourdough tang, leaving a pleasantly subtle bread-like taste in its wake.

~~~~~~

FOR THE DRY INGREDIENTS:

65 g (⅓ cup) caster sugar
60 g (½ cup) tapioca flour
40 g (¼ cup) fine white rice flour
1 teaspoon gluten-free baking powder
½ teaspoon bicarbonate of soda

FOR THE WET INGREDIENTS:

2 extra-large eggs, separated
130 g (½ cup) gluten-free sourdough
  discard, thick (see page 2)
50 g butter, melted
2 tablespoons vegetable or olive oil
1 teaspoon vanilla bean paste

TO FINISH:

butter and/or oil for greasing
pure maple syrup, to serve
berries or whatever else you fancy, to
  serve

1. Combine all the dry ingredients in a large bowl and whisk to combine.

2. Place egg yolks in a small bowl and egg whites into a separate clean and dry large bowl. Add the sourdough discard, butter, oil and vanilla to the egg yolks and whisk to combine.

3. Using electric beaters or stand mixer with whisk attachment, beat egg whites for 5 minutes or until stiff peaks form. Whisk the dry ingredients into the egg yolk and sourdough discard mixture until combined. Using a spatula, gently fold egg whites into egg yolk mixture until just combined.

4. Heat a large non-stick frying pan over low–medium heat and brush with a little melted butter or oil. Add 1–2 tablespoons batter to pan per pancake and cook until bubbles appear on surface. I find that because this mixture is very light and fluffy, it's best to cook them on a lower heat, so adjust accordingly as you go. Gently flip and cook for a further minute or until golden and cooked through. Repeat with remaining batter to make 8 pancakes.

5. Serve with maple syrup and berries, or whatever you enjoy most on your pancakes.

NOTES

This recipe assumes you're using sourdough discard from a well-established, thick and active starter with a consistency akin to a bubbly Greek yoghurt. Sourdough discard, as a quick refresher, is the sourdough starter that you remove before feeding the remainder. Because sourdough discard hasn't been fed in a while, it has a tangy flavour profile and is highly acidic. This is important for these pancakes, because the bicarbonate of soda works in tandem with the discard to neutralise the acidic taste of both ingredients and to provide leavening for fluffy pancakes. For this reason, I don't recommend using discard from a new starter in this recipe.

The flour you're using to feed your starter might affect the flavour of these pancakes, particularly if it's a strong flavour.

For an option free from high-starch flours, use 80 g (½ cup) fine white rice flour.

For a dairy-free option, use a plant-based butter.

Sourdough brown butter brownies

LOW LACTOSE
FODMAP-FRIENDLY OPTION
GLUTEN FREE

Makes: 12 brownies
Prep time: 25 minutes
Cook time: 20–30 minutes

In a telling tale of what I do for fun, I recently made three or four varieties of brownies for some friends to blind test. The result was unanimous support for this sourdough brownie. If a biased anecdote about the casual and unscientific consumption of brownies can't convince you that these are great, I don't know what will.

~~~~~~

100 g butter
75 g (⅓ cup) light brown sugar
110 g (½ cup) caster sugar
200 g dark chocolate (50% cocoa solids for a shiny top, 70% for a serious brownie with a less attractive top)
2 extra-large eggs
2 tablespoons Dutch processed cocoa powder
2 tablespoons boiling water
130 g (½ cup) gluten-free sourdough discard, thick (see page 2)
1 teaspoon vanilla bean paste
generous ¼ teaspoon fine salt
sea salt, to finish (optional)

1. Preheat oven to 180°C. Line a 24 cm square baking tin (base measurement) with baking paper – leave long edges so you have a handle to pull the brownies out.

2. Place the butter in a small saucepan over medium–low heat. Cook, stirring occasionally, until butter is deep brown in colour and smells nutty.

3. Transfer butter to a large bowl or the bowl of your stand mixer. Add the sugar and use electric beaters or stand mixer with whisk attachment to beat until just combined. Set aside to cool slightly.

4. Place chocolate in a small heatproof bowl over a saucepan of simmering water, ensuring base of bowl does not touch the water. Cook, stirring, until chocolate is melted and smooth. Remove from heat.

5. Turn the mixer on to a medium–high speed (I used speed 5 on a KitchenAid) and add the eggs, one at a time. Stop to scrape the sides and bottom of the bowl, before returning to a medium–high speed. Quite quickly, the mixture should lighten in colour and take on a meringue-like appearance and texture. It will be a light brown colour with a sheen to it. Beat the mixture for around 3 minutes or until it is visibly light and fluffy.

6. While the mixer is running, add the cocoa and boiling water to the melted chocolate. Use a spatula to JUST combine – any more and the mixture will stiffen. Boiling water is used to bloom the cocoa and give a more pronounced chocolate flavour.

NOTES

Brownies keep well for 3–4 days in an airtight container in the fridge.

As with the pancakes, I highly recommend using sourdough discard from a well-established, thick and active starter. Because these brownies contain no flour, discard with a thick consistency (akin to Greek yoghurt) is critical to a good result as opposed to an expensive liquid mistake. For this reason, I don't recommend using discard from a new starter in this recipe.

Because these brownies are fudgy, I recommend making them the night before you plan to serve them, to allow them time to set in the fridge before slicing. Doing so gives you the best of both worlds: molten, gooey innards, yet also your sanity intact after trying to cut them.

50% dark chocolate will yield a shinier, more aesthetically pleasing brownie, but it does contain more milk solids. 70% dark chocolate will yield a more matte brownie but it contains less milk solids.

7. Reduce mixer speed to low, add chocolate mixture and beat to combine. Add sourdough discard, vanilla and salt and beat to combine.

8. Pour batter into prepared tin and tap on bench a few times to remove any excess air bubbles. Bake for 20 minutes for an incredibly fudgy brownie. You can cook it a little longer if you prefer your brownie more well done.

9. Once brownies have cooled slightly, place them in the fridge to set for 2–3 hours, or up to overnight. This makes them infinitely easier to slice. When they're set, remove the brownies from the tin and slice into squares. Sprinkle with a little sea salt if you like.

CHAPTER EIGHT

Savoury pastry

Traditional puff pastry

LOW LACTOSE
EGG FREE
FODMAP FRIENDLY
GLUTEN FREE
FREE FROM HIGH-STARCH FLOURS
  OPTION
GUM-FREE OPTION

Makes: base and lid for 1 large pie
Chilling time: 2 hours or overnight
Prep time: 40 minutes

FOR THE PASTRY:

160 g (1 cup) fine white rice flour
60 g (½ cup) tapioca flour
½ teaspoon xanthan gum
1 teaspoon salt or 55 g (¼ cup) caster
    sugar, for a sweet pastry
50 g unsalted butter, cut into cubes
½ cup + 1 tablespoon iced water

FOR THE BEURRAGE:

150 g unsalted butter
tapioca flour, for dusting and rolling out

NOTES

To avoid xanthan gum, use the psyllium paste option for the rough puff on page 39. It's not quite as flaky but is an excellent stand-in.

I have used all manner of different flour combinations in this recipe. I have even made a 100% teff flour recipe to success. If you're new to puff pastry making, consider using an extra ¼ teaspoon xanthan gum if you intend to use a wholegrain (i.e. no starch).

A personal promise: laminating pastry becomes addictively satisfying when you get the hang of it. All up, this pastry takes about a day if you're counting the overnight rest, but it truly is worth the time investment. As with my other pastry recipes, feel free to experiment with the flours you're using.

1. Combine the dry ingredients for the pastry in a small mixing bowl. Using the tips of your fingers, rub in the butter until only small pieces are left and the mixture resembles coarse crumbs.

2. Add the iced water, a ¼ cup at a time, mixing the dough with your hand while you pour. Only add just enough water to bring the pastry together in a ball. There shouldn't be dry bits of flour in the bowl, but the pastry shouldn't be wet.

3. Transfer the pastry into plastic film and wrap tightly. Press it down into a rectangle and refrigerate for 2 hours or overnight.

4. Place butter on a large piece of baking paper and set aside for 10–20 minutes to soften slightly (season dependent). Use your rolling pin to beat it into submission (aka into a rectangle). It should be reasonably thin and approximately 10 cm x 5 cm. Dust rolling pin with flour as required to prevent it from sticking. Place butter rectangle in fridge, and take pastry out of fridge to soften for 10 minutes.

5. Place pastry on a second sheet of well-floured baking paper. Roll pastry into a rectangle about 3 times the length of your butter block. The exact size doesn't matter too much.

6. Place your butter block in the centre of the pastry. Dust off excess flour, then fold the top third of pastry over the butter and the bottom third over the top. Pinch together the seams so the butter is encased. Pick pastry up and turn it so that the short side is facing you. Press down on the pastry in a few spots to secure it, and then gently roll the pastry into a rectangle again, roughly the same length as before. This is your first turn. Wrap pastry in plastic film and refrigerate for 30 minutes.

7. Complete 4–5 more turns in the same fashion, refrigerating between each turn if the butter or dough feels too soft. After the last turn, wrap in plastic film and refrigerate one last time. After this, your puff pastry is ready for use.

Rough puff pastry

LOW LACTOSE
EGG FREE
FODMAP FRIENDLY
GLUTEN FREE
VEGAN OPTION
FREE FROM HIGH-STARCH FLOURS
 OPTION

Makes: enough for 1 large pie base and lid or 1 batch of sausage rolls
Prep time: 20 minutes
Chilling time: 1 hour

240 g (1 ½ cups) fine white rice flour
120 g (1 cup) tapioca flour
1 teaspoon xanthan gum
1 teaspoon fine salt
200 g unsalted butter, cut into cubes
iced water, to bring dough together

NOTES

This recipe works with plant-based butter. I recommend choosing a brand that contains 80% fat per 100 g, as this will help mimic traditional butter. I also recommend freezing the butter for 20 minutes before use, and the pastry between each turn. Plant-based butter softens a lot faster than regular butter, and cold chunks of butter hitting a hot oven are what create the puff in pastry.

As with the other pastry recipes, you can play around with the flours as you see fit. I have successfully made a pastry free from high-starch flours using sorghum in place of the tapioca flour.

Rough puff pastry could also be called puff lite. It's a little less flaky and a little less layered than traditional puff, but a lot easier and quicker to make. You can use plant-based butter to make this pastry vegan. If you'd like a gum-free version, see page 39.

~~~~~~~~

1. Place the dry ingredients in a large bowl and whisk to combine.

2. Add the cubes of butter to the flour and toss to coat. Use your fingertips to rub the butter into the flour until it resembles a coarse crumb. Only small specks of butter should be visible.

3. Add the iced water, a tablespoon at a time, until the dough just comes together. It should come together in a ball without too many dry spots. Don't add too much water as this is the enemy of flaky pastry – add just enough to bring it together.

4. Place the ball of dough in plastic film and then press into a small rectangle. Refrigerate for 30 minutes or until the butter is chilled and pastry slightly hardened.

5. Place the dough on a well-floured sheet of baking paper. Roll out into a 20–30 cm rectangle and complete 2–3 turns as per the instructions on page 166. Cover and chill for another 30 minutes before use.

CURRIED VEGETABLE AND PANEER PIE (PAGE 170)

Curried vegetable and paneer pie

LOW-LACTOSE OPTION
FODMAP FRIENDLY
GLUTEN FREE
EGG-FREE OPTION

Serves: 8–10
Prep time: 1 hour 30 minutes
Cook time: 1 hour 20 minutes

Savoury pie can safely be filed under 'not a 30-minute dinner'. With that said, an afternoon of mostly inactive labour can yield a hearty and delicious dinner for many nights afterward. Better yet, I designed this recipe so that the curry filling makes a standalone meal if you get to the pie-making and realise you can't be bothered. Serve it with the sourdough flatbreads on page 196 and you're good to go.

~~~~~

FOR THE PASTRY:

1 quantity rough puff pastry
   (see page 168)

FOR THE PIE:

500 g potatoes, kept whole
1 large carrot, chopped into small bite-
   sized cubes
1 head of broccoli, cut into small florets
60 ml (¼ cup) oil of choice
2 teaspoons black mustard seeds
2 teaspoons fennel seeds
1 tablespoon cumin seeds
20–30 fresh curry leaves
5–6 spring onions, green part only, sliced
40 g fresh ginger, peeled, finely grated
2 teaspoons curry powder (check to
   ensure it doesn't contain onion or garlic)
3 teaspoons garam masala
2 teaspoons ground cumin
chilli powder, to taste
2–3 teaspoons light brown sugar
pinch of salt
juice of 1 lime
250 ml (1 cup) water
2 tablespoons tomato paste
2 tomatoes, chopped
2 large zucchini, chopped into small bite-
   sized cubes
200 g paneer cheese, cut into cubes (see
   notes)

TO FINISH:

1 egg, lightly beaten

1. To make the pastry, follow instructions in the recipe on page 168. Preheat the oven to 180°C. Divide the block of pastry into 2 pieces by cutting it with a sharp knife.

2. Place one piece of pastry on a large, well-floured piece of baking paper. Gently begin rolling the dough out, aiming for a rectangle approximately 35 x 30 cm. Make sure you regularly 'turn' the dough (pick it up off the baking paper) to ensure it isn't sticking. Dust any sticking points with extra flour whenever necessary.

3. Place your pie dish upside down in the centre of the pastry (so the bottom of the dish is facing upwards). Slide one hand under the baking paper and into the centre of the pie dish, and then place the other on top. Quickly flip the pie dish right side up so that the pastry falls into the dish.

4. Allow the pastry to fall generously into the dish – don't try to stretch it. Gently press it flush up against the dish, patching up any tears as necessary. Trim any pastry overhang and redistribute it to any areas that have none. Using the palm of your hand, press down on the pastry around the rim of the dish. This will create a flat and even pie edge. Line pastry with baking paper and fill with pie weights, dry rice or beans. Blind bake pastry for 30 minutes.

5. Carefully remove paper and (hot!) weights from pastry shell. Brush pastry with beaten egg and return to oven and bake for a further 10–15 minutes or until pastry is golden. Remove from the oven and set aside to cool.

NOTES

If you want a low-lactose option, replace the paneer with cubed firm tofu or add 200 g extra vegetables.

If you have any leftover pastry, you can use it to make some decorative elements for your pie. I like to use my leaf pastry cutters at every possible opportunity.

For an egg-free option, use the vegan egg wash from page 69.

Pie keeps well, covered, in the fridge for 2–3 days.

6. To make the vegetable filling, cook the potatoes in a large saucepan of boiling water for 10–15 minutes or until almost tender. Add the carrot and cook for 3–4 minutes or until carrot is almost tender. Add broccoli and cook for 3 minutes or until broccoli is tender crisp. Drain and set vegetables aside to cool slightly. Cut potatoes into rough cubes.

7. Heat oil in a large saucepan over medium heat. Cook the mustard, fennel and cumin seeds, stirring, for 2 minutes or until seeds start to pop. Add the curry leaves and spring onion greens. Add a splash of water and cook, stirring, for 2 minutes or until fragrant.

8. Add the grated ginger and cook, stirring, for 2 minutes, adding a splash of extra water if necessary. Add the curry powder, garam masala, ground cumin, chilli, sugar and a pinch of salt and cook, stirring, for 2 minutes or until fragrant. Deglaze pan with the lime juice and 250 ml (1 cup) water.

9. Add the tomato paste and chopped tomato and stir to combine. Add the cooked vegetables and zucchini and simmer for 10–15 minutes or until liquid has almost evaporated. Gently stir in paneer. Taste and adjust for seasoning and set aside to cool.

10. Increase oven temperature to 200°C. Roll out second half of pastry using the same method as for the pastry base. Gently spoon cooled vegetable filling into pastry shell and smooth top. It will be heavily domed but try to make sure the top of the dome is smooth. Brush the cooked pastry edges with beaten egg, and quickly but carefully place second sheet of pastry on top, pressing gently to adhere. Trim any edges and brush pastry with beaten egg.

11. Use a fork to poke plenty of air holes in the top of the pie. You can also cut a cross in the centre of the pie for extra ventilation, if you like. Bake for 30–40 minutes or until flaky and golden, finishing with the grill function for extra colour if necessary. Serve pie warm or cold.

Vegetarian or vegan sausage rolls

EGG-FREE OPTION
FODMAP FRIENDLY
GLUTEN FREE
VEGAN OPTION
FREE FROM HIGH-STARCH FLOURS
 OPTION
GUM-FREE OPTION
LACTOSE-FREE OPTION

**Makes: 30–34 mini sausage rolls or
 10 large sausage rolls**
Prep time: 1 hour
Cook time: 20–30 minutes

FOR THE PASTRY:

1 quantity rough puff pastry or vegan
 option (page 168)

FOR THE VEGAN SAUSAGE ROLL
FILLING:

500 g firm tofu, drained and crumbled
1 tablespoon balsamic vinegar
2 tablespoons gluten-free dark soy or
 tamari
2 tablespoons light brown sugar
1 tablespoon gluten-free miso paste
 (I use shiro or genmai)
2 tablespoons olive oil
60 ml (¼ cup) water
2 teaspoons psyllium husk
3 teaspoons dried sage
3 teaspoons dried rosemary
1 teaspoon smoked paprika
½–1 teaspoon ground cloves
pinch of chilli powder

TO FINISH:

1 egg, lightly beaten

NOTES

Leftover sausage rolls can be
kept in an airtight container in
the fridge for 3–4 days. They
also freeze well for up to a
month in an airtight container.

If you're a regular reader of my blog, you'll know how much satisfaction I get from (quite literally) shoving crumbled tofu recipes down your throats. This vegan sausage filling works exceedingly well here, and can also be used as a faux sausage crumble for pizza (page 236) or stirred into fresh egg pasta (page 242).

1. Prepare the pastry as per instructions on page 168. Divide the block of pastry into 2 pieces by cutting it with a sharp knife.

2. To make the vegan sausage filling, place all ingredients in a blender or high-speed food processor. Blend until the mixture is mostly smooth – some small lumps are okay. Season to taste.

3. Preheat oven to 200°C. Line 2 baking trays with baking paper. On a well-floured surface, roll out each piece of pastry into a rectangle. To make small sausage rolls, slice each rectangle down the middle of the short side, creating 4 long rectangles. To make larger sausage rolls, leave each rectangle whole.

4. Spoon a line of filling down each rectangle, aligned to one side, leaving a 2 cm border. Once you've spooned all the mixture out, brush the seam with a little whisked egg or water to help seal it. Working from the seam closest to the filling, roll each rectangle up and press down lightly to secure. Slice each log into 5–8 sausage rolls (5 for big ones, 8 for little ones) and place on prepared trays. Brush with a little more egg wash or plant-based milk with a bit of sugar (for browning) for a vegan option.

5. Using a fork, prick 2 sets of holes on top of each sausage roll. Bake for 20–30 minutes or until golden and cooked through.

Tomato, red pesto, thyme and goat's cheese galette

FODMAP FRIENDLY
GLUTEN FREE
FREE FROM HIGH-STARCH FLOURS
  OPTION
GUM-FREE OPTION

Serves: 6
Prep time: 20 minutes
Cook time: 30–40 minutes

FOR THE PASTRY:

1 quantity puff or rough puff pastry
  (page 166 or 168)

FOR THE RED PESTO:

75 g (½ cup) sun-dried tomatoes
40 g (¼ cup) raw almonds (or pine nuts)
4–5 sprigs fresh thyme
pinch of dried chilli flakes, optional
1–2 tablespoons olive oil, to achieve a
  paste

TO FINISH:

500–600 g vine-ripened tomatoes, thinly
  sliced
50–100 g marinated goat's cheese,
  to your taste
fresh thyme sprigs, to sprinkle
salt and pepper, to taste
1 extra-large egg, lightly beaten

NOTES

Galette keeps well in an
airtight container in the fridge
for up to 3 days.

To my mind, a galette is a lazy person's pie. I am a lazy person. No blind baking, no intricate latticework, just a good old-fashioned buttery, flaky crust (if you know, you know). You can change up the filling based on your mood; fine coins of zucchini and a FODMAP-friendly green pesto would be a great alternative.

～～～～～

1. Preheat the oven to 200°C. Roll out, laminate and chill pastry following instructions for the recipe you have chosen. Roll prepared pastry out into a large rectangle or rough circle, about 20–30 cm across and approximately 1 cm thick, on a large sheet of baking paper. The size doesn't matter too much; it will just dictate how many tomatoes you can fit in your galette. Place pastry in fridge to chill while you make the pesto.

2. To make the pesto, place all ingredients in a food processor and process until you have a thick paste consistency. Alternatively, you can use a mortar and pestle or chop ingredients finely by hand. Season to taste.

3. Gently spread pesto over pastry, leaving a 2 cm border. Top with tomatoes, cheese and thyme and season with salt and pepper. Using the baking paper to assist, flip the bare edges of pastry up over the filling, pressing lightly to secure. If the pastry cracks, allow it to warm up a little. Continue moving around the pastry, flipping edges up and securing them until you've gone all the way around and formed the galette. You can then gently mould the galette with your hands to shape it lightly if it's looking a bit angular. Brush pastry edges with beaten egg and carefully place galette (lifting the baking paper) on a large baking tray.

4. Bake for 30–40 minutes or until pastry is flaky and golden and tomatoes have softened. Serve warm or cold.

Flaky roti

FODMAP-FRIENDLY OPTION
GLUTEN FREE
LOW-LACTOSE OPTION

Makes: 4 roti
Prep time: 20 minutes
Chilling time: 20 minutes
Cook time: 10 minutes

The defining characteristics of roti, for me personally, are the buttery, flaky layers and chewy texture. In the process of developing this recipe, I found that a lot of gluten-free roti recipes online were basically flatbread. Delicious flatbread, I'm sure, but they didn't have the flaky layers and bite I so coveted.

As I was concurrently making ten thousand croissants, I thought to myself: why not make the roti in the same way I'm laminating the croissants – with an almost offensive amount of butter?

The thing about this recipe is you can scale the amount of butter up or down depending on your penchant for decadence. Use the full 75 g plus smearing butter for a real treat, or scale it back to 50 g and a light smear for a more modest affair. Keep in mind though that the butter is what creates the flakiness, so the less you use, the less flaky your roti will be.

30 g dried milk powder (regular, lactose-free or a plant-based milk variety)
90 g tapioca or potato starch, plus extra to dust
40 g fine brown rice flour or sorghum flour
40 g fine white rice flour
½ teaspoon xanthan gum
2 teaspoons psyllium husk
½ teaspoon fine salt (use 1 teaspoon if you use unsalted butter)
75 g chilled butter, cut into cubes
125 ml (½ cup) iced water
50–75 g extra butter, at room temperature, for the layers (see intro)
butter or oil, for the pan

1. Whisk together the dry ingredients in a medium-sized mixing bowl. Add the cold butter cubes and use your fingertips to quickly rub the butter into the flour. The mixture should look like wet sand, with only small chunks of butter visible.

2. Add the iced water and use your hands to gently combine. You don't want to crush the little bits of butter. Once mixture has formed a shaggy ball, cover and place in fridge for 10 minutes to chill.

3. Flour a clean work bench liberally with tapioca flour. Divide dough into 4 pieces. Roll out first piece of dough (keep remaining 3 in fridge) into a rough rectangle. As an option, you can laminate the dough quickly for a bit of extra flakiness. Simply roll the dough out into a rough rectangle, dust off the excess flour and fold it like a business letter. You can repeat this again if you fancy.

RECIPE CONTINUES >

The xanthan gum serves a textural purpose here: it creates the chew that you'd expect from a good roti.

Don't stack the roti on top of each other as you cook them as it deflates their flakiness.

I had moderate success using a plant-based butter, although the roti didn't become quite as flaky.

4. Roll the dough into a roughly 8 cm x 4 cm rectangle. Dust off any excess flour (a little is okay) and use your finger to smear some of the soft butter in little dabs across the pastry. The water content of the extra butter will give the roti extra flakiness and lift as it cooks.

5. Starting from a long side of the rectangle, roll dough into a log and press gently to seal.

6. Now you have a long snake of dough. Take one end of the 'snake' and begin rolling it into a swirl, keeping the seam on the inside of the swirl. When you get to the end, tuck tail under the swirl and press to secure.

7. Flour the bench and gently roll the swirl of dough out into an approximately 10–15 cm diameter circle. Place this roti on a flat plate and into the fridge to set the butter. Repeat with remaining dough to make 4 roti.

8. Preheat a large non-stick frying pan over medium heat. Once hot, add a little butter or oil. Add the first roti – it should sizzle on impact. Pop a lid on the pan and cook roti for 2 minutes or until first side is golden. Flip and cook for a further 2 minutes or until golden. Repeat with the remaining roti, adjusting heat as necessary.

9. To fluff (or buss up) the roti, place one hand on either side of the roti and bring your hands in quickly in a clapping motion. This will help separate the layers. Roti are best served hot.

Chinese scallion pancakes

FODMAP-FRIENDLY OPTION
GLUTEN FREE
LOW-LACTOSE OPTION

Makes: 4 pancakes
Prep time: 30 minutes + 10 minutes
**   resting**
Chilling time: 20 minutes
Cook time: 10 minutes

This recipe is very heavily based on the flaky roti recipe on page 176. The difference is we're using a scalded spring onion (scallion) oil mixture in place of the room-temperature butter. The scalding helps bring out all the flavours and leads to a bolder tasting pancake. Make sure you cut the spring onions really, truly finely, or else you're setting yourself up for a headache when it comes to rolling out the pancakes.

As with the roti recipe, you can scale the amount of butter up or down depending on your penchant for decadence. Use the whole 75 g for a full-on extravagance, or scale it back to 50 g for a more modest affair. Keep in mind though that the butter is what creates the flakiness, so the less you use, the less flaky your pancakes.

~~~~~~~

FOR THE SPRING ONION PASTE:

½ teaspoon Chinese five spice (optional)
½ teaspoon fine salt
8 Sichuan peppercorns, crushed (optional)
white pepper, to taste
6 spring onions, green part only, finely chopped
60 ml (¼ cup) vegetable or peanut oil

FOR THE PANCAKES:

30 g (¼ cup) dried milk powder (regular, lactose-free or a plant-based milk variety)
90 g (¾ cup) tapioca or potato starch, plus extra to dust
40 g (¼ cup) fine brown rice or sorghum flour
40 g (¼ cup) fine white rice flour
½ teaspoon xanthan gum
2 teaspoons ground psyllium husk
75 g chilled butter, cut into cubes
125 ml (½ cup) iced water
butter or oil, for the pan

1. To make the spring onion paste, combine the Chinese five spice, if using, salt, peppercorns, white pepper and spring onion in a small heatproof bowl. Heat the oil in a small saucepan over medium heat. Once hot, carefully pour the hot oil over the spring onion mixture. Stir and set aside.

2. To make the pancakes, place the milk powder, tapioca starch, flours, xanthan gum and psyllium in a medium bowl and whisk to combine. Add the chilled butter and, using clean fingertips, rub butter into flour until mixture resembles coarse crumbs.

3. Add iced water and use your hands to gently combine. You don't want to crush the little bits of butter. Once mixture has formed a shaggy ball, cover and place in fridge for 10 minutes to chill.

4. Liberally flour a clean work bench with tapioca flour and divide dough into 4 pieces. Roll out first piece of dough (keep remaining 3 in fridge) into a rough rectangle. As an option, you can laminate the dough quickly for a bit of extra flakiness. Simply roll the dough out into a rough rectangle, dust off the excess flour and fold it like a business letter. You can repeat this again if you fancy.

RECIPE CONTINUES >

The xanthan gum serves
a textural purpose here: it
creates the chew that you'd
expect from a good scallion
pancake.

Don't stack the pancakes on top
of each other as you cook them
as it condenses their layers.

I had moderate success using
a plant-based butter, although
the pancakes didn't become
quite as flaky.

These pancakes are best served
straight from the pan, but
leftovers can be kept in an
airtight container in the fridge
for 1–2 days.

5. Roll dough out into a small, long rectangle approximately 8 cm x 4 cm. Dust off any excess flour, then use the back of a spoon to gently smear a conservative amount of the scallion paste across the pastry.

6. Starting from a long side of the rectangle, roll dough into a log and press gently to seal.

7. Now you have a long snake of dough. Take one end of the 'snake' and begin rolling it into a swirl, keeping the seam on the inside of the swirl. When you get to the end, tuck tail under the swirl and press to secure.

8. Flour bench and gently roll the swirl of dough out into an approximately 10–15 cm diameter circle. Place this pancake on a flat plate and into the fridge to set the butter. Repeat with remaining dough to make 4 pancakes.

9. Preheat a large non-stick frying pan over medium heat. Once hot, add a little butter or oil. Add the first pancake – it should sizzle on impact. Pop a lid on and cook pancake for 2 minutes or until first side is golden. Flip and cook for a further 2 minutes or until golden. Repeat with the remaining pancakes, adjusting heat as necessary. Serve.

Empanada pastry

LOW LACTOSE
FODMAP FRIENDLY
GLUTEN FREE
EGG-FREE OPTION

**Makes: enough pastry for
    12 empanadas**
**Prep time: 45 minutes + time to prep
    filling**
Cook time: 25 minutes

I have exceedingly fond memories of the bustling empanada stores in San Telmo market, Buenos Aires. Although I couldn't eat them, I wolfed down many a humita while the buttery scent of travel companions' empanadas wafted past. This pastry and its accompanying corn and parmesan filling (page 185) are my ode to that Argentina trip.

~~~~~~~~

160 g (1 cup) fine white rice flour
60 g (½ cup) tapioca flour, plus extra
    to dust
¾ teaspoon xanthan gum
2 teaspoons caster sugar
1 teaspoon fine salt
100 g chilled butter, cut into cubes
½ an extra-large egg (use the other half
    to seal the pastries)
2 teaspoons vinegar
4–5 tablespoons FODMAP-friendly milk
    of choice
enough empanada filling of choice (I like
    corn and parmesan, see page 185) to
    fill 12 empanadas

TO FINISH:
½ egg, lightly beaten (retain from
    empanada pastry)

1. Place flours, xanthan gum, sugar and salt in a medium bowl and whisk to combine. Add butter and, using clean fingertips, rub the butter into the flour until mixture resembles coarse crumbs.

2. Add the egg and vinegar and use a fork to combine. Add the milk, tablespoon by tablespoon, until your dough comes together to form a smooth ball without any dry bits.

3. Wrap dough in plastic film and place in fridge while you prepare your chosen filling.

4. Preheat oven to 170°C. Line a baking tray with baking paper. Tear a golf-ball-sized piece of dough off and cover the remaining dough. Roll dough out on a lightly floured work surface until about 2 mm thick.

5. Cut dough out with a 15 cm round cutter or large glass. Spoon ½–1 tablespoon of filling into the centre of pastry round. Brush the edges of the pastry with the egg wash, before folding to enclose filling and form a semi-circle. You will quickly get a sense of how much you can stuff into each pastry without it bursting. Use pressure to seal the edges of the pastry, ensuring there are no holes for the filling to leak out. Repeat with remaining pastry to make 12 empanadas.

6. Transfer empanadas to a large, lined baking tray and brush with beaten egg. Use a fork with thin prongs to make 3 sets of steam holes in each empanada. Make sure the fork goes right through to the filling. Bake for 25 minutes or until golden. Serve warm or cold.

NOTES

I find that these empanadas are a little prone to leaking a bit of filling if not handled with a reasonable amount of care. Make sure all the edges are well sealed before baking, and keep the oven temperature on the lower side to encourage a more even bake.

Because this dough is fragile, I found that crimping the edges with a fork resulted in more leaks than simply pressing them together with your fingers to seal, so I don't recommend it.

Like my dumpling wrapper and pastry recipes, I daresay you could substitute flours as you see fit. Keep to the ratio of 160 g wholegrain to 60 g starch, or up the xanthan gum content to 1 teaspoon for a completely wholegrain version.

For an egg-free version, use the rough puff pastry recipe (page 168) with 100 g butter. Add more liquid as necessary to compensate. Then, use the vegan egg wash from page 69 to finish.

Empanadas keep well in an airtight container in the fridge for a few days.

Corn empanada filling *(empanadas de humita)*

LOW LACTOSE
FODMAP FRIENDLY
GLUTEN FREE

**Makes: enough filling for
    12 empanadas**
Prep time: 10 minutes
Cook time: 10 minutes

My last trip overseas in ~the before times~ was to Argentina, a country full of good food and great empanadas. I didn't get to try a gluten-free empanada on the trip, so this is my attempt to rectify that cultural faux pas and general injustice.

I chose this corn filling because it's traditional to Argentina, and reminiscent of the humitas I ate there. Canned corn is actually quite FODMAP friendly and it makes for a delectable filling.

~~~~~~~~

2 tablespoons vegetable oil or butter
5–6 spring onions, green part only, chopped
2 tablespoons gluten-free cornflour
60 ml (¼ cup) FODMAP-friendly milk of choice
420 g can corn kernels, drained
200 g creamed corn
75 g vegetarian parmesan cheese, grated
2 teaspoons smoked paprika
½ teaspoon ground nutmeg
pinch of asafoetida (optional)
pinch of chilli powder, to taste
1 teaspoon white vinegar
salt and pepper, to taste

1. Heat the oil (or butter) in a medium saucepan over medium-low heat. Cook the spring onions, stirring, for 5 or 6 minutes or until softened and fragrant. Add the cornflour and milk in quick succession, followed by the corn kernels and creamed corn. Stir really well and cook for two minutes or until the mixture is well combined.

2. Add the cheese, spices and vinegar and cook, whisking constantly, until cheese has melted and the mixture is nice and thick. Season with salt and pepper to taste.

3. Once cooled, use to fill empanadas (page 182).

Yorkshire puddings

GUM FREE
FODMAP FRIENDLY
GLUTEN FREE
DAIRY-FREE OPTION

Makes: 9 Yorkshire puddings
Prep time: 25 minutes
Cook time: 20–25 minutes

generous amount of vegetable oil,
    for greasing
120 g (¾ cup) fine white rice flour
10 g tapioca flour, optional (for a bit
    of stretch and chew)
3 extra-large eggs
½ teaspoon fine salt
250 ml (1 cup) FODMAP-friendly milk of
    choice

My dad is a proud Yorkshireman, so I'm no stranger to the Yorkshire pudding. Sunday roast was a weekly tradition and the wholly addictive carbs were always on the menu. I tested a whole raft of different flour ratios before I settled on this one; which is, I'm pleased to say, Dad-approved.

1. Preheat oven to 200°C. Grease nine 80 ml (⅓ cup) capacity muffin holes with oil. Place muffin tray in oven to preheat for 20–30 minutes or until steaming hot.

2. Meanwhile, combine flours, eggs, salt, milk and water in a blender and blend until smooth and frothy. Transfer mixture to a jug.

3. Open oven (hot oil can sting your eyes so stand back as you open it) and, working quickly, pour the batter into the prepared muffin holes. I like to fill the muffin holes as I find the puddings have a better shape. Bake for 20–25 minutes or until puddings are puffed and golden. Don't open the oven at all during the baking time. Serve immediately for maximum puff (although personally, I quite like eating them cold).

NOTES

Resting the batter overnight in the fridge has a positive impact on the height of Yorkshire puddings. From what I've read, it's best to let it come to room temperature the next day before baking. Resting the batter isn't compulsory, though; using fresh batter will still yield a delightful pud.

The mixture should sizzle on impact with the oil – if it doesn't, you haven't preheated long enough. This isn't the end of the world, but you might not get as much height on your Yorkshire puddings.

A cheap and stale rice flour will be really noticeable in this recipe, so make sure you buy some good quality stuff. I like to get mine at the bulk food store because I know it will be fresh, but I realise this might not be a safe option for coeliacs.

SAVOURY PASTRY

Gum-free 'wheat' tortillas

Makes: 10–14 tortillas
Prep time: 30 minutes
Cook time: 20 minutes

320 g (2 cups) fine white rice flour
120 g (1 cup) tapioca flour, plus extra
   to dust
1 tablespoon caster sugar
1 ¼ teaspoons fine salt
1 ½ tablespoons psyllium husk powder
   (see notes)
50 g butter, at room temperature, cut
   into cubes
375 ml (1 ½ cups) boiling water
oil, to cook tortillas

I like to think that I'm better than wanting a white, sugary tortilla when I could have a more authentic corn one. The truth is I am not at all, so here we are. This recipe can be halved for a smaller crowd, although cooked tortillas freeze and defrost beautifully.

~~~

1. Place the flours, sugar, salt and psyllium in a medium heatproof bowl and whisk to combine. Stir through the cubes of butter. Whisking constantly, gradually add the boiling water. You may not need the whole amount so add it by sight. The mixture should look crumbly and moist, without any dry bits on the bottom of the bowl.

2. Flour a clean work bench with extra tapioca flour. Tear off a golf-ball-sized piece of dough, keeping the rest covered while you work. Roll dough out to a circle, as thin as you would like (it's a very easy dough to work with). You can use a large round cutter or mouth of a bowl to trim edges or leave as is. Personally, I use a 20 cm bowl with a thin edge. Repeat until you have used all the dough.

3. Heat 1 teaspoon oil in a large non-stick frying pan over medium–high heat. Cook the tortilla for 1–2 minutes each side, or until it has some lovely brown spots and is cooked through. Repeat with the remaining tortillas.

NOTES

I recommend psyllium husk powder in this recipe because it doesn't affect the appearance of the tortillas and it gives a bit of extra flexibility. You can grind the husks into a powder using a spice grinder.

You can experiment with the flours you use in this recipe. I chose white rice because I wanted tortillas that were close in taste and appearance to the regular variety. I have also successfully made this recipe with all fine white rice flour – that is, without high-starch flour. The tortillas are a little thicker and slightly less flexible, but still delicious.

You can use a plant-based butter to make these tortillas vegan. I don't recommend omitting the sugar – it results in the lovely caramelised spots and a great flavour.

Leftover tortillas can be stored in an airtight container in the fridge for 3–4 days or frozen and defrosted. Gently microwave or steam bake to reheat.

Vegan taco mince

LACTOSE FREE
FREE FROM HIGH-STARCH FLOURS
GUM FREE
EGG FREE
VEGAN
FODMAP FRIENDLY
GLUTEN FREE

Serves: 4–6
Prep time: 15 minutes
Cook time: 25–35 minutes

What started as an accompanying recipe to the 'wheat' tortillas (page 188) has swiftly become a low-effort, high-reward weeknight dinner and arguably my most requested dish. I like to keep a batch in the fridge for tacos, a protein-filled salad accompaniment, or just to appease my needy, hungry sister.

You can replace the walnuts with tofu or two grated carrots, or simply omit them (but your dish will be extra saucy).

~~~~~~~

FOR THE MINCE:

450 g firm tofu, crumbled
100 g walnuts, finely chopped
60 ml (¼ cup) gluten-free dark soy sauce
    or tamari
1 tablespoon pure maple syrup
80 g (⅓ cup) tomato paste
1 tablespoon olive oil
2 tablespoons nutritional yeast (optional)
1 tablespoon ground cumin
2–3 teaspoons smoked paprika
2 teaspoons dried oregano
2 teaspoons dried sage powder
chilli powder, to taste

FOR THE SALSA:

2 cups shredded red cabbage
juice of ½–1 lime
1 bunch fresh coriander, finely chopped
3–4 large tomatoes, diced
2 Lebanese cucumbers, thinly sliced
2 teaspoons toasted cumin seeds
seasoning, to taste

TO FINISH:

lime juice
tortillas (page 188)

1. To make the mince, preheat the oven to 180°C and combine the tofu and walnuts in a large bowl. In another bowl, combine the remaining ingredients to make the sauce. Taste and adjust according to your preferences.

2. Pour the sauce mixture over the walnut tofu mixture and mix until it's completely coated. Transfer mixture to a 28 cm/1.6 litre baking dish and bake in the oven for 15–20 minutes. Stir the mince and cook for an additional 10–15 minutes or until browned on top and fragrant.

3. While the mince is cooking, combine all the ingredients for the salsa in a large bowl. Stir to meld the flavours and adjust to suit your taste.

4. Remove the mince from the oven and serve with tortillas, salsa and lime.

Wholegrain cacio e pepe scones

LOW-LACTOSE OPTION
GUM FREE
FREE FROM HIGH-STARCH FLOURS
FODMAP-FRIENDLY OPTION
GLUTEN FREE

Makes: 6 scones
Prep time: 20 minutes
Cook time: 25 minutes

280 g (1 ¾ cups) sorghum flour or
   240 g (1 ½ cups) fine white rice flour
2 teaspoons gluten-free baking powder
1 teaspoon bicarbonate of soda
20 g (¼ cup) psyllium husk or
   1 ½ tablespoons psyllium husk powder
¾ teaspoon to 1 tablespoon
   freshly cracked black pepper
¼ teaspoon fine salt
150 g vegetarian parmesan cheese, finely
   grated
200 g chilled butter, cut into cubes
250 g thick Greek yoghurt
   (lactose free if needed)
2 tablespoons vinegar of choice
   (white or apple cider work well)
1 extra-large egg

TO FINISH:

1 egg, lightly beaten (or milk of choice)

Given my love for both the cacio and the pepe, it seemed inevitable that the flavour combination would appear at least twice in this book. These scones are 100% wholegrain and use only one flour. They hold together like a dream courtesy of the freshly grated parmesan.

1. Preheat oven to 180°C. Line a 28 cm/1.6 litre baking dish with baking paper. Place flour, baking powder, bicarbonate of soda, psyllium, seasoning and parmesan in a medium bowl and whisk to combine. Add the chilled butter and, using clean fingertips, rub in butter until mixture resembles coarse breadcrumbs.

2. Combine yoghurt and vinegar in a small bowl. Add the egg and whisk to combine. Add the yoghurt mixture to the flour mixture and, using a fork, stir to combine. I find it best to finish mixing using my hands.

3. Press dough out until approximately 3–4 cm thick, dusting with a little extra flour as required. Using a round cutter, cut dough into 6 pieces, or alternatively shape into rounds, and place them snugly in the prepared dish.

4. Brush scones with beaten egg or milk and bake for 25 minutes or until golden and firm to the touch. Set aside to cool slightly before serving.

NOTES

Scones are best on the day of baking but will keep in an airtight container at room temperature for 2–3 days. Microwave or steam bake to re-warm them.

CHAPTER NINE

Savoury sourdough

Sourdough flatbread

LOW LACTOSE
FREE FROM HIGH-STARCH FLOURS
GUM FREE
EGG FREE
VEGAN
FODMAP FRIENDLY
GLUTEN FREE

Makes: 4 flatbreads
Prep time: 30 minutes
Proofing time: 2+ hours fermentation
    (optional)
Cook time: 10 minutes

FOR THE BINDER:

1 tablespoon psyllium husk
1 tablespoon oil
80 ml (⅓ cup) boiling water

FOR THE DRY INGREDIENTS:

80 g (½ cup) fine white rice flour
80 g (½ cup) buckwheat flour
5 g (1 teaspoon) fine salt

FOR THE WET INGREDIENTS:

65 g (¼ cup) gluten-free sourdough
    starter, fed or unfed
1 tablespoon vegetable or olive oil
180 ml (¾ cup) warm water

NOTES

You can experiment with different wholegrain flours, bearing in mind that you might need to adjust the hydration of the dough.

Flatbreads can be stored in an airtight container on the bench for 2 days.

If you're looking for an easy entry point to the world of gluten-free sourdough, you're in the right place. These flatbreads can be rolled as thin as a tortilla (and make for a great sourdough version, incidentally) or as thick as roti. You can also ferment them according to your preference: cook them instantly for a very subtle sour flavour, or leave them overnight on the bench for some serious tang.

This recipe can easily be scaled up, and leftover dough can be kept in the fridge, covered, for 2–3 days.

1. To make the binder, place the psyllium, oil and boiling water in a small bowl and whisk until well combined. Set aside for 5 minutes or until mixture thickens and forms a gel.

2. Place dry ingredients in a medium bowl and whisk to combine. Add the sourdough starter, oil, warm water and binder. Stir to combine then, using clean hands, squelch the dough through your fingers, evenly distributing and dispersing the psyllium gel. Add a little extra water if dough seems dry.

3. You can cook the dough immediately, or cover and leave in a warm draught-free spot to ferment for a couple of hours or up to overnight. This will develop the sourdough flavour and create extra air pockets in the dough.

4. Lightly flour a clean work surface. I like to use tapioca because it's inexpensive and soft. Divide dough into 4 pieces. Use your rolling pin to roll each piece into a circular (or not) flatbread.

5. Heat a large frying pan over medium–high heat. You can use a little oil or dry fry the flatbreads. Cook the flatbread for 2 minutes each side, or until it has golden spots and is cooked through. Repeat with remaining flatbreads. Serve warm or cold.

'White bread' sourdough

VEGAN
GLUTEN FREE
FODMAP FRIENDLY
GUM FREE

Makes: 1 loaf
Prep time: 30 minutes
Proofing time: overnight fermentation
   + 2–4 hours
Cook time: 1 hour 20 minutes

Let it be known that I'm not a fan of attaching judgement to food, but I consider this to be more of a 'treat' loaf. This is due to the higher starch content, which is a delightfully easy source of food for a bacterial overgrowth in your small intestine (ask me how I know that). With that said, starches do create a beautiful elastic crumb and the value of finding joy in baking and eating cannot be overlooked.

This dough can be used to make baguettes, bread rolls or hot dog buns as well. Note that you'll need a banneton (or bowl lined with a tea towel) and a Dutch oven for this recipe.

~~~~~

FOR THE PRE-FERMENT:

130 g gluten-free sourdough starter, thick and active, fed 3–4 hours before
100 g water, plus 50 g more if needed
100 g sorghum or millet flour

FOR THE LOAF:

25 g psyllium husk
400 g water
150 g sorghum flour
100 g tapioca flour
100 g potato starch
13 g (2 ¼ teaspoons) fine salt
¼ teaspoon ground ginger
¼ teaspoon vitamin C powder (or substitute with apple cider vinegar, added to psyllium liquid mix)
1 tablespoon olive oil (optional, makes for a softer crust)
fine white rice flour, for dusting

THE NIGHT BEFORE:

1. To make the pre-ferment, combine the starter and 100 g water in a large bowl. Add the flour and whisk until well combined. The pre-ferment should have the consistency of a smooth paste or yoghurt. If it looks dry, add 50 g more water to achieve the right consistency. Cover and set aside in a warm, draught-free place overnight.

THE NEXT MORNING:

2. The pre-ferment should look like a starter that has begun to fall after not being fed for a while. The top should have some popped bubbles, but will still look quite watery. Even if you think it has 'failed' it should still strengthen both the flavour and the physical properties of the dough.

3. Combine the psyllium and 400 g water (and apple cider vinegar, if using) in a large bowl, and whisk to combine. Set aside for 5–10 minutes or until a thick gel forms.

4. Meanwhile, place flours, potato starch, salt, ginger and vitamin C powder, if using, in a large non-reactive bowl and whisk to combine.

RECIPE CONTINUES >

You can store the loaf in a bag or freeze it in slices.

HOW I SHAPE MY DOUGH

Drop the dough onto the floured bench 2 or 3 times to create a smooth surface on the bottom. Any cracks in your dough will be exacerbated in the oven, so you want to create a smooth ball of dough.

Using your hands, flatten the dough into a rough oblong shape approximately the size of your banneton, short side facing you. Check the bottom is smooth, then fold the long edges in to the middle of the dough. Then, roll up from the short side until it resembles a cinnamon scroll. If you're using a rectangular banneton, tuck just the edges under to create a loaf shape. If you're using a circular banneton, tuck the edges under all the way around to form a circular shape.

Flip the loaf smooth side up and place it on the counter. Use both hands to spin it in one direction on the bench. This helps to seal any seams on the underside of the dough. Once you're happy, gently pick up the dough with one hand and lower the banneton over the top. Flip them over so the loaf falls into the banneton. Check that the seams are closed and pinch together any that aren't. Your loaf is now ready for proofing.

5. Whisk the psyllium gel and oil, if using, into the pre-ferment. Add the pre-ferment mixture to bowl with the flour mixture. Use a spoon to stir the dough until it starts to look like scone dough, then get your hands in there and squelch the dough through your fingers until you have a mostly smooth ball of dough. You could also use a stand mixer with a dough hook, but I find this easier and quicker.

6. Place dough onto a lightly floured surface and shape it to fit your banneton (proofing basket). Lightly flour your banneton with fine white rice flour. Place dough, nice side (aka the side with no seams) down, into the banneton. The base of the loaf (with all the seams) should be facing upwards.

7. Place banneton into a giant ziplock bag, then into the fridge or onto bench top to proof. If you proof it on the bench, it will take anywhere from 2–4 hours, climate dependent. This is a high-starch loaf, so it will proof quicker than other loaves. If you use the fridge, you can leave it overnight, but it will need to bake first thing in the morning.

8. 30 minutes before the loaf is ready, preheat your oven with your Dutch oven inside to the highest setting possible. Note that some Dutch ovens are not designed for high temperatures so only go as high as you can without damaging it. Dough is properly proofed when you poke it and the indent bounces back partially, but not all the way. It should have tangibly risen and feel airy and light.

9. Take a rectangular piece of baking paper (I like the reusable variety for this) and lay it on a damp bench. Carefully invert the loaf onto the centre of the baking paper, leaving the edges free so you can use them as handles. Use a lame (sharp scoring blade) or a sharp knife to score the loaf.

10. Carefully and quickly remove the super-hot Dutch oven from oven. Quickly lower in bread (being careful not to touch the sides), gently replace lid to trap the steam and return to oven.

11. For a blonder crust, reduce oven temperature to 220°C and bake for 1 hour. For a darker crust, keep oven at the highest setting (no hotter than 300°C) for 30 minutes, before lowering to 220°C for the next 30 minutes. Remove lid and continue to bake for 20 minutes, or until the crust sounds hollow when you knock on it. For a blonder crust, reduce heat to 180°C.

12. Take loaf out of oven, remove baking paper and place on a wire rack. Allow to cool completely (3–4 hours, ideally overnight) before slicing, as you can compress all the air in the loaf and end up with gummy bread.

Everything dough

LACTOSE FREE
GUM FREE
EGG FREE
VEGAN
FODMAP FRIENDLY
GLUTEN FREE

Makes: 1 loaf
Prep time: 30 minutes
Proofing time: overnight fermentation + 3–6 hours
Cook time: 1 hour 30 minutes

FOR THE PRE-FERMENT:

130 g gluten-free sourdough starter, thick and active, fed 3–4 hours before
130 g water
75 g sorghum flour

FOR THE LOAF:

100 g sorghum flour
100 g tapioca flour
75 g millet flour (or extra buckwheat flour)
50 g buckwheat flour
50 g potato starch (or extra tapioca flour)
13 g (2 ¼ teaspoons) fine salt
¼ teaspoon ground ginger
¼ teaspoon vitamin C powder (or substitute with apple cider vinegar, added to psyllium liquid mix)
fine white rice flour, for dusting the bench

FOR THE BINDER GEL:

370 g water
25 g psyllium husk
1 tablespoon olive oil
1 tablespoon pure maple syrup

This is one of my earlier sourdough recipes that I never got around to posting online. What I love about this recipe is that it's endlessly versatile once you get a sense of the hydration required for each purpose – I've made focaccia, pizza, Vegemite rolls, fougasse, baguettes and bread rolls using this recipe. Note that you'll need a banneton (or bowl lined with a tea towel) and a Dutch oven for this recipe.

~~~~~~

THE NIGHT BEFORE:

1. Combine the starter and 130 g water in a large bowl. Add the flour and whisk until well combined. Cover and set aside in a warm, draught-free place overnight.

THE NEXT MORNING:

2. The pre-ferment should look like a starter that has begun to fall after not being fed for a while. The top should have some popped bubbles but will still look quite watery. Even if you think it has 'failed' it should still strengthen both the flavour and the physical properties of the dough.

3. In a small mixing bowl, combine the 370 g water and psyllium husk. Leave it to completely thicken and gel (around 10–15 minutes, maybe a little longer).

4. While you're waiting, place the flours, potato starch, salt, ginger and vitamin C powder, if using, in a large, non-reactive mixing bowl. Whisk to thoroughly combine.

5. Once the psyllium has thickened, whisk in the olive oil and maple syrup (and apple cider vinegar, if using). Add the gel mixture to the pre-ferment and whisk to combine. Add the wet ingredients to flour mixture and stir until it begins to look a bit like a scone dough. Using clean hands, continue to mix until a dough forms.

NOTES

Bread keeps well stored in a clean tea towel for 2 days. Alternatively, it makes great toast and freezes well in slices.

6. Place dough onto a lightly floured surface and shape it to fit your banneton (proofing basket). Lightly flour banneton with white rice flour. Place dough, nice side (aka the side with no seams) down, into the banneton.

7. Place banneton in a giant ziplock bag and seal. Proof the loaf for 2–3 hours on the bench, noting that the temperature of your kitchen and the season is critically important in proofing times (see page 159). When you start to see tangible rising action, transfer loaf to fridge for 1–3 hours to finish proofing. I find this an easy, almost foolproof way to ensure the loaf proofs nicely without over-proofing.

8. 30 minutes before the loaf is ready, preheat your oven with your Dutch oven inside to the highest setting possible. Note that some Dutch ovens are not designed for high temperatures so only go as high as you can without damaging it. Dough is properly proofed when you poke it and the indent bounces back partially, but not all the way. It should be tangibly risen and feel light and puffy.

9. Take a rectangular piece of baking paper and lay it on a damp bench. Invert the loaf onto the centre of the baking paper, leaving the edges to use as handles. Use a lame (sharp scoring blade) or a sharp knife to score the loaf.

10. Carefully and quickly remove the super-hot Dutch oven from oven. Quickly lower in bread (being careful not to touch the sides), gently replace lid to trap the steam and return to oven.

11. Reduce oven to 220°C and bake for 1 hour. Remove lid and continue to bake for 25–30 minutes (with the option to turn the oven down to 180°C for a blonder crust) or until the crust sounds hollow when you knock on it.

12. Once cooked to your liking, take loaf out of oven, remove baking paper and set on a cooling rack. I find this loaf only needs to cool for a couple of hours before you slice it, but it might be a little wet inside. Ideally, slice it the day after baking.

THIS DOUGH IS THE *white shirt*
OF THE GLUTEN-FREE
sourdough – IT WORKS FOR
PRETTY MUCH *everything*.
WITH THE RIGHT *hydration,*
YOU CAN USE THIS RECIPE FOR
pizzas, scrolls, focaccia AND
(OF COURSE) AN *excellent*
LOAF OF BREAD.

Starch-free sourdough

LACTOSE FREE
FREE FROM HIGH-STARCH FLOURS
GUM FREE
EGG FREE
VEGAN
FODMAP FRIENDLY
GLUTEN FREE

Makes: 1 loaf
Prep time: 45 minutes
**Proofing time: overnight fermentation
    + 3–5 hours**
Cook time: 1 hour 30 minutes

FOR THE DRY INGREDIENTS:

150 g sorghum flour
150 g buckwheat flour
150 g fine brown rice flour
⅛ teaspoon vitamin C powder (or apple
    cider vinegar)
⅛ teaspoon ground ginger

FOR THE WET INGREDIENTS:

130 g gluten-free sourdough starter,
    thick and active, fed 3–4 hours before
750 g water
2 tablespoons oil (any type)
1 tablespoon pure maple syrup

TO FINISH:

13 g (2 ¼ teaspoons) fine salt
20–30 g psyllium husk

Starches are generally added to gluten-free breads to give them a light, chewy and more flexible crumb. This loaf uses an overnight autolyse (see page 4) and high hydration to achieve this with only wholegrain flours.

Because this is a high-hydration formula without any stretch from starches, I highly recommend using a steel loaf pan.

～～～～～

THE NIGHT BEFORE:

1. Combine dry ingredients and divide between two large non-reactive bowls. Add the starter and 300 g water to the first bowl (the pre-ferment) and whisk to combine. Add the oil, maple syrup (and apple cider vinegar, if using) and the remaining 350 g water to the second bowl (the autolyse) and whisk to combine. Cover both bowls and leave to ferment on bench overnight.

THE NEXT DAY:

2. Add salt to the bowl with oil. It should have a thin layer of water on top, which will dissolve the salt.

3. Combine contents of both bowls and whisk well. Add 20 g psyllium husk and whisk again until combined. The mixture will still look wet, but don't panic! Cover it and set aside to thicken for 20 minutes.

4. Assess the dough. Because it will bake in a loaf pan, it doesn't need too much structure. If you are unable to pick dough up and transfer to a 21.5 cm x 11.5 cm (base measurement) steel loaf pan, add an additional 5 g psyllium and wait 10 minutes before trying again. Keep in mind that higher psyllium husk content can equate to a gummy loaf, so try not to add too much.

5. Transfer the dough to tin and cover it well (I like to put mine in a reusable giant ziplock bag). Set aside to proof for approximately 3–5 hours, climate dependent. Keep in mind that there is no starch in this loaf, so it will take longer than the starchier loaves in this book.

NOTES

Bread is best the day after baking but keeps well with the cut-side down on the bench or in an airtight container. It can be sliced and frozen for future toast.

6. Place oven rack in middle of oven and preheat oven to highest possible setting for 30 minutes. Half fill a small baking dish with boiling water and place in base of oven 10 minutes before baking.

7. Reduce oven temperature to 220°C and bake loaf for 20 minutes. Reduce oven temperature again to 180°C and cook for an additional 40 minutes. You can take the steam bath out at this point if you like. I generally keep it in for a softer crust. Lightly tent top of loaf with foil if it's taking on too much colour. Continue cooking for a final 20–30 minutes or until the crust is firm to the touch and sounds hollow if you tap on it.

8. Remove loaf from the oven and place on a wire rack to cool completely (3–4 hours, ideally overnight) or remove loaf from tin and cool in oven (on rack) with door ajar. Allow to cool completely before slicing to prevent a gummy loaf.

Sourdough fougasse

LACTOSE FREE
GUM FREE
EGG FREE
VEGAN
FODMAP FRIENDLY
GLUTEN FREE

Makes: 1 large fougasse
Prep time: 30 minutes
Proofing time: overnight fermentation
    + 2–5 hours
Cook time: 40 minutes

This is my favourite sort of sourdough recipe – one that's basically impossible to stuff up. Unlike many of the other loaves that require a watchful eye during proofing, this fougasse couldn't be lower maintenance. Simply whip up the dough the night before and leave to ferment overnight before shaping and baking whenever you get around to it the next day. This recipe also works for pizza bases and buns. If you can't find brown teff flour, use ivory teff. Otherwise, use 200 g sorghum and 100 g buckwheat flour. You can stud your fougasse with olives, sun-dried tomatoes or rosemary sprigs (or, you know, all of the above).

~~~~~~~

FOR THE DRY INGREDIENTS:

200 g brown teff flour
100 g sorghum flour
100 g potato starch
25 g psyllium husk
13 g (2 ¼ teaspoons) fine salt
⅛ teaspoon ground ginger
⅛ teaspoon vitamin C powder or apple
    cider vinegar

FOR THE WET INGREDIENTS:

475 g water
2 tablespoons olive oil
130 g gluten-free sourdough starter,
    thick and active, fed 3–4 hours before

NOTES

Fougasse can be stored in an airtight container on the bench for 2–3 days.

THE NIGHT BEFORE:

1. Place all dry ingredients in a large non-reactive bowl and whisk to combine. Add the wet ingredients and whisk until well combined. Cover and leave on bench overnight, or in the fridge if it's hot and humid where you live.

THE NEXT DAY:

2. You can make 1 large fougasse or 2 medium ones. Line 1 or 2 baking trays accordingly. Lightly grease the baking paper and place the dough on top. Use your hands to spread the dough into an oval shape, roughly 3–4 cm thick. Use a knife to slice through the dough in a decorative fashion. The internet has some dazzling fougasse shape ideas.

3. Cover fougasse and proof in a warm draught-free place until puffy, anywhere from 2–5 hours or more. It is extremely low maintenance and can handle an extended proof.

4. Place oven rack in middle of oven and preheat oven to highest possible setting for 30 minutes. Half fill a small baking dish with boiling water and place in base of oven. Set the timer for 10 minutes.

5. Reduce oven temperature to 220°C and bake fougasse for 20 minutes. Reduce oven temperature again to 180°C and bake for a further 20 minutes. The fougasse should be browned and feel firm to the touch. Set aside to cool on a wire rack for 1 hour before eating.

Pickled jalapeño and cheddar sourdough

LOW LACTOSE
GUM FREE
EGG FREE
FODMAP FRIENDLY
GLUTEN FREE

Makes: 1 loaf
Prep time: 30 minutes
Proofing time: overnight fermentation
    + 2–4 hours
Cook time: 1 hour 30 minutes

I dub this recipe the savoury counterpart to the offensively good cinnamon and raisin loaf on page 150. There's something about the combination of pickled jalapeño and a good sharp cheddar that just echoes throughout every inch of this loaf, elevating it to another level.

I find this loaf works best in a Pullman pan, as less cheddar is exposed to the oven, preventing the cheese from leaking out and burning. The pan I use for all sourdough loaves is a steel Pullman pan – 21.5 cm × 11.5 cm – without the lid.

~~~~~~~

FOR THE PRE-FERMENT:

130 g gluten-free sourdough starter,
    thick and active, fed 3–4 hours before
150 g water
100 g buckwheat flour

FOR THE DRY INGREDIENTS:

150 g buckwheat flour
100 g sorghum flour
100 g potato starch
25 g psyllium husk
13 g (2 ¼ teaspoons) fine salt
pinch of ground ginger
pinch of vitamin C powder

TO FINISH:

75 g good quality cheddar cheese,
    chopped into 1 cm cubes
75 g pickled jalapeños, chopped
440 g water
1 tablespoon olive or vegetable oil
1 tablespoon pure maple syrup

THE NIGHT BEFORE:

1. Combine the starter and 150 g water in a large bowl. Add the flour and whisk until well combined. Cover and set aside in a warm, draught-free place overnight.

THE NEXT MORNING:

2. The pre-ferment should look like a starter that has begun to fall after not being fed for a while. The top should have some popped bubbles but will still look quite watery. Even if you think it has 'failed' it will still strengthen both the flavour and the physical properties of the dough.

3. Combine all the dry ingredients in a large non-reactive bowl. Add the pre-ferment and finishing ingredients and whisk until well combined. The mixture will be very wet. Cover and set aside to thicken for 20 minutes. By the time you return, you should have a cohesive and thick dough that you can scoop out of the bowl with your hands.

NOTES

This loaf keeps well stored cut-side down on the bench. It can also be sliced and frozen.

I have used cheddar because it's a flavourful, easily acquired low-lactose cheese. You can use a firm cheese of your choice, but keep in mind that the lactose content might change.

4. Transfer dough to 21.5 cm x 11.5 cm (base measurement) steel bread tin. Use a moistened hand to smooth down top of the loaf and cover. Set aside in a warm draught-free spot for 2–4 hours, weather dependent. It's proofed when it has risen considerably and is light and airy to the touch.

5. When the loaf is nearly proofed, gently put it flat in the fridge to slow the fermentation and firm it up.

6. Place oven rack in middle of oven and preheat oven to highest possible setting for 30 minutes. Half fill a small baking dish with boiling water and place in base of oven. Set the timer for 10 minutes.

7. Reduce oven temperature to 220°C and bake for 20 minutes. Check on loaf and tent very lightly with foil if you feel it's browning too quickly. Reduce oven temperature again to 180°C and bake for a further 60–70 minutes or until the top is deeply golden and the loaf sounds hollow if you knock on the crust.

8. Remove loaf from the oven and place on a wire rack to cool completely (3–4 hours, ideally overnight) or remove loaf from tin and cool in oven (on rack) with door ajar. Allow to cool for at least 2 hours before slicing.

THERE'S SOMETHING
ABOUT THE COMBINATION OF
pickled jalapeño AND A
GOOD *sharp cheddar* THAT
JUST *echoes* THROUGHOUT
EVERY INCH OF THIS LOAF,
elevating IT TO *another level*.

Olive and rosemary 'supermarket' sourdough

LACTOSE FREE
GUM FREE
EGG FREE
VEGAN
FODMAP FRIENDLY
GLUTEN FREE

Makes: 1 loaf
Prep time: 30 minutes
Proofing time: overnight fermentation
+ 3–6 hours
Cook time: 1 hour 30 minutes

This loaf is so named because it contains only flours you can buy at the supermarket. I'm very lucky to have access to a number of bulk and health food stores that carry more niche flours, but I realise that not everyone is in the same boat. If you're in the market for an everyday loaf, this bread can be made without olives and rosemary, too. Note that you'll need a banneton (or bowl lined with a tea towel) and a Dutch oven for this recipe.

~~~~~~~~

FOR THE PRE-FERMENT:

130 g gluten-free sourdough starter,
    thick and active, fed 3–4 hours before
150 g water
100 g buckwheat flour

FOR THE DRY INGREDIENTS:

150 g tapioca flour
100 g buckwheat flour
100 g toasted quinoa flour
25 g psyllium husk
13 g (2 ¼ teaspoons) fine salt
¼ teaspoon ground ginger
¼ teaspoon vitamin C powder
    (or apple cider vinegar)
fine white rice flour, for dusting

FOR THE ADD-INS:

3–4 sprigs of rosemary, woody
    parts removed and chopped (or
    1 tablespoon dried rosemary)
75 g pitted olives (kalamata or Sicilian),
    chopped
350–400 g water
2 tablespoons olive oil
1 tablespoon maple syrup

THE NIGHT BEFORE:

1. Combine the starter and 150 g water in a large bowl. Add the flour and whisk until well combined. Cover and set aside in a warm, draught-free place overnight.

THE NEXT MORNING:

2. The pre-ferment should look like a starter that has begun to fall after not being fed for a while. The top should have some popped bubbles but will still look quite watery. Even if you think it has 'failed' it should still strengthen both the flavour and the physical properties of the dough.

3. Combine all the dry ingredients in a large non-reactive bowl. Add the add-ins and whisk until well combined. The mixture will be very wet. Cover and set aside to thicken for 20 minutes. By the time you return, you should have a cohesive and thick dough that you can scoop out of the bowl with your hands.

4. Lightly flour your banneton (proofing basket) with fine white rice flour. Place dough, nice side (aka the side with no seams) down into the banneton. The base of the loaf (with all the seams) should be facing upwards.

RECIPE CONTINUES >

5. Place banneton in a giant ziplock bag either in the fridge or on the bench top to proof. If you proof it on the bench, it will take anywhere from 3–6 hours, weather dependent. It's proofed when it has risen considerably and is light and airy to the touch.

6. When the loaf is nearly proofed, gently put it flat in the fridge to slow the process and firm it up.

7. 30 minutes before the loaf is ready, preheat your oven with your Dutch oven inside to the highest setting possible. Note that some Dutch ovens are not designed for high temperatures so only go as high as you can without damaging it.

8. When the loaf is proofed and ready for the oven, dampen your kitchen bench slightly and lay down some durable baking paper. I like the reusable stuff because it doesn't break apart when damp. Invert your loaf very gently onto the baking paper, and score using your lame or a very sharp blade.

9. Carefully remove the very hot Dutch oven from the oven and take the lid off. Gently lower the loaf on the baking paper into the Dutch oven, and very gently place the lid back on. Any jolting can knock the air out of the loaf. Return to oven.

10. Reduce oven temperature to 220°C and bake for 1 hour. Reduce oven temperature again to 180°C, remove the lid of the Dutch oven and bake for a further 20–30 minutes or until the top of the loaf is golden and the loaf sounds hollow when you knock on it.

11. Remove loaf from the oven and place on a wire rack to cool (3–4 hours, ideally overnight). Allow to cool completely before slicing to prevent a gummy loaf.

Sourdough Vegemite scrolls

LOW LACTOSE
GUM FREE
EGG FREE
FODMAP FRIENDLY
GLUTEN FREE
VEGAN OPTION

Makes: 12 scrolls
Prep time: 45 minutes
Proofing time: overnight fermentation
**   + 1–3 hours**
Cook time: 40 minutes

FOR THE DRY INGREDIENTS:

200 g sorghum flour
150 g tapioca flour
100 g buckwheat flour
13 g (2 ¼ teaspoons) fine salt
¼ teaspoon ground ginger
¼ teaspoon vitamin C powder or apple
    cider vinegar
20 g psyllium husk

FOR THE WET INGREDIENTS:

525 g water
1 tablespoon olive oil
1 tablespoon pure maple syrup
130 g gluten-free sourdough starter,
    thick and active, fed 3–4 hours before

FOR THE FILLING:

75–100 g gluten-free Vegemite
    (75 g for regular people, 100 g plus
    for Vegemite fiends)
1 ½ tablespoons boiling water
150–200 g sharp vegetarian cheddar
    cheese, grated (vegan if necessary)

FOR ROLLING OUT:

vegetable oil
a long piece of thread or very fine string,
    for cutting rolls

While the house was brimming with baked goods during the making of this book, it was commonplace that I would try to palm off all my experiments onto unsuspecting guests or family members. Not a single one of these Vegemite scrolls made it out of the house. They're easy, delicious, vegan with an alternative cheese, and keep well for a number of days.

NB: You can add as much cheese as you like, I just didn't want to scare you off.

~~~~~~~~

THE NIGHT BEFORE:

1. Combine all the dry ingredients (not the filling ingredients) and wet ingredients in a large, non-reactive bowl and whisk until well combined. Cover and set aside on bench overnight.

THE NEXT MORNING:

2. Oil or butter a 30 cm × 20 cm (base measurement) baking dish. Check your dough – it should be noticeably bubbly and light. You should be able to pick it up in a ball with your hands.

3. Grease a large piece of baking paper. Divide dough into 2 even-sized balls. Cover one, and place other ball of dough onto prepared baking paper. Use your hands to spread it into a large, relatively thin rectangle, about 1 cm thick, with smooth edges and sides approximately 30 cm x 35–40 cm.

4. To make the filling, combine Vegemite and 1 ½ tablespoons boiling water in a medium bowl, whisking until smooth. You can add a little extra water if necessary. Use an offset spatula or the back of a spoon to gently spread half the Vegemite paste across the dough, leaving a 1 cm border on long edges of the rectangle. Sprinkle half the grated cheddar evenly atop the Vegemite.

RECIPE CONTINUES >

NOTES

If you're not a Vegemite fiend, you could use pizza sauce or a FODMAP-friendly pesto in its place.

You cannot taste the buckwheat flour in this recipe. You could try using fine white rice flour if necessary, but you will have to adjust the hydration to suit.

I have used cheddar because it's a flavourful, easily acquired low-lactose cheese. You can use a firm cheese of your choice, but keep in mind that the lactose content might change.

Scrolls keep well in an airtight container for 3–4 days.

5. Turn the baking paper so that a long edge is facing you. Starting from the side closest to you, roll the dough over itself, using the baking paper to help you keep the roll nice and tight. Once you get 80% of the way there, roll the furthest edge back towards you to create the full log. Turn the dough over so that it sits seam side down.

6. Gently thread your piece of string underneath the log. Roughly eyeball or measure the dough into six even pieces. Think of the thread as your knife and, holding one end of the string in each hand, pull in opposing directions to slice through the dough. Sit that first scroll upright and gently mould it with your hands by pressing down gently. Place roll into prepared dish and repeat to make 6 scrolls. Tuck the seam of each scroll against the side of the dish or another scroll, to prevent them from unfurling during the baking process.

7. Repeat with second ball of dough to make 12 scrolls in total.

8. Cover the tray of scrolls (I like to use and reuse a giant ziplock bag) and allow to proof for 1–3 hours (climate dependent) until a little puffy to the touch. They will not have doubled, but should look a little bigger.

9. Preheat oven to 180°C. Bake scrolls for 40 minutes or until cooked through and lightly golden on top. You can brush them with a little melted butter once baked for a bit of added moisture and sheen, if you like, but it is not strictly necessary.

Sourdough baguettes

LACTOSE FREE
GUM FREE
EGG FREE
VEGAN
FODMAP FRIENDLY
GLUTEN FREE

Makes: 2 baguettes
Prep time: 40 minutes
Proofing time: overnight fermentation
    + 2–4 hours
Cook time: 50–60 minutes

When you're approaching 30, not much beats the excitement of waiting for your new baguette pan to arrive in the mail. (Except, potentially, the thought of investing in a good vacuum cleaner.) Although you don't strictly need a baguette pan, the tiny little holes on the bottom of your loaves will bring a tear to the gluten-free baker's eye.

Realistically, you can make a baguette with a plain old baking tray and with any sourdough recipe in this book or beyond. That said, I like to use the 'white bread' sourdough recipe for an authentic, hole-filled baguette. To make the crumb as baguette-like as possible, you can also experiment with an autolyse.

FOR THE PRE-FERMENT:

130 g gluten-free sourdough starter, thick and active, fed 3–4 hours before
100 g water
100 g sorghum flour

FOR THE LOAF:

25 g psyllium husk
400 g water
150 g sorghum flour
100 g tapioca flour
100 g potato starch
13 g (2 ¼ teaspoons) fine salt
¼ teaspoon ground ginger
¼ teaspoon vitamin C powder (or apple cider vinegar)
1 tablespoon olive oil
white rice flour, for dusting

NOTES

Baguettes keep well for 2 days and make for great toast thereafter. They can also be frozen.

THE NIGHT BEFORE:

1. Combine the starter and 100 g water in a large bowl. Add the flour and whisk until well combined. Cover and set aside in a warm, draught-free place overnight.

THE NEXT DAY:

2. The pre-ferment should look like a starter that has begun to fall after not being fed for a while. The top should have some popped bubbles but will still look quite watery. Even if you think it has 'failed' it should still strengthen both the flavour and the physical properties of the dough.

3. Combine the psyllium and 400 g water (and apple cider vinegar, if using) in a large bowl, and whisk to combine. Set aside for 5–10 minutes or until a thick gel forms.

4. Meanwhile, place flours, potato starch, salt, ginger and vitamin C powder, if using, in a large non-reactive bowl and whisk to combine.

5. Whisk the psyllium gel and oil into the pre-ferment. Add the pre-ferment mixture to bowl with the flour mixture. Using a spoon, stir to combine and then use your hands to mix, until you have a hydrated, smooth-ish ball of dough. You could also use a stand mixer with a dough hook, but I find this easier and quicker.

6. Place dough onto a lightly floured work surface and shape it, best as you can, into 2 baguettes. When the dough is shaped, lightly flour your baguette tray and gently lift the baguettes onto the tray. If you don't have a baguette tray, place both baguettes on a lined baking tray. Cover tray and place in a plastic bag either in the fridge or on the benchtop to proof. If you proof it on the bench, it will take anywhere from 2–4 hours, weather dependent. If you use the fridge, you can leave them overnight.

7. Place oven rack in middle of oven and preheat oven to highest possible setting for 30 minutes. Place a small baking dish of boiling water in base of oven 10 minutes before baking. Score baguettes using a lame or sharp knife.

8. Place baguette tray in the oven and reduce heat to 220°C. Bake baguettes for 20 minutes. Reduce oven again to 180°C and bake for a further 30–40 minutes, or until baguettes are golden brown and sound hollow if you tap them. Lightly tent them with foil if becoming too golden at any point.

9. Cool baguettes on tray for 30 minutes before transferring to a wire rack to cool for a further hour before slicing.

Wholegrain sourdough pizza bases

GLUTEN FREE
FODMAP FRIENDLY
VEGAN
FREE FROM HIGH-STARCH FLOURS

**Makes: 4 large or 5–6 medium-large
    pizza bases**
Prep time: 20 minutes
Proofing time: overnight fermentation
Cook time: 10–20 minutes (per pizza)

When I first made sourdough pizza bases, I was struck by how incredibly low maintenance they are, especially compared to bread. You can mix up a batch of dough on a Thursday evening, keep it in the fridge and make pizza every night of the weekend. The bonus of a recipe free from high-starch flours is that the dough will ferment at a slower pace, leaving you with even more time to enjoy it.

FOR THE DRY INGREDIENTS:

200 g sorghum flour
150 g fine brown rice flour
100 g buckwheat flour
13 g (2 ¼ teaspoons) fine salt
¼ teaspoon ground ginger (optional)
20 g psyllium husk

FOR THE WET INGREDIENTS:

130 g gluten-free sourdough starter,
  thick and active, fed 3–4 hours before
580 g water
2 tablespoons olive oil

NOTES

Leftover pizzas keep well in an airtight container in the fridge. They are best reheated in the microwave or a steamy oven.

THE NIGHT BEFORE:

1. Combine all the dry ingredients in a large non-reactive bowl.

2. Add the wet ingredients to the dry ingredients and whisk thoroughly to combine. The mixture will still be very runny but will continue to thicken over the next 10–15 minutes.

3. Once dough has thickened, cover and either leave on the bench or place in fridge to ferment overnight.

THE NEXT MORNING:

4. Place dough in fridge until you need to use it (if you left it on the bench overnight).

5. When you're nearly ready to bake, take the dough from the bowl and divide it into 4–6 equal balls. Lightly flour a sheet of baking paper, and use the palm of your hand to flatten each ball into a pizza base just smaller than a dinner plate. The dough rises as it cooks, so you can make the bases quite thin. If you fancy, fold the edge of the pizza up onto itself and press to secure. Flip the pizza over so the seams are hidden and you have a lovely raised crust.

6. Preheat a large oven-proof frying pan, pizza stone or pizza tray in oven at highest possible setting for 30 minutes. Nothing with any plastic parts though, please.

7. You can top your pizza base lightly or par-bake the dough first. Either way, reduce oven temperature to 200°C and place the pizza (on sheet of baking paper) on your preheated pan, stone or tray.

8. Bake pizza for 10 minutes to par-bake, for 15–20 minutes with toppings or possibly longer if your toppings need to cook too.

CHAPTER TEN

Yeasted breads

Everyday yeasted bread

LACTOSE FREE
GUM FREE
EGG FREE
VEGAN
FODMAP FRIENDLY
GLUTEN FREE

Makes: 1 loaf
Prep time: 20 minutes
Proofing time: 2 hours
Cook time: 1 hour 10 minutes

This bread does what it says on the packet. Not too wholesome and not too starchy, it's an easy, everyday loaf of bread.

~~~~~~

FOR THE DRY INGREDIENTS:

150 g sorghum flour
100 g buckwheat flour
150 g potato starch
7.5 g (1 sachet) dried yeast (see note)
20 g psyllium husk
10 g fine salt

FOR THE WET INGREDIENTS:

470 g water
2 tablespoons olive oil
1 tablespoon maple syrup

1. Combine all the dry ingredients in a large non-reactive bowl. Add the wet ingredients (and yeast mixture if you went that route – see notes) to the dry ingredients and stir until well combined, adding a little extra water if necessary. The dough should be quite runny at this stage. Cover the bowl of dough with a plate and set aside in a warm, non-draughty place for 1 hour to proof. When proofed, the dough should form a cohesive ball that is light and airy.

2. Transfer mixture to a 21.5 cm x 11.5 cm (base measurement) loaf pan. Use a moistened hand to smooth the top of the bread before covering to proof for another hour, season dependent.

3. When your bread is nearly finished proofing, move your oven rack to the middle and preheat oven to 200°C. Place a small baking dish of boiling water in the base of oven 10 minutes before baking. Steam helps the bread to rise and keeps the crust softer.

4. Bake bread for 20 minutes, then reduce oven temperature to 180°C and bake for a further 40–50 minutes or until the loaf is firm and golden.

5. Set aside to cool in tin before transferring to a wire rack to cool completely before slicing.

NOTES

The bread keeps well stored cut-side down on the bench for a few days. I find yeasted bread gets stale a lot more quickly than sourdough, so I recommend slicing it and freezing if you do not intend to eat it within a few days.

If you are concerned that your yeast is old, take 75 g of the water and heat it gently. Add the sachet of yeast and a splash of maple syrup and allow the yeast to bubble up. This step isn't necessary (you can simply add the yeast dry) but it can be helpful if you're unsure how long the yeast has been sitting in your cupboard. If it doesn't bubble up, discard the mixture and start again.

Seeded wholegrain bread

LACTOSE FREE
FREE FROM HIGH-STARCH FLOURS
GUM FREE
EGG FREE
VEGAN
FODMAP FRIENDLY
GLUTEN FREE

Makes: 1 loaf
Prep time: 20 minutes
Proofing time: 1 hour 30 minutes
Cook time: 1 hour 10 minutes

FOR THE DRY INGREDIENTS:

150 g sorghum flour
150 g ivory teff flour
100 g buckwheat flour
40 g (¼ cup) pepitas (pumpkin seeds)
35 g (¼ cup) linseeds (flaxseeds)
35 g (¼ cup) sunflower seeds
2 teaspoons fennel seeds (optional)
2 teaspoons caraway seeds (optional)
7.5 g (1 sachet) dried yeast (see note)
10 g fine salt

FOR THE WET INGREDIENTS:

675 g water
25 g psyllium husk
1 tablespoon olive oil
1 tablespoon pure maple syrup

This recipe was affectionately titled by my household 'not quite Burgen bread'. Full of wholegrains and seeds, it is a wholesome yet satisfyingly good and sturdy little loaf. I find seeded loaves are best with a single rise in the loaf tin, as opposed to two rises for a non-seeded loaf (see page 226).

1. Combine all the dry ingredients in a large non-reactive bowl. Add the wet ingredients (and yeast mixture if you went that route – see notes) to the dry ingredients and stir until well combined. The dough will be quite runny at this stage.

2. Transfer mixture to a 21.5 cm x 11.5 cm (base measurement) loaf pan. Use a moistened hand to smooth the top of the bread before covering to proof in a warm, non-draughty place for 1 ½ hours, weather dependent.

3. When your bread is nearly finished proofing, move your oven rack to the middle and preheat the oven to 200°C. Place a small baking dish of boiling water in the base of oven 10 minutes before baking. Steam helps the bread to rise and keeps the crust softer.

4. Bake bread for 20 minutes, then reduce oven temperature to 180°C and bake for a further 40–50 minutes or until the loaf is firm and golden.

5. Set aside to cool in tin before transferring to a wire rack to cool completely before slicing.

The bread keeps well stored cut-side down on the bench for a few days. I find yeasted bread gets stale a lot more quickly than sourdough, so I recommend slicing it and freezing if you do not intend to eat it within a few days.

If you are concerned that your yeast is old, take 75 g of the water and heat it gently. Add the sachet of yeast and a splash of maple syrup or honey and allow the yeast to bubble up. This step isn't necessary (you can simply add the yeast dry) but it can be helpful if you're unsure how long the yeast has been sitting in your cupboard. If it doesn't bubble up, discard the mixture and start again.

Enriched bread

LOW-LACTOSE OPTION
GUM FREE
FODMAP-FRIENDLY OPTION
GLUTEN FREE

Makes: 1 loaf
Prep time: 20 minutes
Proofing time: 2–3 hours
Cook time: 1 hour 10 minutes

This chapter wouldn't be complete without a quick foray into the world of enriched bread dough. This one uses milk powder for a tender crumb as well as eggs for binding and an additional flavour boost. It has the softness and sweetness of white bread but without an inordinate amount of starch. If you're looking for a yeasted loaf to prove to someone that gluten-free bread isn't always as dense as a brick, this is it.

~~~~~~

FOR THE DRY INGREDIENTS:

300 g sorghum flour
100 g potato starch
30 g (¼ cup) dried milk powder (regular, lactose-free or a plant-based milk variety)
20 g psyllium husk
10–12 g fine salt
7.5 g (1 sachet) instant yeast (see note)

FOR THE WET INGREDIENTS:

470 g water
2 tablespoons olive oil
1 tablespoon pure maple syrup
2 extra-large eggs

1. Combine all the dry ingredients in a large non-reactive bowl. Add the wet ingredients (and yeast mixture if you went that route – see notes) to the dry ingredients and stir until well combined. Cover the bowl of dough with a plate and set aside to rise in a warm, non-draughty place for 1 hour or until it is significantly risen and is airy to the touch. It is a high-hydration dough, so it will be a little too sticky to pick up.

2. Transfer mixture to a 21.5 cm x 11.5 cm (base measurement) loaf pan. Use a moistened hand to smooth the top of the bread before covering to proof for another 1–2 hours, season dependent. The dough is proofed when you can tell it has risen quite significantly up the sides of the tin.

3. When your bread is nearly finished proofing, move your oven rack to the middle and preheat oven to 200°C. Place a small baking dish of boiling water in the base of oven 10 minutes before baking. Steam helps the bread to rise and keeps the crust softer.

4. Bake bread for 20 minutes, then reduce oven temperature to 180°C and bake for a further 40–50 minutes or until the loaf is firm and golden.

5. Set aside to cool in tin before transferring to a wire rack to cool completely before slicing.

NOTES

The bread keeps well stored cut-side down on the bench for a few days. I find yeasted bread goes stale a lot more quickly than sourdough, so I recommend slicing it and freezing if you don't intend to eat it within a few days.

If you're using old yeast sachets, see note on page 229.

Yeasted pizza bases

LACTOSE FREE
GUM FREE
EGG FREE
VEGAN
FODMAP FRIENDLY
GLUTEN FREE
FREE FROM HIGH-STARCH FLOURS
 OPTION

**Makes: 2 large or 4 medium pizza
  bases**
Prep time: 20 minutes
Proofing time: 1 hour
Cook time: 15–20 minutes (per pizza)

Sourdough is great and all, but sometimes you need pizza and you need it in a hurry. These pizza bases are risen and ready in under 2 hours (a feat that I as a person have never managed to achieve) and thus perfect for such pizza emergencies. In this instance, I like to include a bit of starch for elasticity and chew, but there's an option free from high-starch flours if you'd prefer it (see notes).

~~~~~~

FOR THE YEAST MIXTURE:

100 g warm water
2 teaspoons caster sugar
7.5 g (1 sachet) dried yeast

FOR THE PIZZA BASES:

120 g (¾ cup) fine white rice flour
60 g (½ cup) tapioca flour
60 g (½ cup) sorghum flour
1 ½ teaspoons fine salt
¼ teaspoon ground ginger
15 g psyllium husk
60 ml (¼ cup) olive oil
300 g warm water

1. To make the yeast mixture, combine 100 g warm water, the sugar and yeast in a small bowl. Set aside in a warm spot for 10–20 minutes. The top of the mixture should be slightly domed and very bubbly. If this doesn't happen, discard the mixture and start again (as yeast is inactive).

2. Meanwhile, combine flours, salt, ginger and psyllium in a large non-reactive bowl. Add the bloomed yeast, olive oil and 300 g warm water and use a spoon to stir thoroughly until no lumps remain. The dough should look a bit like thick porridge. Cover and set aside to rise in a warm, non-draughty place for 1 hour or until doubled in size.

3. Preheat oven to 200°C. Line 2 baking trays with baking paper. Divide dough into 2 large or 4 medium portions. Using thoroughly oiled hands, place one piece of dough on a prepared tray and use your hands to press it out into a circular pizza shape, about 20 cm in diameter for small pizzas or 30 cm for large. You can make the pizza thinner or thicker depending on how you like it but remember that this will affect cooking time. I like to leave the edges a little thicker than the body of the pizza to mimic a traditional pizza crust. Repeat with remaining dough.

4. You can top your pizza base lightly or par-bake the dough first. Bake pizza for 10 minutes to par-bake, for 15–20 minutes with toppings or possibly longer if your toppings need to cook too. I like to put a small baking dish of boiling water in base of oven to give dough a bit of lift (the steam will help the dough puff up), but this is optional.

NOTES

You can make this dough the night before and leave it, covered, in the fridge until use. Ideally, use within 24 hours.

You can play around with different flours for this recipe. Note that hydration levels will change, too.

Spread the pizza bases a little thinner than you'd like them to end up, as they do puff a little in the oven.

These pizza bases can be made without starch by using all sorghum in place of the tapioca flour. I found they were a little fragile the next day, but still delicious.

FODMAP-friendly pizza sauce

LOW LACTOSE
EGG FREE
FODMAP FRIENDLY
GLUTEN FREE
VEGAN OPTION

Makes: 500 g pizza sauce (enough for 6–8 large pizzas)
Prep time: 5 minutes

400 g can diced tomatoes (no flavourings)
2 tablespoons tomato paste
50 g vegetarian parmesan (omit for vegan), freshly and finely grated
1 teaspoon pure maple syrup (optional)
½ teaspoon asafoetida (optional, see page 11)
¼ teaspoon dried oregano
4–5 basil leaves (keep the rest of the bunch for finishing the pizza)
small pinch of dried chilli flakes
salt and freshly ground pepper, to taste

Where there's smoke there's fire, and where there's pizza, there's pizza sauce. I only figured out recently that a smear of tomato paste is the lazy man's topping and not the norm. Luckily for me (the lazy man), this pizza sauce is ready in about the time it takes to pry the lid off a jar of tomato paste.

~~~~~~

1. Place all ingredients in a food processor and process until smooth. Season with sea salt and freshly ground black pepper.

2. Spread sauce on par-baked gluten-free pizza bases (see page 222 for sourdough bases or 232 for regular ones).

NOTES

Sauce keeps in an airtight container in the fridge for 2–3 days.

'Sausage' and caramelised fennel pizzas

LOW LACTOSE
GUM FREE
FREE FROM HIGH-STARCH FLOURS
 OPTION
EGG FREE
VEGAN OPTION
FODMAP FRIENDLY
GLUTEN FREE

Makes: 4 large pizzas
Prep time: 1 hour
Cook time: 15–20 minutes (per pizza)

1 quantity pizza dough (regular on page
    232 or sourdough on page 222)
1 quantity pizza sauce (page 235)
1 quantity vegan 'sausage' (page 172)

FOR THE CARAMELISED FENNEL:

25 g butter, regular or plant based
1–2 tablespoons olive oil
1 large bulb fennel, mandolined or finely
    sliced
½ teaspoon fine salt
1–2 tablespoon pure maple syrup, to taste
1 tablespoon gluten-free miso paste
    (I use shiro or genmai)
3–4 tablespoons balsamic vinegar, to taste
¼ teaspoon asafoetida (optional)
½ teaspoon sage powder, optional

TO FINISH:

grated mozzarella cheese (I like to use
    smoked mozzarella) or vegan/dairy-
    free alternative
a micro-grating of parmesan or a vegan
    alternative
any other pizza toppings you fancy (I like
    this pizza as is, but some pitted olives
    never go astray)

You'd think I owned a tofu factory at the rate I spruik tofu recipes. I don't, but I'd be open to discussion if you're selling. These pizzas are my rebuttal to the sausage and caramelised onion variety of my distant past. If you can find smoked mozzarella, it goes a long way towards creating the illusion of meat and general FODMAP mischief. The asafoetida provides an onion- and garlic-like flavour while the sage gives a meaty richness of flavour.

〜〜〜〜〜〜

1. To make the fennel, heat the butter and oil in a large frying pan or saucepan over medium–low heat. Cook the fennel, stirring occasionally, for 20 minutes or until soft and caramelised. Add a splash of water whenever necessary to keep the fennel from sticking.

2. Meanwhile, whisk together the salt, maple syrup, miso, vinegar, asafoetida and sage, if using, until miso is dissolved.

3. Add sauce mixture to fennel and quickly stir to combine. It should sizzle up and thicken quite quickly. You should be left with a sweet, jammy and aromatic fennel topping.

4. Preheat oven to 200°C and place your pizza stone or tray in oven to heat. Shape your pizza bases on individual sheets of baking paper and decide if you would like to par-bake them or cook as is. I find par-baked pizza bases are crispier, while pizzas topped raw are doughier.

5. Either way, top pizza bases with a few spoons of pizza sauce, according to taste. Top with caramelised fennel and crumble over the raw 'sausage' mixture. Finish with the cheeses and any other toppings you fancy.

6. Baking one at a time, place a pizza on the preheated stone (or tray) and bake for 15–20 minutes or until mozzarella is melted and golden. Repeat with remaining pizzas. Leftover pizza keeps well in an airtight container in the fridge for a number of days. Microwave or steam bake it to reheat.

Yeast-free buckwheat seed bread

LACTOSE FREE
GUM FREE
FREE FROM HIGH-STARCH FLOURS
EGG FREE
VEGAN
FODMAP FRIENDLY
GLUTEN FREE

Makes: 1 loaf
Prep time: 30 minutes
Cook time: 30–40 minutes

In the interest of making this book as inclusive as possible, I had to include a yeast-free bread. This recipe uses naught but buckwheat for flour, but the result is soft and surprisingly fluffy. It also happens to be vegan.

Weirdly, this loaf actually works beautifully with a 7.5 g sachet of yeast added to the flour mixture. Follow the recipe as written, but let the dough proof for 2 hours before steps 4 and 5.

FOR THE BINDER:

35 g (¼ cup) linseeds (flaxseeds) ground into a meal
15 g psyllium husk
650 g water

FOR THE SEED LOAF:

350 g (2 ¼ cups) buckwheat flour
3 teaspoons gluten-free baking powder
½ teaspoon bicarbonate of soda
7.5 g (1 ¼ teaspoons) fine salt
2 teaspoons apple cider vinegar
1 tablespoon pure maple syrup
1 tablespoon oil of choice
40 g (¼ cup) pepitas (pumpkin seeds)
35 g (¼ cup) hemp or sesame seeds

1. Preheat oven to 180°C. To make the binder, combine linseeds, psyllium and water in a medium bowl and whisk to combine. Set aside to gel, about 15–20 minutes.

2. Meanwhile, combine the flour, baking powder, bicarbonate of soda and salt in a large bowl.

3. Add the binder, vinegar, maple syrup and oil to the flour mixture and mix well to combine. I find it helps to get your hands in there and squish the dough through your fingers to eliminate any lingering dry spots.

4. Transfer dough to a 21.5 cm x 11.5 cm (base measurement) loaf pan. Use a moistened hand to smooth the top of the bread and sprinkle with the seeds. Press lightly to secure them to the loaf.

5. Bake loaf for 30–40 minutes or until light golden and cooked through. Set aside to cool in tin for 5 minutes before transferring to a wire rack to cool completely.

NOTES

This loaf stays lovely and moist for a number of days but can also be sliced and frozen.

I recommend turning this loaf upside down when slicing – it's easier!

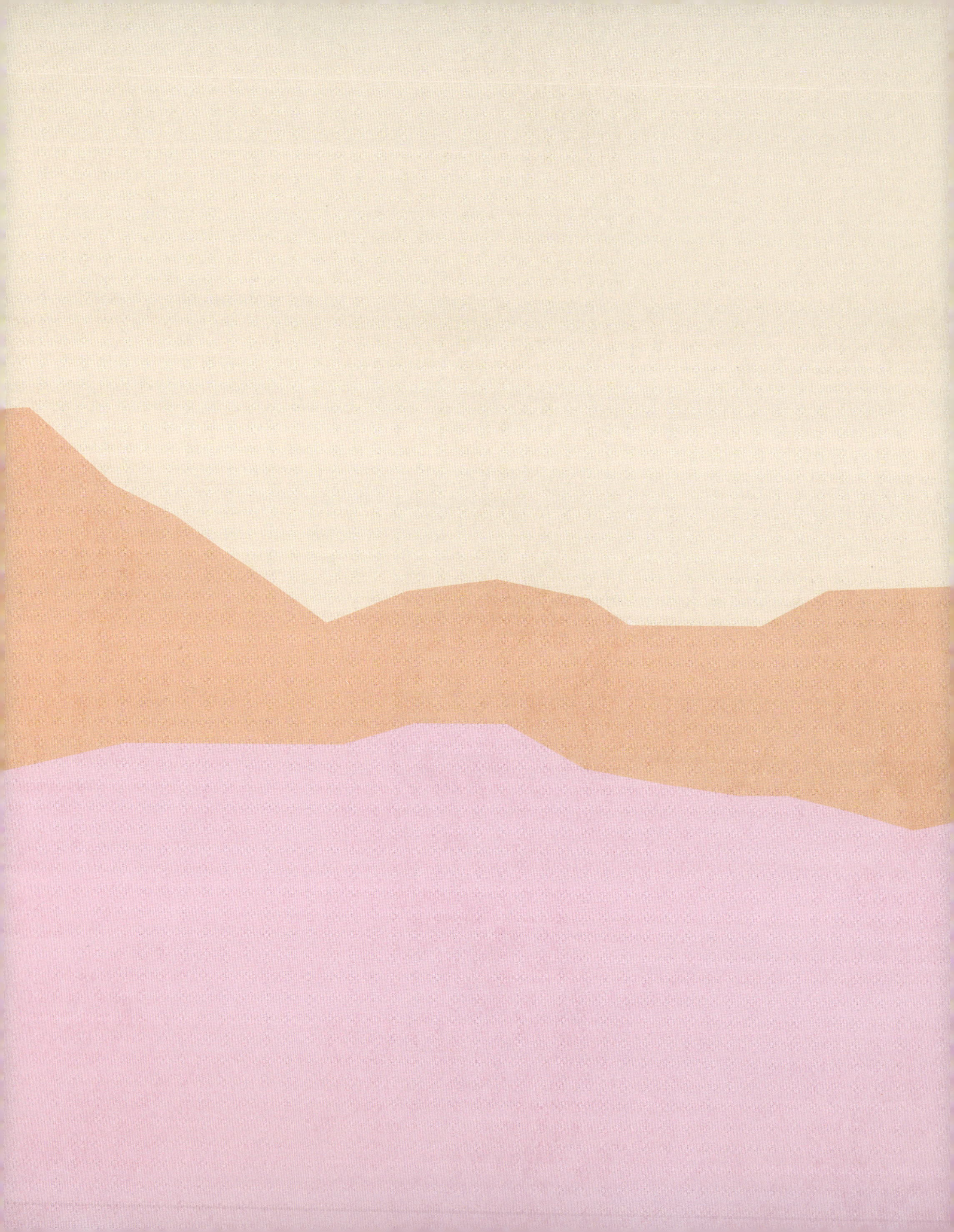

CHAPTER ELEVEN

Pasta and noodles

Egg pasta *without xanthan gum*

LACTOSE FREE
GUM FREE
FODMAP FRIENDLY
GLUTEN FREE

Serves: 4–5
Prep time: 40–60 minutes
Cook time: 2–3 minutes

A word of warning: gluten-free pasta dough without xanthan gum can be quite sensitive. If gums are not your friend, though, the good news is it is still possible to whip up a lovely homemade egg pasta. I recommend cooking it only briefly, on a low boil, and ideally using a sauce that you can pour over the top instead of stirring through.

～～～～

FOR THE SCALD:

2 tablespoons psyllium husk powder
1 tablespoon fine white rice flour
1 teaspoon vegetable oil
125 ml (½ cup) boiling water

FOR THE PASTA:

200 g (1¼ cups) fine white rice flour
90 g (¾ cup) tapioca flour, plus extra to dust
3 extra-large eggs
1–2 teaspoons water, just to form a ball

1. To make the scald, combine the psyllium powder, fine white rice flour and oil in a small bowl. Have a whisk at the ready as you add the boiling water. The mixture should quite quickly gel up and become a grainy paste as you whisk it. Set aside to cool.

2. To make the pasta, place the flours in a large bowl and use a fork to whisk. Using clean fingertips, rub the cooled scald into the flour, until it resembles coarse crumbs.

3. Using a fork, whisk in the eggs and mix until most of the egg has combined. Get your hands in there and thoroughly squelch the dough through until mostly smooth. Add 1–2 teaspoons water, a teaspoon at a time, until you have a firm ball of dough.

4. Turn the dough out onto a well-floured work surface and knead for about 5 minutes. This is to disperse the scald through the dough. Cover dough with a clean, damp tea towel and set aside to rest for 5–10 minutes.

5. Flour your workbench and rolling pin with tapioca flour. Tear off about a quarter of the dough and cover the remainder. Use your rolling pin to roll dough thin enough to get through the thickest setting of your pasta machine. After getting it through the thickest setting (mine is a 7) run it through the machine again. Continue rolling it through on decreasing settings until your desired thickness, noting that it swells during cooking (so go a little thinner than you think). I like to get mine through smoothly at setting 3 on my machine. Thread pasta through your pasta cutter. This dough works well through both the regular and angel hair cutters. Repeat this process until you have used all the dough.

6. Cook pasta in a large saucepan of well-salted boiling water for only 2–3 minutes, depending on the thickness and shape of your pasta. Drain and serve with a sauce of your choice.

NOTES

Cooked pasta will keep in an airtight container in the fridge for 2 days or uncooked pasta can be piled into nests and frozen in an airtight container. Cook straight from frozen, allowing a little extra cooking time.

Cacio e pepe ravioli and brown butter sage sauce

LOW LACTOSE
FODMAP FRIENDLY
GLUTEN FREE
FREE FROM HIGH-STARCH FLOURS
 OPTION

Serves: 6–8
Prep time: 1 hour 30 minutes
Cook time: 15 minutes

Cacio e pepe and brown butter sage sauce: catnip for the millennial with a food Instagram. Clichés aside, this is one of my favourite savoury recipes in the book. Paired with a homemade lactose-free ricotta, this ravioli is a bit of a faff to make but somewhat therapeutic and thoroughly delicious all at the same time.

~~~~~

FOR THE RICOTTA FILLING:

450–500 g lactose-free ricotta (see page 100)
200 g vegetarian parmesan cheese (yes, it exists!), finely grated (I use my blender)
½–1 tablespoon freshly cracked pepper

FOR THE PASTA DOUGH:

320 g (2 cups) fine white or brown rice flour
60 g (½ cup) tapioca flour, plus extra to dust (see notes)
1 teaspoon xanthan gum
4 extra-large eggs
water as needed to bring dough together

FOR THE BROWN BUTTER:

100 g butter
1–2 small bunches fresh sage, leaves picked

1. To make the ricotta filling, combine ricotta, parmesan and pepper in a medium bowl. Taste and adjust seasoning according to your preferences. Place in the fridge while you make your pasta.

2. To make the pasta dough, combine flours and xanthan gum in a large bowl.

3. Add the eggs to the flour and use a fork to break them up. Mix the eggs into the flour, using the fork and then your hands. Add water only as necessary to bring the mixture together into a stiff but smooth ball of pasta dough. There shouldn't be flour left over in the bowl.

4. Once dough is smooth, tear off about a quarter and cover remaining pasta with a slightly dampened tea towel or place in a ziplock bag. Lightly flour the bench with tapioca flour. Roll out dough thin enough to get through the thickest setting of your pasta machine. After getting it through the thickest setting (mine is a 7) run it through the machine again. Continue rolling it through on decreasing settings until desired thickness, noting that it swells during cooking (so go a little thinner than you think). I like to get mine through smoothly at setting 2 or 3 on my machine. The thinner the better, to avoid chewiness.

NOTES

You can replace the tapioca flour with equal weight of a wholegrain flour (such as sorghum or buckwheat) to make this pasta free from high-starch flours. It will be a stiffer dough to work with, but should still be easy enough to roll out.

5. Once you have 2 long, thin sheets of even-width pasta, place scant teaspoons of ricotta mixture evenly across one sheet of pasta, leaving a couple of centimetres between them. Use a finger or pastry brush to lightly brush the pasta around the ricotta with water. Lay the second sheet of pasta on top. Working around slowly, seal the top pasta sheet onto the bottom around each individual ravioli, pushing all the air out as you go. If you leave air in the ravioli it will float as it cooks and is more likely to pop open. Repeat steps 4 and 5 until you run out of dough or filling.

6. Trim ravioli into squares or use a scone cutter to make circular ravioli. If you have any leftover pasta dough, you can make it into fettuccine and freeze it for later.

7. Bring a large saucepan of well-salted water to the boil. Meanwhile, to make the brown butter, place the butter in a large frying pan or saucepan over a medium–low heat. Cook, stirring occasionally, until the butter is deep brown in colour and smells nutty. Add the sage leaves and cook for 1 minute, or until crisp. Remove from heat.

8. Working in batches, gently lower ravioli into the boiling water and cook for 2–3 minutes or until pasta floats and is soft and almost translucent. Transfer to serving plates with a slotted spoon. Drizzle with the brown butter and top with crisp sage leaves. Serve immediately.

Brown butter AND *sage* WITH *ravioli*
IS AKIN TO *florals* FOR SPRING:
NOT EXACTLY GROUND-BREAKING.
BUT YOU KNOW WHAT THEY SAY
ABOUT THINGS THAT AREN'T BROKEN,
AND THIS *flavour combination*
IS IRONCLAD.

Tantanmen-style ramen

LACTOSE FREE
VEGAN
FODMAP FRIENDLY
GLUTEN FREE

Serves: 4
Prep time: 20 minutes
Cook time: 15 minutes

Tantanmen ramen is a creamy, rich and nutty ramen with a toasted sesame and soy milk broth. My take on the delicacy could be considered Tantanmen style, namely because it doesn't contain the traditional pork. I have tried to retain the spirit as much as possible within a FODMAP-friendly, gluten-free and vegan framework.

~~~~~~

FOR THE SOUP:

20 g (2 sachets) kombu dashi powder, dissolved in 250 ml (1 cup) boiling water
50 g (⅓ cup) deeply toasted white sesame seeds
2–3 tablespoons toasted sesame oil
60 g fresh ginger, peeled, finely grated
5–6 spring onions, green part only, sliced
1 tablespoon gluten-free white miso paste (I use genmai or shiro)
60 ml (¼ cup) dry sherry, optional (see notes on page 255)
1.5 litres (6 cups) unsweetened low-FODMAP soy milk
1–2 tablespoons gluten-free dark soy or tamari
white pepper and salt, to taste
pinch of asafoetida powder, optional (see notes)
2 teaspoons caster sugar (optional, to balance out the flavours)
3–4 tablespoons chilli oil (page 270) or pinch of dried chilli, to your taste
1–2 tablespoons rice wine vinegar (see notes)

1. Use a mortar and pestle or spice grinder to grind the toasted sesame seeds to a paste.

2. Heat the sesame oil in a medium-sized saucepan. Add the ginger and spring onions, stirring well to coat them in the oil. Cook for 2–3 minutes or until softened and fragrant.

3. Add the white miso and use a spoon to keep it moving as it cooks. Add the sesame seed paste and cook briefly until fragrant. Deglaze the pan with the sherry before adding the soy milk and dashi broth. Add the dark soy according to your taste, as there is already salt from the miso and dashi. Season to taste with white pepper and salt if necessary, and add the asafoetida powder and/or caster sugar, if using. Cook the broth for 5–10 minutes to meld the flavours. Add the chilli oil or a pinch of dried chilli and rice wine vinegar, if using.

4. Add the cooked egg noodles to the base of each serving bowl and pour the broth over the top. Add toppings of choice and serve.

FOR THE RAMEN:

1 quantity Chinese egg noodles (page 250), slightly undercooked (1–2 minutes) in boiling water with ½ teaspoon kansui (see notes on page 251 and below)

TO FINISH:

Any toppings you fancy (I used canned corn, smoked tofu, pak choi, another chopped spring onion, green part only, some nori sheets and some chilli oil (page 270)

NOTES

Kansui powder is what gives ramen noodles their bouncy, slippery texture and flavour. You can buy it from Asian grocers or make your own using baking powder. It is optional but it does give the noodles a more authentic texture and taste.

Asafoetida powder will give your ramen an added depth of flavour with its cooked-onion-and-garlic taste. It is entirely optional but a very handy thing to have on hand in a FODMAP-friendly kitchen.

Adding rice vinegar to the broth helps with complexity of flavour. Adding vinegar to milk will also start to curdle it, so proceed with caution. At 2 tablespoons, the ramen broth will thicken considerably (which I personally like). I would not recommend adding more than that unless you enjoy buttermilk soup.

Chinese egg noodles

LACTOSE FREE
FODMAP FRIENDLY
GLUTEN FREE

**Serves: 3–4 (approximately
400 g noodles)**
Prep time: 40 minutes
Cook time: 2–3 minutes

Growing up, egg noodles with toasted sesame oil and tamari were a common after-school snack at my house. The combination is nostalgic, and I'm glad to report these egg noodles live up to my impeccably high nostalgia noodle standards.

I highly recommend the millet flour addition if you can. It adds a lightly sweet but kind of wheat-like flavour that reminds me of the packet noodles of my youth. Another thing I highly recommend is a pasta machine. While these can technically be cut by hand, I found it offensively tedious, and the result looked akin to a small child's school holiday project. I like to cut reasonably thick (setting 3–5) sheets of pasta using the angel hair cutter – the noodles expand during the cooking process and come out like thin egg noodles.

The xanthan gum in this dough serves not only to strengthen it, but also to provide that chew people look for in a good noodle. If you can't have xanthan gum, see the gum-free pasta recipe on page 242.

~~~~~~~~

160 g (1 cup) fine white rice flour
60 g (½ cup) tapioca flour, plus extra to dust
1 tablespoon millet flour (optional, see page 8)
1 teaspoon xanthan gum
3 extra-large eggs
1 teaspoon vegetable oil
water, just to bring dough together into a ball

1. Combine flours and xanthan gum in a large bowl. You can also do this on a clean, dry work surface. Either way, form a well in the flour and break in the eggs. Use a whisk to break up the yolks, and then begin to incorporate eggs into the flour.

2. Once eggs are mostly combined (mix will look clumpy) add the oil and a little water, 1 teaspoon at a time, just until it comes together. The dough is much easier to roll out the stiffer it is, so only add just as much water as you need to bring it into a smooth, firm ball (I generally need 1–4 tablespoons, as a guide). Cover dough and set aside to rest for 5–10 minutes.

3. Once dough is smooth, tear off a golf-ball-sized piece and cover remainder in a slightly dampened tea towel or place in a ziplock bag. Liberally flour bench and rolling pin with tapioca flour.

4. Roll out dough thin enough to get through the thickest setting of your pasta machine.

NOTES

Cooked noodles will keep in an airtight container in the fridge for 2 days or uncooked noodles can be piled into nests and frozen in an airtight container. Cook straight from frozen, allowing a little extra cooking time.

These noodles are suitable for a whole host of preparations. If you'd like to use them in ramen, you can experiment with adding a little kansui powder (an alkaline substance that gives ramen noodles extra bounce, shine and flavour). You can also cook them in a scant amount of bicarbonate of soda to achieve a similar taste and effect.

If you have overshot the hydration of the dough and are finding it tricky to roll out, add 1 tablespoon of tapioca flour and 1 tablespoon of rice flour, knead well, and try again.

5. After getting it through the thickest setting (mine is a 7) run it through the machine again. Continue rolling it through on decreasing settings until you reach your desired thickness, keeping in mind that the noodles expand a little as they cook. I like to cut this dough reasonably thickly so that my noodles are thicker. When you are happy with the width, thread the sheet through your angel hair cutter. Repeat this process until you have used all the dough.

6. Cook noodles in a large saucepan of well-salted boiling water for 2–3 minutes, depending upon the thickness of your noodles. Keep a close eye on things, as the noodles go mushy when overcooked. Drain and you're ready to use!

Leftover laksa can be stored in an airtight container in the fridge for up to 2 days. I do recommend taking the noodles out if you're using the psyllium noodles (as they tend to disintegrate if left in liquid for long periods).

Traditional laksa often uses both hokkien and vermicelli noodles. I've used a half-batch of my Chinese egg noodles and half vermicelli. If you'd prefer, you can use all vermicelli to make it vegan.

Canned coconut milk often contains gums and thickeners, so read the label before buying.

If you can't find galangal, use a little more ginger and lemongrass (around 25 g of each).

Laksa

LACTOSE FREE
GUM FREE
EGG-FREE OPTION
VEGAN OPTION
FODMAP FRIENDLY
GLUTEN FREE

Serves: 4
Prep time: 30 minutes
Cook time: 20 minutes

Laksa is a spicy noodle soup that hails from South-East Asia. Traditionally, it uses prawn stock as a base, garlic and onion in the spice paste and wheat noodles to finish. This version is vegan, FODMAP friendly and gluten free courtesy of a few simple substitutions.

~~~~~~~~

FOR THE LAKSA PASTE:

5–6 fresh birds eye chillies, (depending on your taste for heat), seeds removed, chopped
3 sticks lemongrass, trimmed, finely grated
50 g (1 small–medium piece) galangal, peeled, finely grated (see notes)
50 g (1 small–medium piece) ginger, peeled, finely grated
20 g (1 small piece) fresh turmeric, peeled, finely grated
2 teaspoons sweet paprika (optional, for colour)
2 tablespoons vegetable oil

FOR THE BROTH:

2 tablespoons vegetable oil
5–6 spring onions, green parts only, chopped
20–30 fresh curry leaves, stalks removed
60 ml (¼ cup) vegan fish sauce
1 tablespoon light brown sugar
1 tablespoon tamarind paste
1 tablespoon gluten-free tamari or dark soy
1.5 litres (6 cups) water or vegan stock
400 ml can coconut milk (see notes)
400 g gluten-free tofu puffs or cubed, pan-fried tofu

TO FINISH:

½ quantity (200 g) gluten-free Chinese egg noodles (page 250)
100 g vermicelli noodles (see notes)
1 bunch Vietnamese mint, leaves picked, to serve
trimmed bean sprouts, to serve
1 long red chilli, deseeded, sliced, to serve

1. To make the laksa paste, use a mortar and pestle or food processor to grind the chilli, lemongrass, galangal, ginger and turmeric until smooth. Add the paprika and oil and mix to combine.

2. For the broth, heat the oil in a large saucepan over a medium heat. Cook the spring onion greens and curry leaves, stirring, for 2 minutes or until fragrant and softened. Add the laksa paste and cook, stirring, for 2–3 minutes or until fragrant. Add a splash of water if it sticks at any point. Add the vegan fish sauce, sugar, tamarind paste and tamari and stir to combine. Stir in the water or stock and coconut milk. Add the tofu, then reduce heat to low and simmer, uncovered, for 10 minutes to allow flavours to infuse.

3. Meanwhile, par-cook the Chinese egg noodles (1–2 minutes instead of 2–3) following instructions on page 251. Pour boiling water over the vermicelli in a heatproof bowl and leave to soften for about 2–3 minutes. Drain and set aside.

4. Taste and adjust broth according to your preferences. Add a little extra stock or water if necessary.

5. To serve, divide noodles between serving bowls. Ladle over the hot broth and finish with the Vietnamese mint, bean sprouts and chilli.

Not quite Dan Dan noodles

LACTOSE FREE
VEGETARIAN
FODMAP-FRIENDLY OPTION
GLUTEN-FREE OPTION
EGG-FREE OPTION
VEGAN OPTION

Serves: 4–6
Prep time: 30 minutes
Cook time: 15 minutes

FOR THE SAUCE:

95 g (⅓ cup) smooth natural peanut
    butter
80 ml (⅓ cup) chilli oil (page 270)
¼ cup black rice vinegar (or white rice
    vinegar to taste)
2 tablespoons gluten-free dark soy sauce
    or tamari, plus more to taste
2 tablespoons dry sherry (see notes)
1 tablespoon light brown sugar
1 teaspoon Sichuan peppercorns,
    dry fried and ground
extra chilli powder, to taste

FOR THE MINCE:

2 tablespoons vegetable oil
40 g ginger, microplaned
6–7 spring onions, green parts only, chopped
2 bunches choy sum or Chinese broccoli,
    washed and chopped into bite-size pieces
400 g smoked firm tofu (regular firm tofu is
    fine too), crumbled into small pieces
1 teaspoon Chinese five spice
1 teaspoon dried sage powder
2 tablespoons gluten-free dark soy sauce
    or tamari

TO FINISH:

1 quantity (400 g) egg noodles (page
    250 with xanthan gum or 242 without)
    or a vegan alternative
2 tablespoons toasted sesame oil
45 g (⅓ cup) toasted chopped peanuts
    (optional)
1–2 spring onions, green part only, finely
    chopped

Dan Dan noodles are a hearty noodle dish from the Sichuan province of China. Traditionally they include meat, along with some condiments and general additions that are off limits to FODMAPpers. I have tried my best to retain the spirit of the dish while adjusting it for FODMAP purposes. Use Chinese sesame paste or tahini instead of peanut butter and omit the extra peanuts if you wish.

~~~~~~~~~

1. To make the sauce, place all ingredients in a medium-sized bowl and whisk until well combined and smooth. Adjust according to taste. Set aside.

2. For the mince, heat the oil in a large wok over medium–low heat. Cook ginger and spring onions, stirring, for 2 minutes or until softened and fragrant. Add the chopped greens and cook for 2–3 minutes or until they begin to soften. Add the crumbled tofu, spices and tamari and stir to combine. When the greens are cooked and the mince is light brown in colour, remove from the heat.

3. Cook the noodles in a large saucepan of well-salted boiling water following the instructions on page 251. Drain, place in the wok and drizzle over the toasted sesame oil.

4. Gently toss the noodles with the mince and greens – be particularly gentle if you're using gum-free noodles. Pour over the sauce and toss gently until evenly coated. Divide into 4 serving bowls, top with the peanuts and extra spring onion greens and serve.

NOTES

If you can find sui mi ya cai (a finely chopped pickled vegetable with an umami funkiness) at your local Asian grocer or online, add 2–3 tablespoons to the mince mixture.

Dry sherry is a gluten-free replacement for Shaoxing wine. If you'd prefer an alcohol-free version, you can omit it.

Vegetarian chow mein

LACTOSE FREE
FODMAP-FRIENDLY OPTION
VEGETARIAN
VEGAN OPTION
GLUTEN-FREE OPTION

Serves: 4–6
Prep time: 20 minutes
Cook time: 15 minutes

Chow mein is a Chinese stir-fry noodle dish, traditionally made with a number of ingredients that aren't overly friendly to the digestively challenged. This is my take on a FODMAP-friendly, gluten-free and vegetarian version. Adding fresh ginger isn't traditional, but I find it helps compensate for the lack of garlic. You can use any vegetables you like or have on hand.

FOR THE SAUCE:

2 teaspoons gluten-free cornflour
1 tablespoon hot water
4 tablespoons gluten-free dark soy sauce
  or tamari
2 tablespoons gluten-free vegetarian
  oyster sauce
2 tablespoons rice wine vinegar
2 tablespoons chilli oil (page 270)
2 teaspoons caster or light brown sugar
white pepper, to taste

FOR THE NOODLES:

1 quantity (400 g) gluten-free Chinese egg
  noodles (page 250) or a vegan alternative

FOR THE VEGETABLES:

2 tablespoons vegetable or peanut oil
2 teaspoons fresh ginger, peeled, finely
  grated
5–6 spring onions, green part only, finely
  chopped
2 carrots, julienned (cut into matchsticks)
1 head broccoli or broccolini, chopped
  into small florets
1 red capsicum, thinly sliced
450 g firm tofu, torn into small chunks
80 g (1 cup) bean sprouts

1. To make the sauce, whisk the cornflour and hot water in a medium-sized bowl until smooth. Add remaining sauce ingredients and whisk to combine. Taste and adjust according to your preferences. Set aside.

2. Par-cook noodles for 1–2 minutes in a large saucepan of well-salted water. I recommend the xanthan gum ones from page 250 here, because they hold up well to being tossed in sauce. Drain.

3. Heat oil in a large wok over a medium heat. Add the ginger and spring onions and cook for 2–3 minutes or until soft and fragrant. Add the carrots and stir-fry for 2–3 minutes, before adding the broccoli and then capsicum. Cook until tender crisp. Add the chunks of tofu and stir to combine. Reduce heat, add the sauce mixture and stir-fry for 1 minute. Add the noodles and stir-fry for another 1–2 minutes or until warmed through and coated in the sauce. Add the bean sprouts and toss to combine. Serve.

NOTES

Leftover chow mein can be stored in an airtight container in the fridge for up to 2 days.

PASTA AND NOODLES

CHAPTER TWELVE

Mostly dumplings

Dumpling wrappers

LACTOSE FREE
GUM FREE
EGG FREE
VEGAN
FODMAP FRIENDLY
GLUTEN FREE
FREE FROM HIGH-STARCH FLOURS
 OPTION

Makes: about 44 dumpling wrappers
Prep time: 35 minutes

Thanks to the combined magic of psyllium husk and the scald (see page 2), these dumpling wrappers are a total breeze to work with. They can be rolled as thin as you can feasibly manage and can be crimped without drama. I have fried them, baked them and boiled them and they stand up remarkably well.

I've done a lot of mixing and matching of flours and I can say that these wrappers work with almost everything you throw at them. You can also make them without starches – replace the 120 g tapioca flour with a wholegrain gluten-free flour of your choice, add an extra 1 tablespoon of psyllium husk and more boiling water as necessary.

~~~~~~~~

240 g (1 ½ cups) fine white rice flour
120 g (1 cup) tapioca flour
2 tablespoons psyllium husk
2 tablespoons oil (vegetable or peanut
  work well, but really any oil will work)
250–375 ml (1–1 ½ cups) boiling water,
  just enough to form a dough
extra tapioca flour, for rolling

1. Combine flours and psyllium in a large bowl. Whisk in the oil and enough boiling water to form a damp but crumbly dough. If in doubt, err on the side of caution – you can always add more water later.

2. Turn mixture out onto a clean, dry benchtop. Allow it to cool for a minute or two before beginning to knead with your hands. It will be hot, so be careful. Continue kneading until a smooth and pliable dough forms. If it doesn't, add half a tablespoon of hot water at a time until you reach a good consistency.

3. Tear off a golf-ball-sized piece of dough and cover the remainder. Roll dough out on a well-floured surface until it is as thin as you want it, keeping in mind that it swells a little during cooking. Use a medium-sized circular cookie cutter (or an upside-down glass) to cut out rounds of dough. Mine is 9.5 cm. I like to fill and shape the dumplings as I work (see the next 2 recipes for filling ideas) but you can roll them all out before filling, if you prefer. Just make sure to flour in between the rolled-out wrappers well and keep them covered if you choose the latter option. Re-roll any excess dough as you work. You might need to moisten trimmings with wet fingers to return it to its pliable glory. Repeat with the remaining dough until it is all used.

NOTES

Keep plenty of extra flour on hand for rolling the wrappers out. I like to use starches here because they're soft and minimise grittiness or the potential for tearing the dough.

If any offcuts of dough become dry or difficult to work with, moisten them with your hand and knead them until pliable again.

Tofu and ginger dumpling filling

LACTOSE FREE
GUM FREE
EGG FREE
VEGAN
FODMAP FRIENDLY
GLUTEN FREE

**Makes: enough for around
60 dumplings, depending on how
much you stuff into each wrapper**
Cook time: 15–20 minutes

I never truly got into dumplings until after my digestive system decided to take a permanent holiday. I just never really grasped why everyone was so mad about dumplings. That is, of course, until I figured out a way to make some I could eat. Dumplings have very quickly shot up into my list of favourite foods, and this filling has followed suit.

I find it hard to quantify how many dumplings one will garner from a batch of dumpling filling because it depends on a lot of things. How big are your wrappers? How much are you stuffing? Are you crimping or doing a simple fold? I recommend keeping enough ingredients for a second batch of dumpling dough on hand, just in case.

250 g common white cabbage, finely shredded (about ⅛th of a medium cabbage)
250 g carrots, grated (about 2 medium)
1 teaspoon fine salt
60 ml (¼ cup) vegetable oil
40 g fresh ginger, peeled, finely grated
5–6 spring onions, green parts only, thinly sliced
250 g firm tofu, crumbled into very small pieces
2 tablespoons gluten-free dark soy or tamari
1 teaspoon Chinese five spice (optional)
1–2 tablespoons toasted sesame oil
salt and white pepper, to taste

1. Place the shredded cabbage and carrot in a large sieve over the sink. Make sure these are very finely shredded or torn, as chunky pieces in the filling make it harder to get a good amount into each wrapper, and they also increase the risk of tearing. Sprinkle over salt and massage into the vegetables until they begin to soften and expel liquid. Continue massaging and squeezing the mixture for around 5–10 minutes, or until vegetables are considerably smaller in mass. The more liquid you expel, the better your dumplings will be. Set aside to continue draining while you prepare the rest of the filling.

2. Heat the vegetable oil in a large frying pan or skillet over medium-low heat. Cook ginger and spring onions, stirring, for 2–3 minutes or until softened and fragrant. Add a splash of water if they begin to stick at any time.

3. Add the tofu, carrot and cabbage and stir to combine. Stir in soy or tamari and sprinkle over the Chinese five spice powder, if you're using it. Add sesame oil near the end of the cooking time and season to taste with salt and white pepper. Set mixture aside to cool. Go forth and make dumplings! (See page 264 for how to fill and cook your dumplings.)

Spinach, water chestnut and tofu dumplings

LACTOSE FREE
GUM FREE
VEGAN
FODMAP FRIENDLY
GLUTEN FREE
EGG FREE

Makes: enough filling for about 60 dumplings
Prep time: 1 hour
Cook time: 2–3 minutes per batch (20–30 minutes total)

500 g frozen chopped spinach, defrosted
60 ml (¼ cup) vegetable or peanut oil
40–50 g fresh ginger, peeled, finely grated
3–4 large spring onions, green part only, thinly sliced
2 teaspoons Chinese five spice
150 g firm tofu, crumbled finely
200 g water chestnuts, finely chopped
2 tablespoons gluten-free dark soy or tamari
2 tablespoons toasted sesame oil
salt and freshly ground black pepper, to taste
60 dumpling wrappers (1–2 quantities of dumpling dough, see page 260)

I am fully aware that I have a problem with trying to stuff tofu into everything I make. This dumpling filling recipe was my attempt to rectify that, until I decided it 'could use some added protein'. You could omit it and add extra spinach or water chestnut if you wish, or you could relax into it with some smoked firm tofu for an added flavour hit.

~~~~~

1. Thoroughly defrost and wring out your spinach. A wet mixture will wreak havoc on your dumpling skins.

2. Heat the oil in a large frying pan or saucepan over a medium–low heat. Cook ginger and spring onion greens for 2–3 minutes or until softened and fragrant. Add a splash of water if anything starts to stick.

3. Add the spinach, Chinese five spice, tofu and water chestnuts and stir to combine. Stir in the dark soy or tamari. Add sesame oil and season to taste with salt and freshly ground black pepper. Set mixture aside to cool.

4. To fill your dumpling wrappers, place a teaspoon or two of filling in the centre of each wrapper. Using your finger, moisten the outer edge of the wrapper. There are a number of different ways to shape a dumpling, and I'm an expert on zero of them. The simplest way is a half-moon shape, made by folding one half of the circular wrapper onto the other and pressing thoroughly to seal the edge. For other methods, I recommend watching tutorials from experts online.

5. You are now ready to boil or steam fry! To boil the dumplings, bring a medium pot of water to the boil. Reduce it to a very gentle simmer and lower in 4–5 dumplings at a time. Move them around to ensure they don't stick to the bottom or each other. Cook for 2–3 minutes or until the wrappers start to look a bit translucent. Remove and drain. I like to sprinkle my colander and cooked dumplings with a little toasted sesame oil to stop them sticking.

6. To steam fry, follow the instructions for the skirt dumpling (without making the skirt) on page 269.

Dumpling soup

LACTOSE FREE
GUM FREE
VEGAN
EGG FREE
FODMAP FRIENDLY
GLUTEN FREE

Serves: 4
Prep time: 10 minutes
Cook time: 30 minutes

2 tablespoons vegetable oil
60 g fresh ginger, peeled, finely grated
5–6 spring onions, green parts only, thinly sliced
2 medium carrots, sliced on a bias
1 tablespoon gluten-free dark soy or tamari
60 ml (¼ cup) dry sherry (see notes)
2 litres (8 cups) FODMAP-friendly stock
25 vegan dumplings (tofu and ginger on page 263 or spinach, water chestnut and tofu on 264)
30 g (1 cup) baby spinach leaves
toasted sesame oil and chilli oil (page 270), to serve

I have to say, I think I would eat a lot more soup if there were always dumplings waiting at the bottom. This dumpling soup is the sort of fresh and delicious thing I could eat every day.

~~~~~

1. Heat the oil in a large saucepan over medium–low heat. Cook ginger and spring onions, stirring, for 2–3 minutes or until softened and fragrant. Add a splash of water if anything starts to stick.

2. Add carrots and cook, stirring occasionally, for 2–3 minutes or until they get a little bit of colour. Deglaze the pan with the dark soy or tamari and dry sherry, then add the stock. Reduce heat to low and simmer for 10–15 minutes or until the carrot has softened and the flavours have melded.

3. While the stock is simmering, cook the dumplings. Unlike regular dumplings, I find gluten-free ones become gummy and break apart when cooked in the broth. So, boil the dumplings in batches in a separate large saucepan of simmering water and set them aside.

4. You can add the dumplings to the broth right before serving or add them to individual bowls. Either way, be very gentle with them.

5. Add the spinach to broth and allow it to wilt. Serve with a drizzle of sesame oil, a spoonful of chilli oil and maybe even a little dumpling dipping sauce (see page 271), if you have some left over.

NOTES

If you have leftover dumpling soup, I recommend keeping the dumplings and broth separate, and adding the dumplings back into reheated broth at the last minute. This will ensure they don't disintegrate.

I like to make my own stock by throwing sad vegetables in the pot and adding some ginger and spring onion. I also like to save vegetable scraps in the freezer for this purpose. I used carrots, fennel and a scant number of mushrooms here, but work with what you have and can eat without issue.

If you're short on time, there are lots of pre-made FODMAP-friendly stock brands out there these days. Try to choose one with an Asian flavour profile as opposed to a Mediterranean/tomato-based stock. This will better complement the dumpling soup.

I use dry cooking sherry as a gluten-free replacement for Shaoxing wine, traditionally added to Chinese dishes. The sherry adds a unique and robust flavour so I highly recommend sourcing some, but it can be omitted if you don't want to use alcohol.

Skirt dumplings

LACTOSE FREE
GUM FREE
VEGAN
EGG FREE
FODMAP FRIENDLY
GLUTEN FREE

**Makes: 1 plate of skirt dumplings
(6–8 dumplings, enough for
1–2 people)**
Prep time: 5 minutes
Cook time: 15 minutes

FOR THE SKIRT SLURRY:

2 teaspoons buckwheat flour
½ teaspoon tapioca flour
½ teaspoon white rice vinegar
pinch of fine salt
125 ml (½ cup) water

TO FINISH:

2 teaspoons vegetable or peanut oil
6–8 uncooked vegan dumplings (tofu and
ginger on page 263 or spinach, water
chestnut and tofu on 264)
60 ml (¼ cup) water

Aesthetics aside, adding a skirt to your dumplings brings
a whole new world of crispy delightfulness to an already
delicious dish. The skirt is easy to make and impressive to serve,
whether or not it slides out in one piece.

1. To make the skirt slurry, combine the flours, vinegar, salt and
    water in a medium jug. Set aside.

2. Heat the oil in a large non-stick frying pan over a medium heat.
    Once hot, add the dumplings and cook, moving them around
    the pan intermittently, until the bottom of each dumpling is
    golden, about 2–3 minutes. Flip and repeat on the other side.

3. Arrange the dumplings in a tight circular fan, leaving enough
    space to put a lid over them. Add ¼ cup (60ml) water to pan
    and quickly top with a lid, ideally see-through so you can see
    how the evaporation is going. Once the liquid has evaporated,
    give your dumpling skirt slurry one final stir. Pour it into pan,
    concentrating on the centre of the dumpling formation. Pop
    the lid back on and reduce heat to low.

4. Continue to steam dumplings, lid on, until most of the liquid
    has evaporated. By now, you should be able to see the slurry
    slowly drying out on the bottom of the pan. Be patient and
    allow it to dry bit by bit. It's honestly quite cool to watch.

5. When it's completely dry, the edges should start to peel away
    from the pan. Take the dumplings off the heat. Using oven-
    gloved hands, invert a large plate over the top of the pan.
    Very carefully (the pan will be hot!) flip the pan so that the
    plate ends up on the bottom. Hopefully, the dumplings should
    have peeled away with the skirt intact. Either way, they will be
    crispy and absolutely delicious.

6. Serve with dumpling dipping sauce (page 271) and chilli sauce
    (page 270). I recommend eating skirt dumplings immediately
    upon making, when the skirt is crispy. Leftovers can be stored in
    the fridge for a day or so, but the skirt is likely to become chewy.

Chilli oil

VEGAN
FODMAP FRIENDLY
GLUTEN FREE

Makes: about 500 ml (2 cups)
Prep time: 10 minutes
Cook time: 10 minutes

Chilli oil is one of those things that is infinitely better homemade. Better yet, you know exactly what is in it and can customise based on your digestive system's demands. I used ¼ cup of milder chilli flakes for this oil so it is suitable for the special breed known as the chilli pleb. Use more if your tastebuds prefer.

~~~~~~~~~

375 ml (1 ½ cups) peanut or vegetable oil
1 teaspoon Sichuan peppercorns
1 teaspoon fennel seeds
2 cinnamon sticks
2–3 star anise
3 slices fresh ginger
2–3 bay leaves
1 black cardamom pod, optional

TO FINISH:

¼ cup dried chilli flakes (see notes)
2–3 teaspoons freshly toasted sesame seeds (optional)
1 teaspoon Chinese five spice
½ teaspoon fine salt

1. Combine the oil, peppercorns, fennel seeds, cinnamon, star anise, ginger, bay leaves and cardamom, if using, in a medium saucepan and place over medium heat. Cook until the oil is shimmery and the ginger is starting to brown and sizzle, about 5 minutes.

2. Meanwhile, combine the chilli flakes, sesame seeds, if using, Chinese five spice and salt in a heatproof bowl on a tea towel. The oil will be very hot, so the tea towel is to prevent any slippages and protect the bench.

3. Once the oil is really hot, carefully pour it over the ingredients in the bowl. They should sizzle up and instantly become fragrant. The bowl will be really hot, so keep your hands clear. Allow to cool completely in the bowl. Adjust the seasoning for taste and transfer to a sterilised glass jar.

NOTES

Chilli oil keeps well for a few weeks on the bench or a few months in the fridge.

Try to find Chinese, Korean or Aleppo chilli flakes. They are a brighter red and milder than the dull, cheap stuff you buy at the shops, and will make for a more beautiful, well-rounded and tasty chilli oil.

Dumpling dipping sauce

VEGAN
FODMAP FRIENDLY
GLUTEN FREE

Serves: 4–6
Prep time: 5 minutes

80 ml (⅓ cup) gluten-free dark soy sauce
　　or tamari
1 ½ tablespoons rice wine vinegar
1 tablespoon chilli oil (opposite)
1 tablespoon toasted sesame oil
2 teaspoons caster or light brown sugar
fresh ginger, peeled and finely grated,
　　to taste

NOTES

Dipping sauce keeps well in an airtight container in the fridge for up to 1 week.

Every dumpling needs a dipping sauce and this one is particularly low effort yet high reward. I like to use extra ginger as a substitute for garlic in this instance.

~~~~~~~

1. Combine all ingredients in a small bowl and adjust flavours according to your taste. Serve alongside dumplings in this chapter or dumpling soup (page 266).

Potato and pea samosas

LOW LACTOSE
EGG FREE
FODMAP FRIENDLY
GLUTEN FREE
VEGAN OPTION

Makes: 22 medium samosas
Prep time: 1 hour
Cook time: 20 minutes for fried
   samosas, 30–40 minutes for baked
   samosas

FOR THE WRAPPERS:

240 g (1 ½ cups) fine white rice flour
120 g (1 cup) glutinous rice or tapioca
   flour
1 ½ tablespoons psyllium husk powder
1 teaspoon baking powder
1 teaspoon fine salt
¼ teaspoon ground turmeric (optional)
1 teaspoon caster sugar (optional)
50 g butter, regular or plant based
375 ml (1 ½ cups) boiling water

FOR THE FILLING:

500 g all-rounder potatoes
2–3 tablespoons butter, ghee or oil,
   plus extra to brush
20–30 fresh curry leaves (optional)
40 g fresh ginger, peeled, finely grated
2–3 spring onions, green parts only,
   chopped (optional)
2 teaspoons ground cumin
2 teaspoons cumin seeds
1 teaspoon garam masala
1 teaspoon black mustard seeds
   (optional)
1 teaspoon fennel seeds
½ teaspoon fine salt
1 teaspoon caster sugar
½ teaspoon ground chilli, or to taste
½ teaspoon ground turmeric
good squeeze of lime juice
55 g (⅓ cup) canned peas, drained
   (optional, see notes)
sliced coriander root and stem (optional)
vegetable or peanut oil, for frying
   (optional)

These samosas use a delicious traditional-style potato and pea filling. Where they deviate from tradition is the gluten-free pastry. I found that dough made in a similar style to the dumpling wrappers (page 260) worked best, albeit with a few tweaks. They can be fried or baked, but either way I recommend serving them with the cheat's imli chutney (page 275).

~~~~~

1. Prepare the samosa pastry as you would the dumpling wrappers on page 260. Knead until you have a smooth, juicy ball of dough. Wrap tightly in cling film or place in a ziplock bag and set aside.

2. Cook potatoes in a medium saucepan of boiling water until really well cooked. Drain. Once cool enough to handle, cut into small bite-sized pieces.

3. Heat the butter, ghee or oil in a large non-stick frying pan over medium heat. Cook the curry leaves, ginger and spring onions, if using, stirring, for 2–3 minutes or until soft and fragrant. Add the spices, seasoning and lime juice and cook, stirring, for 1 minute. Add a splash of water if necessary.

4. Add the peas and coriander, if using. Cook for 2–3 minutes before adding the potatoes. Stir thoroughly to coat in the spices – the mixture should be a pale turmeric hue. Taste and adjust according to your preferences and set aside to cool.

5. Generously flour a clean, dry work bench with tapioca flour. Take a golf-ball-sized piece of dough and roll into a thin 15–20 cm round sheet. Use a sharp, non-serrated knife to cut a 15 cm circle, then cut the circle in half.

6. Take one of the pastry semi-circles and brush the cut edge with water. Flip one cut side over onto the other and use a bit of pressure to seal the two moistened sides together. When you pick it up, you should have a little cone-shaped pastry.

RECIPE CONTINUES >

NOTES

These samosas are easily made vegan by using plant-based butter.

Canned peas are deemed FODMAP friendly in 45 g (¼ cup) serves because the canning process leeches out some of the FODMAP content. If you'd prefer, you can omit them completely without issue.

Uncooked samosas can be frozen and keep well for months in the freezer. To freeze them, arrange the uncooked samosas, not touching, on a lined baking tray that will fit in the freezer. Freeze for a few hours or until frozen through before transferring to a ziplock bag or container. Freezing them this way means they won't get stuck to one another and form mutant samosas upon retrieval from the freezer.

Rice paper rolls are a particularly easy makeshift samosa pastry if you're not in the mood for too much effort. They can be fried or baked, too, although the times may differ a little.

7. Holding the pastry cone upright, spoon ½–1 tablespoon or so of samosa filling into the cone. Do not overstuff it – I recommend a conservative amount of filling while you get the hang of it. Form a little crimp in one top side of the unsealed pastry. Now moisten the top sides of the cone and stick them together, applying a little pressure. Ta-da! Your first samosa. Repeat this process with the remaining dough and filling.

8. These samosas can be baked or fried. To bake them, preheat the oven to 180°C. Line a large baking tray with baking paper. Arrange samosas on prepared tray and brush well on both sides with extra butter, ghee or oil. Bake for 15 minutes, flip the samosas and bake for another 15 minutes or until the pastry is crunchy and golden.

9. To fry, pour in enough vegetable or peanut oil to come halfway up the sides of a small–medium saucepan. Place over medium–high heat and heat for 5–10 minutes or until a samosa edge dipped in the oil sizzles immediately.

10. Cook samosas in the hot oil until pastry is golden and crisp. Drain on a cooling rack placed over a large plate and blot with kitchen paper before serving.

Cheat's imli chutney

LACTOSE FREE
VEGAN
FODMAP FRIENDLY
GLUTEN FREE

Makes: ¾ cup
Prep time: 5 minutes
Cook time: 10 minutes

2 ½ tablespoons tamarind paste
70 g (⅓ cup) jaggery or light brown sugar
½ teaspoon cumin seeds or ground cumin
½ teaspoon black salt or fine salt, to taste
80 ml (⅓ cup) water

My quick, cheat take on a tamarind chutney. The perfect accompaniment to samosas, this is a replacement for more authentic imli chutney, which is often made with tamarind pulp (which is less accessible than the paste) and sometimes dates (which aren't very friendly to the fructose averse).

～～～～～

1. Combine tamarind, sugar, cumin, salt and water in a small saucepan over a medium-low heat. Cook, stirring occasionally, for 10 minutes or until thickened to your desired consistency.

2. Taste and adjust seasoning according to your preference. Serve.

NOTES

Chutney keeps well in an airtight container in the fridge for 3–4 days.

Vegetarian okonomiyaki

FREE FROM HIGH-STARCH FLOURS
GUM FREE
FODMAP FRIENDLY

**Makes: 4 pancakes, enough for 2
   people**
Prep time: 20 minutes
Cook time: 15 minutes

300 g common white cabbage, shredded
200 g (roughly 2 medium) carrots,
   grated
1 teaspoon fine salt
80 g (½ cup) fine brown rice flour
   (see notes)
1 extra-large egg
1 sachet (10 g) kombu dashi powder
   dissolved in 1 tablespoon warm water
   (see notes)
pinch of salt
pinch of white pepper
2 spring onions, green part only, sliced
2–3 tablespoons benishoga (Japanese
   red pickled ginger, optional, see notes)

TO FINISH:

vegetable oil, for cooking
Japanese mayonnaise, for topping
okonomiyaki sauce, for topping
   (see notes)
additional spring onion greens, for
   topping (optional, see page 13)

Okonomiyaki is a Japanese pancake traditionally made with nagaimo, a type of sticky Japanese yam. I had no luck finding any, so this take on the delicacy uses flour and eggs to form the batter. Carrot isn't always included, but I've done so to keep the cabbage within acceptable FODMAP limits. Each pancake contains around 75 g common white cabbage.

~~~~~~~~

1. Place the cabbage and grated carrot in a sieve over the sink. Sprinkle over salt, then use your hands to begin massaging the salt in. The vegetables will start to expel liquid. Squeeze as much liquid out as possible, until the vegetables almost look like cooked, shrivelled ones. The process should take about 10–15 minutes of intermittent squeezing. Once you're happy with them, set them aside.

2. Place flour, egg, dashi powder, salt, white pepper and spring onions in a large bowl and whisk to combine. Stir in the squeezed vegetables and benishoga, if you're using it. It should be quite a firm batter. Use your hands to divide the mixture into 4 portions and shape them into pancakes.

3. Heat 1 tablespoon oil in a large non-stick frypan over medium heat. Add a pancake to your pan and reduce heat to medium-low. Cover pancake with a lid and cook for 2–3 minutes before gently flipping. Cover with the lid and continue cooking and flipping until the pancake is completely cooked through, about 5–6 minutes. Repeat with the remaining 3 pancakes.

4. To serve, top the okonomiyaki with Japanese mayonnaise, okonomiyaki sauce and the spring onion greens, if you're using them.

NOTES

I have successfully used fine white rice flour and sorghum flour in place of the brown rice flour in this recipe. Note that sorghum flour is less absorbent, so you may need to add extra cabbage to compensate.

I have found kombu dashi and benishoga at various boutique grocers. If you can't find them, you can use vegetable stock cubes in place of dashi and a little grating of fresh ginger in place of the benishoga.

One thing I haven't found in any mainstream groceries is okonomiyaki sauce. There are lots of recipes to make your own online, and I have read that kecap manis works in an (inauthentic) pinch.

Okonomiyaki keep well in an airtight container in the fridge for 2–3 days and make a great lunch the next day.

Vietnamese spring rolls

LACTOSE FREE
GUM FREE
VEGAN
EGG FREE
FODMAP FRIENDLY
GLUTEN FREE

Makes: 12 spring rolls
Prep time: 30 minutes
Cook time: 30 minutes

Firstly, if you don't feel like an excitable child watching the rice paper puff up in the hot oil, you're a liar. Secondly, no, I did not make the rice paper wrappers from scratch. Some things, like rice noodles, buckwheat soba and rice paper wrappers, are best left to the experts. Rice paper wrappers are incredibly versatile and can be used, in a pinch, for essentially anything you'd like to wrap, dumplings and samosas included. It is worth noting that you can eat these as rice paper rolls – frying is optional!

~~~~~~~

16–20 rice paper wrappers, 22 cm diameter (it's helpful to have extra on hand in case some crack)
vegetable oil, to half fill a medium–large saucepan, for frying

FOR THE VEGAN NUOC MAM DRESSING:

60 ml (¼ cup) lime juice
60 ml (¼ cup) vegan fish sauce
2 tablespoons caster sugar
½–1 teaspoon gluten-free soy sauce or tamari, to taste
chopped fresh red chilli, to taste
½ bunch Thai basil, leaves picked, chopped
½ bunch Vietnamese mint, leaves picked, chopped (remainder used in filling)

FOR THE FILLING:

2 medium carrots, grated
1 teaspoon fine salt
2 tablespoons vegetable or peanut oil
50 g fresh ginger, peeled, finely grated
5 spring onions, green parts only, sliced
450 g firm tofu, crumbled into very small pieces
leftover ½ bunches herbs, finely chopped
2 tablespoons gluten-free dark soy sauce or tamari
2 tablespoons vegan fish sauce
chilli flakes, to taste
50 g rice vermicelli noodles, cooked in boiling water, chopped
zest of ½ makrut lime, grated

1. To make the nuoc mam dressing, place all ingredients in a small bowl or jar and stir to dissolve the sugar. Adjust seasoning to taste. Set aside to allow the flavours to meld.

2. Grate the carrots and place them in a sieve over the sink. Sprinkle with fine salt and massage it into the carrots. Over the course of about 10 minutes, periodically squeeze as much liquid out of them as possible. This will prevent soggy roll innards.

3. To make the filling, heat the oil in a large non-stick frying pan over medium-low heat. Cook the ginger, stirring, for 2–3 minutes or until fragrant. Add the spring onion greens and cook, stirring occasionally, for 2 minutes or until softened. Add the well-drained carrot, tofu, herbs, sauces, chilli flakes, vermicelli noodles and lime zest and stir well to combine. Taste and adjust seasoning as necessary. Set aside to cool to room temperature.

4. Fill a shallow bowl with warm or hot water and clear some clean bench space. Lightly grease a large piece of baking paper atop a large tray. Dip a rice paper wrapper in the water until it softens and becomes malleable. Lay it flat on the bench.

5. Spoon 3 tablespoons of filling in a log across the third of the rice paper closest to you. Roll the rice paper up over the filling, tucking it in as you roll, completing one revolution. Press the sides of the paper in to remove any air, then fold in tightly over the filling. Continue rolling forward, tucking tightly as you go, until the last bit of rice paper adheres to the roll. Repeat the dipping and rolling process with the remaining rice paper and filling. Place each finished roll onto the greased baking paper, ensuring they don't touch (or they will stick). Place the rolls in the fridge for at least an hour to dry and set (this is critical for frying).

NOTES

If fried, these rolls are best on the day of making, as they lose their crispiness. However, fried or not, leftovers can be stored in an airtight container in the fridge for a few days.

Some rice paper wrappers contain tapioca flour as the primary ingredient. Make sure you choose a rice-only variety if you need these to be free from high-starch flours.

6. To fry, place enough oil in a medium-large saucepan to come halfway up the side. Place saucepan over a high heat until oil is hot; this will take 5–10 minutes. To test if it's ready, you can dip the corner of a roll into the oil or drop in a small piece of rice paper. If it starts bubbling up immediately, it's ready.

7. Reduce heat a little and fry rolls 1 or 2 at a time, until they are bubbly, crispy and golden, about 5 minutes. Transfer to a cooling rack with kitchen towel or a large plate underneath. Leave space between them so they don't stick to each other. Repeat with remaining rolls and serve warm with the nuoc mam.

Acknowledgements

Thank you to my family, who have wholeheartedly supported this dream of mine ever since they caught me covertly photographing my breakfast on the front lawn.

To my cat, Arthur, who kept me company during the long days of recipe testing and shooting: thank you for (mostly) indulging me as I grapple with my unhealthy levels of emotional attachment to you, Ginger Prince.

To my friends (who come in third after the cat, sorry): thank you for continually being so understanding as I disappear for months at a time. One day my 3–5+ day response time will improve, I promise.

To Amanda and Izzy from Penguin Random House: thank you for your enthusiasm and support for this book. Your passion, hard work and expertise made the process as easy and fun as writing a (gluten-free) cookbook can be. I could have not asked for a better team, nor could I have asked for a better result.

To James Rendall and Sonja Heijn, thank you for your invaluable contributions and for making this book what it is.

To my designer, Andy Warren: a more aesthetically pleasing package for this book couldn't possibly exist and I'm beyond grateful for your talent.

To Chrissy Freer, my recipe editor: thank you for bearing with my eclectic note-taking style and for imparting your wisdom into the book.

Finally, to everyone reading this book and following along at home: none of this would be possible without you. From poorly lit, edible flower-laden smoothie bowls to a second cookbook, your support has changed the course of my life and I am forever grateful.

Note: Pages in italics denote tips

LANTERN AUSTRALIA

UK | USA | Canada | Ireland | Australia
India | New Zealand | South Africa | China

Lantern Australia is part of the Penguin Random House group of companies
whose addresses can be found at global.penguinrandomhouse.com.

Penguin
Random House
Australia

First published by Lantern Australia, 2022

Cover and internal photography, prop and food styling and recipe development by Georgia McDermott
Cover and internal design by Andy Warren Design
Recipes edited by Chrissy Freer
Typeset by Post Pre-press Group, Australia
Printed and bound in China by RR Donnelley

A catalogue record for this
book is available from the
National Library of Australia

ISBN 978 176104 393 2

penguin.com.au